See Naples and Die

See Naples and Die

*A World War II Memoir of a
United States Army Ski Trooper
in the Mountains of Italy*

Robert B. Ellis

McFarland & Company, Inc., Publishers
Jefferson, North Carolina, and London

Permission granted by the following:
Page 115, "Suicide in the Trenches," Siegfried Sassoon (Viking Penguin).
Page 147, "Beaucort Revisited," A.P. Herbert (A.P. Watt, Ltd.).
Page 210, "A Lament," Wilfrid Wilson Gibson (Macmillan General Books).

British Library Cataloguing-in-Publication data are available

Library of Congress Cataloguing-in-Publication Data

Ellis, Robert B., 1924–
    See Naples and die : a World War II memoir of a United States
Army ski trooper in the mountains of Italy / Robert B. Ellis.
    p. cm.
    Includes index.
    ISBN 0-7864-0199-0 (library binding: 50# alk. paper)
    1. Ellis, Robert B., 1924–   . 2. United States. Army
Mountain Division, 10th—History. 3. United States. Army—
Ski troops—History. 4. World War, 1939–1945—Campaigns—
Italy. 5. World War, 1939–1945—Personal narratives,
American. 6. United States. Army—Biography.
7. Soldiers—United States—Biography. I. Title.
D763.I8E37 1996
940.54'8173—dc20   96-22230
                                                                CIP

Manufactured in the United States of America

McFarland & Company, Inc., Publishers
  Box 611, Jefferson, North Carolina 28640

We must all thank God that we have been allowed,
each of us according to our stations, to play a part in
making these days memorable in the history of our race.

—Winston S. Churchill
Address to the Boys of Harrow School, October 29, 1941

Table of Contents

Preface

No one who has experienced the looks, sounds, and smells of infantry combat and the brotherhood of others facing death ever forgets that part of his life, however many years have passed. To recall specific individuals and events after the passage of some fifty years is quite another thing, unless you have the gift of total recall or have kept some written record of what transpired. I am not blessed with the former, but was favored by having a mother who saved hundreds of the letters I wrote both before and after my entry into military service. In addition, I kept a skeletal diary from the time our division set sail for Italy until our arrival home after Germany's surrender.

What prompted this book were two things: the recent discovery of these writings and a need to share with my children what their father thought and felt as he came of age in a time before the laptop computer and global television displays of genocide. Perhaps this account will help them realize that the aging relic they see today was himself young once, with dreams about the future, and that while circumstances change, the challenges we face in dealing with each other and with life's calamities remain much the same.

Since we are all influenced by the continuum of life stretching back through the lives of our parents and beyond, I have tried to provide some insight into how my mother and father prepared me for the trials to come. This includes a brief summary of my background as the son of a missionary surgeon and his strong-willed missionary-teacher-wife and some of their accounts of the horrors they witnessed in Persia (Iran) during and after World War I— horrors similar to those that have recently occurred in Bosnia and Rwanda. Their training and counsel largely shaped my beliefs and attitudes as I bore the shock of military service and battle.

This book is a personal memoir and does not pretend to be a completely balanced history of the ski troops in training or in combat. Those who wish a more general description of the actions of our division must look elsewhere. My focus is on the individual units in which I served, and to a lesser extent their parent organizations. This in no sense is meant to disparage the deeds performed by other elements of the 10th Mountain Division, all of whom served with great distinction.

The story is mainly chronological to preserve for the reader how a naive and relatively sheltered youth of eighteen gradually learned to accept life's disappointments and the Army's follies—even while he was somewhat embittered by them. To keep the book a reasonable length, I have omitted some letters and reduced the length of others when the content did not seem to add much to the story. Regrettably, the letters written to the woman who was the light of my life during the war were not available for this book.

Certain gaps between letters sent home exist presumably because some letters were lost by the military's mail system, my mother, or others in the family with whom they were habitually shared. All letters from the battle zone reflect the censor's hand, while those to my parents in particular—especially from the front lines—reflect self-censorship in order to spare them the more gruesome details of what I had undergone.

In writing this narrative, I have consulted such secondary sources as the accounts of military historians, a few records and personal letters supplied by fellow combatants, company morning reports, civilian and military magazine and newspaper stories, scrapbook records, military orders, and published and unpublished books on the history of the 10th. I did not rely (with a few notable exceptions) on the recollections of participants some four or five decades later. That technique, used in many World War II combat accounts, may offer a dramatic narrative, but the accuracy of the resultant product is questionable. Too often actions are embellished, and exhibitions of human weakness and mistakes are forgotten, with the result that everyone appears to emerge a hero.

The principal foundation underlying what I have written here is what I said and wrote at the time. (Only four names have been changed where it seemed necessary to respect the privacy of the men and their families.) I have expanded on the narrative only to explain the context within which an event occurred or to provide details about the action mentioned as supplied by our company morning reports and other reliable sources. In this recounting, not everyone performs valiantly all of the time, including the author. The actions and judgment of commanders are questioned where appropriate, as well as the conduct of some in the lowest ranks.

I am grateful to the Kitsap County, Washington, library system staff and to Cindy Harrison in particular for help in obtaining research materials pertinent to the story. I would also like to express the gratitude and affection all 10th Division veterans feel for the Italian people of the Apennine mountain villages who have shown us friendship and acts of kindness both during those terrible days of war and since. Most of all I must thank my wife, Susan, without whose encouragement and editorial assistance this account of actions and events, which continue to haunt my psyche and arouse deep emotions, would never have been brought to fruition.

I entered the military service of my country full of optimism and gulli-bility. I left it embittered in many ways and ambivalent about the army and whether the horror we had experienced and the losses undergone—whatever the iniquities of the Hitler and Japanese regimes—were worth the price paid. The advent of nuclear weapons has only increased this doubt.

Preamble

A Rendezvous with Death

It was 9:45 A.M., H-Hour. The Germans knew we were coming because they had just emerged from a terrible onslaught, beginning with a 40-minute aerial bombardment by our P-47 fighter-bombers. As we watched, streams of flame shot from these "Thunderbolts" when they released their rockets, and one fire bomb alone enveloped an acre of ground around a cluster of houses off to our right. Next our artillery opened up, delivering some 75,000 shells on the German positions. This cannon fire was accompanied by bullets from 50-caliber machine guns, positioned near us only 30 yards apart, sending their tracers arcing over our heads to the other side of the valley. The German hillsides, as well as our own, seemed enveloped in dust and smoke as an endless stream of shots from a number of guns converged on one house. Then a single stream cut in two a five-inch tree which slowly toppled on to the scarred earth.

Our commander in chief, Franklin D. Roosevelt, had died less than 48 hours earlier, and as we emerged from our foxholes and began walking fearfully down the exposed hillside to the road and the German lines in the woods, the rain of death from incoming artillery and mortars seemed to foretell that we would follow our president and father-figure shortly. "Let's get the bastards," a rifleman near me yelled as he jogged through the smoke and shell bursts pockmarking the slope.

As usual in the attack, our two machine gun squads were separated, each being attached to a different rifle platoon to provide fire support. Not that we were doing much firing as we hurried forward, for there was rarely any enemy to be seen in such circumstances, and our principal concern was to escape the shrapnel flying all about us.

The terror was real, and very quickly the ground around us was bloodied by dead and wounded ski troopers, those unable to seek help awaiting the medics and hoping they would be evacuated in time to save their lives. A number of them were from my own platoon. They included "Mother" Eyer, one of our three 60mm mortar squad leaders. Eyer wrote me later he had been lying in a ditch when he heard a mortar shell hit in front of him and then another land behind him. He knew that "the third would be on target," and it was. Shrapnel from the shell struck him in the back, drenching his shirt and mountain jacket in blood, but he was still able to walk. As he headed back through the smoke and fury, he found another wounded GI who had been hit by a rock—changed into a missile by another shell burst—and the two helped each other get back to the aid station.

Other casualties included our platoon sergeant, Jim Orwig, hit in the shoulder; a private whom I will call George Olsen, stunned by the near explosion of a shell—he was a member of my squad who had been my foxhole companion our first night in battle two months earlier; and Private Turman Oldham, who had been helping me try to hack a slit trench into the unyielding soil near Monte della Torrachia, when our much-detested battalion commander, Lieutenant Colonel Roche, arrived and had his own hole dynamited open by an aide.

Looking to right and left, I saw an irregular line of troopers stretching all across the valley. A signal flare burst over the Jerry positions, leaving floating lanterns of flame drifting across the sky. We began stepping more cautiously, trying to avoid any ground that appeared disturbed, signifying the placement of the dreaded "Bouncing Betty" mines. When these mines were set off by someone stubbing a trip wire or tiny exposed detonator, they bounded into the air about chest high and exploded, scattering marble-sized steel pellets some 50 feet in all directions.

Working our way out of the valley towards the stark, shell-burnt woods, we began to come across the bodies of many Company G men who had preceded us in the attack and had been killed by exploding mines. The Germans had used the past month effectively to prepare for the spring offensive they knew we would initiate; they had seeded all the logical avenues of approach with these terrible instruments of death and disfigurement. It also became clear as the shells dropped among us that they had figured out with great accuracy what trails, draws, and hiding places we might use to approach their positions.

Larry Boyajian—one of the mortar men—and I suddenly found ourselves lying together on a rock ledge cowering under a rain of shells from what we later learned were 120mm mortars whistling over our heads. As we had found too often before in these rock-infested hills, there was no way we could dig down for cover because no shovel could penetrate the ground, so we simply lay there crimping our bodies together into as small a space as possible, expecting any moment to receive a fatal hit.

Then Larry said: "Bob, I think I see a dugout under the road down there. Do you think we should make a run for it?" Looking back at the road the attack plan had designated as our so-called "line of departure" (LD), I had to admit it appeared to offer a good-sized culvert of some kind. Borrowing a pair of field glasses from another GI nearby, I got a better look and said, "It sure as hell looks better than where we are."

Larry, however, now had second thoughts. As we hugged the trembling rock on which we lay, we heard the familiar whooshing sound of more than one incoming projectile overhead, the noise stemming from the shells' movement, which created a vacuum into which the air rushed. Fortunately, most of the missiles were landing either in the valley or on the steep slope behind us, but their effect was frightening to behold. In addition to those coming from 120mm field pieces, some rounds came from 170mm mortars, almost twice the caliber of the German 88mm artillery that we all feared so much. Awestruck, we saw their explosions felling trees at least 100 feet tall, and when the trees came down with a terrible crash on the hillside, it left little to our imagination as to what the shell bursts might do to our bodies if the shots fell the least bit short.

Larry's reasoning for staying put was that the supposed refuge by the road was not only some distance across open ground, but also its location in the bottom of the valley was where most of the incoming mail being lobbed over our heads was landing. Unfortunately, some of it was falling nearby and, as we both knew, even if a shell missed you by fifty feet it could still kill you.

Lying in tandem, arms outstretched to achieve the flattest attitude possible, we stared wide-eyed about us. Suddenly something struck my arm, and I turned my head to see what damage had been done. I saw none, but the object that hit me turned out to be an irregular piece of sharp-edged steel some three inches in length. I picked it up, and it burned my fingers.

For a few seconds I seemed incapable of thought. Fear washed over me, and I tensed waiting for the next blow. When my panic momentarily subsided and reason returned, I placed the spent shrapnel in Larry's hand. It was still warm, and I said, "We'd better take off now or the next one could go right through us."

Larry was convinced, and we leaped up and ran like mad down the rock-strewn slope to the road. The dugout, however, turned out to be a small slit trench with a flimsy box over it, and we saw immediately it would offer no real security. As I later described the situation in a letter home, "There we were with shells raining all around and our comparative former safety—on the reverse slope of a steep hill facing the enemy—a long way off."

Having no alternative, we ran back to our previous positions and sought protection under rock ledges and in water-filled shell holes while sweating out more barrages. We later learned we had run directly through a mine field going down the hill and coming back up. When I wrote Larry some 47 years later and asked whether he remembered the experience we had shared—one I had described in a letter to Mother, a copy of which I enclosed—he said he recalled the incident only too well and added: "As to those mine fields, wow! [There was an] entire platoon with its officer and noncoms blown up just above and to the left of the spot you mentioned. I think 48 men were blown up."[1]

By the middle of the afternoon, after hours of running, crawling, digging, and creeping, we had worked our way in a somewhat disorganized line part way up the slopes of our Company F's initial objective: another hill with only a number (Hill 909) and no name. Some Jerries came toward us carrying a wounded German whose intestines bulged from his stomach. They looked frightened and stopped, the lead German waving a white rag hung from the end of a stick. We waved them to our rear and, as they struggled off, some seemingly dazed ski troopers with bandaged arm and leg wounds followed after.

There was heavy fire from German "burp guns" (machine pistols) and snipers hiding in stone farm buildings and bunkers, fighting to the last trying to maintain their defensive line. Many such strong points we purposefully bypassed, but some continued to inflict casualties until they were cleaned out days later.

As we advanced cautiously, the whistle of a bullet coming from somewhere to our right sang between us. It had the unmistakable whine of rifle fire—fire which snapped off twigs just above our heads—and I and other members of my machine gun squad hit the ground, seeking safety behind scattered boulders or nearby embankments. One of our men I will call Allen Paulsen, who was some 20 feet from me in the shattered vegetation, sounded the cry for help which always meant tragedy and pain: "Medic! Medic!"

I later learned that he was wounded by a bullet in the foot and might have shot himself,* but for once I was more angered than frightened in the heat of battle and emboldened to respond in kind. I crawled forward through the underbrush to try and determine where the shot came from. Ahead some 20 yards in front of me lay two large log bunkers. Peering through the trees, I tried to determine if the first was occupied. An unearthly hush seemed to have descended over the woods where I lay, but my insides were churning with excitement. Clearly nothing so stimulates one's sense of alertness and anticipation as the prospect of a bullet in the head.

After eyeing the nearest redoubt from different sides and seeing no movement, I crawled by one of its openings and headed for the second bunker. Scattered about were Jerry grenades, abandoned guns, and other weapons which increased my concern about the kind of fire I might anticipate from the log-covered entrenchment ahead. Taking care to approach it from what I thought was a blind side, hoping the occupant (if any) could not see my crawling form, I gradually edged towards an opening.

---

*Self-inflicted wounds, as a means of avoiding battle, were not that unusual, although they were hard to verify. Such injuries were most often inflicted on a toe, and the claim was commonly made, when the individual had not been in combat, "I was cleaning my gun." At least one nonbattle injury, however, that occurred in our company, whether premeditated or not, seemed unusually careless as well as excessive. According to one of our daily "morning reports," it involved a man who "stumbled on a foxhole and fell against his own bayonet."

Pressure was mounting in my chest, and I was scarcely breathing when suddenly I saw him. Only his head and shoulders could be seen from my prostrate position, and fortunately his back was partially toward me. This was the first German I had seen at close quarters in combat. His manner seemed agitated. He was either trembling or bobbing up and down in a peculiar way; perhaps he had been frightened by the oncoming American troops or had been injured. I could not see a weapon, but if his comrades had left him behind because of wounds, why was he not making an offer to surrender apparent? And could I take the chance to call out to him "*Hände hoch*" ("Hands up"), have him turn and see where I was, and toss a grenade or fire at me?

All the conditioning and guidance I'd received from my medical missionary parents argued for me not to assume the worst about another human being and to determine first what his true condition and attitude was before taking further action. But my army training, not to mention my fear and excitement, were both too great. As he heard my movements and turned toward me, I rested both elbows on the ground, steadied the .45-caliber pistol I carried in both hands, and shot him in the head.

He dropped immediately out of sight. I considered crawling forward to get a better view of the situation or even to enter his hiding place, but we were under orders to continue our advance to capture the hill. Also, if he were still alive, caution dictated leaving the investigation to those who would come after, so I signaled the others and we moved on.

If my parents disapproved of my action, which I described in a private letter some weeks later to my brother Edwin—he subsequently shared it with them—they never made an issue of it. Perhaps they were so relieved I had survived the encounter, they could not make their true feelings known. It was not that they were pacifists, nor unfamiliar with the terrible cruelties members of our species are capable of inflicting on one another. They had seen war in all its savagery firsthand. They were also practical-minded people and often advised their children that "God helps those who help themselves." But their own lives had been dedicated to serving others—whatever the hardships they encountered—and they had tried to instill that same "missionary" spirit in me.

1

From a Middle East
Inferno to World War II

Persia to the United States, 1915–1943

Like the writer St. Clair McKelway, who described his Presbyterian forebears as forming an inverted pyramid, the sharp point of which pressed into the top of his head, my genealogy too was filled with Presbyterians stretching back in time.[1] My mother, Jessie, and father, Wilder, were both children of Presbyterian ministers who served as pioneer home missionaries, one in Utah and the other in the Montana Territory. After finishing college and surviving a five-year engagement while awaiting my father's completion of medical training, they married in July of 1915 and immediately set off for service as Presbyterian missionaries in the city of Urumia, Persia. Europe, Russia, and the Middle East were engulfed in World War I, and Urumia's situation was similar to that of Bosnia today. It was a battleground for Turkish and Russian troops, Kurdish tribesmen, Assyrians, Armenians, and other native partisans. Massacres and epidemics were the order of the day. My father's medical services as a surgeon were desperately needed, as the sick and wounded numbered in the thousands.

Following a long and dangerous journey, my parents arrived in Urumia on November 10, 1915, and three days later my father wrote home:

> Yesterday I took a long ride into the mountains to bury some 60 Christians who, last May, the Turks and Kurds had forced to carry burdens for them, then tied them together, led them off to this lonely gulch, and told them to sit down and rest. After going off a little ways, they then shot into them, killing all but three who escaped by feigning death and hiding under the dead bodies of their comrades. These poor people had lain out there all this time—months under the summer sun—and no service had been held over them. It was a ghastly sight, indeed, not to go into any further details.

11

Jessie Ellis, about 1910.

My mother began language lessons, helped in the hospital and the children's school, and by the spring of 1916 was pregnant. Many Kurdish and other Moslem inhabitants of surrounding villages had taken refuge in the mission compound. She wrote:

It would be difficult for a Westerner to imagine the scene that was enacted there daily. About 1,000 Kurds and Moslems occupied these yards, and therein each family set up village life on an abbreviated scale on its own little spot. The huge ungainly water buffalo always occupied the drawing room, together with his bed and bath. If there were cow or donkey members, as there generally were, plus sheep, goats, hens and horses, these stood in what might be considered the family living room. They made fine musical instruments for the early morning orchestra which was never lacking. In the little space that remained, the family squatted around a small hearth made of two stones placed together.

By June of 1918, the young couple were parents of Edwin, age 2, and newborn Paul. The revolutionary Kerensky government had withdrawn all Russian forces from Persia, Moslem Turks had occupied Urumia, and the Moslem Kurds were attacking their Christian neighbors.

Soon some 80,000 Christian refugees crowded the Urumia plain and the mission compounds. The senior American missionary, Rev. William Shedd, decided to lead an exodus of refugees and missionaries from Urumia to central Iran. My parents chose to stay, feeling that neither Edwin nor Paul could survive the trip. (Edwin was seriously ill with malaria and dysentery.) My mother also said, "Our carriage was very old and our horse aged 20," and the flight, based on her initial view of it, was going to be a nightmare.

> The small avenue was crowded with nearly every type of transportation from cows to camels, from carts to phaetons, with thousands on foot. Little children huddled on oxen, which would afford food as well as transportation; mothers had babies tied to their backs, and 50 babies were abandoned to us because of the inability of the mothers to carry two children. As we had no milk or food for them, we could only brood over them as they died.

Half of the wretched 80,000, including the Rev. Shedd, perished from slaughter and disease before they reached their destination.

Immediately after the exodus, armed and fearsome Kurdish tribesmen invaded the building where the missionaries who stayed had gathered. When the Kurds couldn't shoot open the mission safe, they searched the missionaries for money and jewelry. One Kurd seized the two-weeks bride of a young missionary and tried to drag her away. My mother noted, "She and Ned were pacifists, but she put up a fierce resistance and, although a mite for strength, wrestled with that Kurd amazingly." She was saved when Turkish soldiers charged through the door.

The Kurds murdered several missionaries and carried out brutal massacres in the French mission and in a local orphanage. In the latter they separated the Christian children from the Moslems and slaughtered all the Christian children.

As the Turkish occupation proceeded, my father wrote that the death rate approached 50 percent. Dysentery, malaria, typhoid, typhus, influenza, smallpox, and diphtheria were rampant, and food was scarce. Before the summer was over, all children under 10 had died except for my brothers, Edwin and Paul, and the children of another missionary physician. My mother

Missionary auto caravan on Syrian desert en route to Persia, 1932.

mourned, "There was no place one could step that one did not see the sick, the dying, the sorrowing and starving."

On October 8, 1918, the Turkish commandant ordered the missionaries to leave Urumia for Tabriz. After a grueling six-day trek, they reached the latter city, where they expected to be prisoners of war. Instead, they were treated well and set free eight days later upon news of the upcoming armistice.

After a furlough in the United States, the family was allowed to return to Urumia, where in 1931, my father completed and opened the new Cochran Memorial Hospital, named for three generations of Joseph Cochrans who had served as missionaries in Persia. That same year he was joined by the latest Dr. Joseph Cochran, and their work often took them into surrounding villages and mountains. On one occasion, my father was persuaded to go to a mountain stronghold to treat one of the wives of the principal Kurdish chieftain, the redoubtable Ismail Agha, familiarly known as Simko. Simko was not averse to killing Christians, but Dad returned from that venture unharmed.

The Persian government began to restrict missionary activity. A former Persian army colonel, Reza Khan, had been crowned Reza Shah Pahlavi, beginning the Pahlavi dynasty. He was determined to modernize the country, weaken the influence of the Moslem clergy, and strengthen the power of the central government. In 1934, only three years after the opening of the new hospital in Urumia, Reza declared the Urumia district a military zone, changed the city's name to Rezaieh after himself (and the country's name to Iran), and ordered the missionaries to leave the area.

So ended 100 years of medical work in Urumia, work that has never been resumed. The Ellis and Cochran families were reassigned to the mission station in Tabriz, where the mission hospital was now the only medical facility with Western-trained physicians and nurses in all of Iranian Azerbaijan.

Jessie and Robert Ellis, Urumia, Persia, 1926.

By 1935, Edwin and Paul had been in the United States attending school for three years, and Margaret, now 14, and I, now 11, had rounded out the tribe. It was time for Margaret and me also to return stateside for more formal schooling, so Mother set out with us, leaving behind our forlorn father, who was not due a furlough for three years. As the Presbyterian Board of Foreign Missions had funds to cover travel for education of missionary children approaching or in their teens, Mother decided that we would spend a

Center, standing, Kurdish chieftain Simko, flanked on left by Wilder Ellis and on right by a French priest later killed by Simko.

Left to right: front, Margaret and Robert; back, Wilder, Paul, Jessie, and Edwin, 1931.

year in Switzerland to broaden our understanding of other cultures and languages.

Once we were settled in Geneva, Paul joined us (Edwin was now in college in North Carolina), and he and Margaret enrolled in the International School. I had the unenviable task of entering a Swiss public school where only French was spoken. As a missionary's son, I had experienced many different schools during our home furloughs. I had learned to make new friends quickly and adapt to a variety of customs and social practices, but doing so through the medium of an unfamiliar language was a new trial. An affectionate but complaining letter to Dad brought this quick response:

> Your delightful note of Sept. 12 arrived yesterday.... I am glad to know that you feel a vital connection with your Dad, even though far away, for my heart often feels so close to you, especially when I get such letters as this one. I trust that our connection will be intimate all our lives.
>
> I was surprised to hear you say that you cannot talk French, only you can understand it well. Do not be afraid of making mistakes. If you do and they laugh, just laugh too. It will be fun then, and something to laugh about. I remember a Chinese boy in America learning English. When he made mistakes, we laughed and he did too. He then saw his mistakes and so was able to correct them. If you talked along making mistakes and no one laughed or told you about it, you would learn wrong. Talk, talk, make mistakes, and then when you have found them out and the right way, you can correct them.

Mother was a loving parent, generous in her praise and affection, but she believed firmly in perfecting all of one's gifts and was convinced that an idle child would come to no good. On October 24, I wrote to Dad:

> I have started playing the piano now. Our schedule for the day is like this: get up at 6:30, get dressed, eat breakfast at 7, finish at half past, and then practice the piano till 8 or half past, and then fifteen minutes on the violin. At 20 minutes of 9 I go to school and stay till 12 o'clock. Then I come home and play on the violin for 30 minutes. That finishes my violin practicing. Then I go to school at 2 and stay till 4 o'clock. Then home again. I play for an hour, do my homework till 6:30, eat supper till 7 and then to bed.

That winter I learned to ski at a resort near Mont Blanc, and in the spring of 1936, Mother suggested that she and I bicycle around Lake Geneva, a trip of some 132 miles. The route offered spectacular mountain scenery, but included high Alpine passes that demanded a lot of any bicyclist in the days before multiple gears, and Mother was 48 years old. Moreover, it rained continuously during the trip.

In spite of the extreme physical demands, Mother kept up with her 11-year-old son until her brakes gave out near the top of one mountain.

"What do we do now?" I asked.

"Why don't I just hang on to your jacket as we go down?"

Since I could think of no better solution, we followed her suggestion and—somehow avoiding entanglement of the two bicycles—coasted some 14 miles with her desperately gripping my back and arm until we reached flatter terrain. We continued this way to Lausanne, more than half way around the lake. There we decided to end the cycling part of the journey and return to Geneva by train.

Three days shy of my twelfth birthday, on June 30, 1936, I had the memorable experience of sitting with Mother in the great hall of the General Assembly of the League of Nations in Geneva, to hear Haile Selassie, Lion of Judah, Emperor of Ethiopia, address the League. His backward country—the only independent state in all Africa—had been invaded by Italian dictator Benito Mussolini's armored tank columns, supported by planes bombing and spraying mustard gas on helpless tribal villages. One of the Italian pilots—a son of Mussolini—was quoted as saying what a thrill it gave him when the bombs he dropped exploded like beautiful flowers.

I watched in awe as the tiny figure of the emperor came to the podium. In an impassioned cry for help, he gave one of the great speeches of history. He came "to bear witness against the crime perpetrated against my people and give Europe a warning of the doom that awaits it, if it should bow before the accomplished fact." He exhorted his listeners: "I assert that the problem submitted to the Assembly today is not merely a question of the settlement of Italian aggression. It is collective security; it is the very existence of the League of Nations.... What reply shall I have to take back to my people?"[2]

Alas, the great powers were too concerned with "peace at any price" to rescue Selassie. The Assembly voted to lift sanctions against Italy, collective security was doomed, and World War II became inevitable. In ensuing years, I never forgot that failure of the great powers to stand against tyranny.

Once back in the U.S., Mother settled in her college town of Wooster, Ohio, and I entered the eighth grade of the local junior high. I played basketball and baseball for the first time and was hooked. I wrote to Dad that I had almost fainted after getting hit on the end of a finger with a ball. He responded:

> Being the son of a missionary does not fit one very well to play baseball, but I have an idea that you will soon get onto it. Tough in that finger getting the ball on the end of it. That is a bad place for a ball to hit, but it is part of the game to catch the ball in the glove, and if you don't, then you have to take the consequences and so get the lesson beaten in pretty strongly.

By 1938, Dad could no longer endure the separation from his family; he resigned from the mission field and joined us in Wooster, Ohio, where he began practice as a country doctor. In the same year, I became a scholarship student at nearby Western Reserve Academy, a college preparatory boarding school whose academic standards were excruciatingly high. WRA exercised

Left to right: Jessie, Robert, Edwin, Margaret, and Paul Ellis, 1936.

strict control over all phases of behavior. Coats and ties were required in classes, the dining hall, and chapel. Students could not drive cars, drinking and smoking were banned, and pinups of movie stars were not permitted. We felt deprived, but the Academy's superb teachers and its insistence on serious study habits offered a great advantage upon entry into college and other benefits that lasted all our lives.

During those high school years, I was very aware of the imminence of war. The Japanese had invaded Manchuria and taken control of most of China's major ports and industrial centers. Hitler's armies seized Austria in March 1938, the remainder of Czechoslovakia in March 1939, and then attacked Poland in September 1939, Western Europe in April 1940, and finally the USSR in June 1941. That same month I graduated from the Academy at age 16.

I had decided on a career in international relations, hoping that in such a field, I might help stave off future wars. With this in mind, in the fall of 1941, I entered the University of North Carolina, where training in international affairs was reputedly the best. On November 12, I wrote this glowing report:

> Wonderful news. I have been admitted into the International Relations Club (IRC). It brings the finest political speakers and international relations experts here—the Roosevelts (Franklin and Eleanor), Ambassador Bullitt, Wendell Wilkie, etc.* Yesterday the IRC brought Ambas-

William Bullitt was our ambassador to France; Wendell Wilkie was the Republican candidate for president in 1940.

sador Gaston Henri-Haye (appointed by Pétain) from France.* I met him and all his attachés. One of the attachés had shot down 25 German planes.

When the Ambassador spoke to us, it was a delicate situation because Hitler's thumb is on him, and he confined his remarks to a plea for food, etc. During questions following the speech, one student exploded: "Everyone knows the glory of France, but how do you explain Pétain's alliance with Hitler?" The Ambassador responded: "The answer is too easy. Your statements are not true." He also said that "Jewish, Communistic or any other 'conflicting' forces in France must be dealt with to preserve unity so necessary at this time."

In contrast, Eleanor Roosevelt's visit impressed us all. She had dinner with us in the student cafeteria, and I wrote: "She spoke to 3,000 students, and was witty, to the point, and interesting. Someone shouted at her if Franklin was going to run for a fourth term. She laughed and said she didn't know, but hoped he wouldn't. When asked what North Carolina girls could do for defense, she said that 60 percent of North Carolina boys are undernourished, and the girls had better learn home economics!"

Less than two weeks before Pearl Harbor, Mother showed remarkable prescience about the Japanese threat, writing: "I wonder if we are on the eve of war with Japan. I do hope that may be averted. I think Japan has bluffed about as long as she can and if she only shows some sense now, it will be best for her. She knows it too, but her old war lords are so war bent." When the Japanese did attack, she advised me to continue my education, while indicating, at the same time, "We are very glad you are ready to serve your country."

On February 28, 1942, I wrote: "Bad news. The University has been selected as a student pilot training center, and soon 1,875 men will take over nine dormitories. I will have to find new quarters." A week later I described the trials and tribulations of that exercise:

> I've been going through hell trying to get a place to live. One place the husband was drunk; in another the baby vomited all over the floor. Many wanted too high rent, and before I could make up my mind, some desperate boy would take the room. Yesterday I went to five places—three had 12 people to one bathroom—imagine! The other two had no single rooms. Today the first place I went to was wonderful, and I took it. I am trying, through all this, to get a "B" average so that I can enter [the University of] Chicago, which is no cinch to get into, especially transferring.

My interest in leaving North Carolina was prompted by the reputation of Chicago's political science department, as well as by a desire to escape the military's impact on life where I was. Chicago finally accepted my application, but as the school year neared its end, I began to dream of becoming a fighter

*Marshal Henri Phillippe Pétain was the German-supported French chief of state in 1940, governing from Vichy the part of southern France under nominal French control after France's defeat by Germany. In November 1942, German troops occupied southern France. Pétain was imprisoned for treason after the war.

pilot and considered enlisting in the Army Air Corps. "With your permission," I wrote home, "I'll enlist as soon as I am 18. You take the physical and mental exams, and if you pass you are placed on reserve and deferred until you graduate from college. However, the major explained that if the situation warrants it, you can be called up at any time."

As it happened, the Air Corps didn't call me at all. After passing all the mental and most of the physical exams required for pilot training, I was found to be red-green color-blind. So ended my dreams of becoming a dashing flyer à la Eddie Rickenbacker.

To help pay for the next year's college expenses, I worked in a steel mill that summer with my brother Paul, who was now studying for the ministry at a Chicago seminary. We cleaned, painted, and assembled corrugated steel igloos for military use, and Paul irritated management by having some success as a union organizer. When he was lucky enough to be injured due to unsafe working conditions, he proceeded to go on workers' compensation for the rest of the season.

In the fall I took a room with a nice young family who lived near the University of Chicago campus. In return for room and breakfast, I fed and maintained their coal furnace and occasionally served as baby-sitter. The shadow of induction into the military was always present.

> *October 8, 1942*
> They tell us the draft age will be lowered, and we should get into some Reserve Corps. I have to get in fast because after November 1, sophomores won't be accepted by any Reserves, but will be drafted instead. I am trying for the Army Enlisted Reserve Corps, and enclose things you should sign and send back to me as fast as possible.

Feeling somewhat isolated because I wasn't living in a dormitory, I joined the Phi Kappa Psi fraternity and ate noon and evening meals at the fraternity house. The strain of trying to continue an education, with the military lusting for my services and my friends fast disappearing, was not lessened by the fact that Congress and the War Department kept changing the rules.

> I'm enjoying fraternity life greatly, and am glad that I joined. One of our members who graduated last year was just killed on Guadalcanal. His wife was heartbroken and, to top it all, her baby died. She is a lovely girl, and the Phi Psi brothers are trying to keep her time occupied so she won't brood too much. I don't believe in war marriages very much.
> I suppose you have seen the new draft bill. From what I read, students can't be deferred beyond July 1943, so I guess I'll be in as soon as the school year ends.

I had met a number of attractive women at the university, but soon zeroed in on the 15-year-old sister of a fraternity brother. Her name was Pat Millar, and her brother Jack was one of my closest friends. Pat had already graduated from high school, but had decided to work for a year before entering college.

Mother was still having difficulty comprehending when and if I was going into the military, and I tried to clarify the situation.

> *November 15, 1942*
> Here is the total explanation of my Army status. I am in the Enlisted Reserve Corps of the Army. This defers me temporarily. According to President Hutchins, we will be called by July 1943, so I should be able to finish this college year. Otherwise I would be drafted earlier, and would go in as a private. This way, when I am called to active duty, I leave for nine weeks of basic training, and then am automatically sent to Officer's Training School, where I can choose my field of specialization. If I don't wash out, I become a 2nd lieutenant, ready for active duty anywhere. That is the entire story.

A few weeks later, the rules were changed again, as was the "entire story." "The Armed Services Representative now says that all Army Enlisted Reserve Corps men will be called up in February or March. I got sworn in yesterday, and then an infantry captain explained two of the Articles of War to us. They had to do with the penalty for desertion—namely, death."

Many university students, including Pat's brother, Jack, soon found that the military was not going to wait until the end of the year to induct them.

> *February 1, 1943*
> My best friend, Jack Millar, has been called into the Army. He leaves in a week. All my best friends here have gone in, or will within a week. I never expected Jack to go so soon, and it was a big surprise to him and his family. They are quite depressed about it, and I will certainly miss him. We've been practically inseparable all year.

Early in February I read some promotional material about a War Department search for men with ski or mountaineering backgrounds to be trained as mountain infantry at Camp Hale in Colorado. Ski troops had already played a major role during the Russo-Finnish War of 1939-40 and in the German invasion of the USSR, with the Russians using entire ski divisions.[3] Millions of American newsreel viewers had seen daring Finnish skiers in white hoods swoop down on Soviet columns, overwhelm them with their skill, and then speed away to safety before the bumbling Soviets could recover.

The recruitment effort was directed by a civilian organization, the National Ski Patrol System (NSPS). Its founder and head was Charles Minot Dole, an establishment Bostonian and a graduate of Yale. He managed to convince General George Marshall of the need for such forces and also persuaded him that it made more sense to make soldiers out of skiers, rather than the reverse.

To guarantee high quality applicants and to convey the sense of an elite unit to which only the best need apply, only volunteers were accepted by NSPS, and each applicant had to submit three letters of recommendation attesting to his skiing prowess and good character.

I was easily seduced by the glamorous vision of schussing across the snow and engaging the enemy on skis. Admittedly, my skiing experience in Switzerland was limited, but it was enough to encourage me to investigate the mountain troops. On February 9, 1943, I wrote to my parents:

> The boys in the Army Air Corps Reserve are being called to active duty on the 18th of the month. Jack Millar left Monday morning, and is at Camp Grant, Ill.
> Rolf Pacek, Tom Mahoney and I are trying to get into the ski troops. We went downtown this afternoon to see a member of the National Ski Association, and our chances seem bright. No great experience is necessary, merely exceptional physical toughness.

My last two months at the university were spent completing paperwork and testing for acceptance into the ski troops, struggling with speeded-up course work, preparing for exams ending the spring quarter, performing my furnace and baby-sitting responsibilities, competing in various athletic events, and saying goodbye to close friends entering military service.

Information that the ski troops offered higher pay than the regular army was one of many false statements emanating from wartime propaganda mills. I later learned to distrust all War Department releases designed to entice young men to volunteer, but at the time I was still naive and taken in by news stories depicting tanned fellows, dramatically draped in white camouflage, climbing sheer rock cliffs or skiing down sunlit trails in defense of their country.

The November 9, 1942, issue of *Life* magazine carried such a story. Entitled "Mountain Troops," its six-page pictorial featured activities of the first volunteers training near Fort Lewis, Washington. Walter Prager—twice winner of Europe's Gold Kandahar ski race and former coach at Dartmouth College—was shown donning a white parka. Others were being belayed with ropes and pitons across ice crevasses and rappelling down rock cliffs. One photo which I should have taken more seriously showed seven ski troopers mounted on mules riding abreast through a gate with a sign reading "Through These Portals Pass the Most Beautiful Mules in the World."

Warner Brothers, not to be outdone in glamorizing this exciting addition to our armed forces, produced a 20-minute movie entitled "Mountain Fighters," and the ski troops were the topic of many other short films. By early 1942, the mountain troops had probably received more media attention than any other U.S. military unit. A newspaper story which I sent home offered some warning of what might lie ahead when it reported: "The ski troops, after 40 days, have to be able to carry a 75-pound pack 20 miles in 8 hours at 12,000 feet above sea level—this while on snowshoes."

Much of the publicity stemmed from the fact that the ski troop recruits

Robert Ellis just prior to induction, 1943.

included many world-famous skiers and mountaineers. Among them were
Torger Tokle, a Norwegian who held most of the U.S. ski jump records; Paul
Petzoldt, one of our greatest climbers, who held the American record for
Himalayan heights; Peter Gabriel, a famous Swiss mountaineer guide and vet-
eran of difficult ascents from the Alps to Alaska; Olaf Rodegaard, the former
head of the Mount Hood Ski School; and Friedl Pfeiffer from Sun Valley,
Idaho, who was to become the U.S. Olympic ski coach.

On March 11, 1943, I wrote that I had been accepted into the ski troops
and quoted the key passage words in the letter sent me:

Your questionnaire for the Mountain Troops is approved. We are asking the Classification and Enlisted Replacement Branch of the Adjutant General's Office to order you assigned to the Mountain Training Center, Camp Hale, Pando, Colorado, for basic training.

Director of Personnel Selection
National Ski Patrol System

I added, "Our military adviser has told us that our date of induction has been moved ahead to April 28th, and that we should receive our orders around April 14th."

What I didn't know was that the army representatives, as usual, had their facts wrong, and my date of induction had been moved up three weeks. I received my orders in the mail on April 6, and, according to the orders, I learned that I was already five days late in reporting for duty. I had no chance to say goodbye to anyone in the family except brother Paul. He saw me off on the train which departed for the nearest army reception center, Fort Sheridan, Illinois.

2

Ninety Pounds of Rucksack

Camp Hale, Colorado, April–October 1943

By April 1943, when I was finally ordered to report for active duty in the army, ski troop training was being conducted at Camp Hale, a facility opened some four months earlier at Pando, Colorado, about 20 miles from Leadville, high in the Rockies at an altitude of some 9,500 feet. The first unit of what later became the Tenth Mountain Division was the 87th Mountain Infantry Regiment, which had spent the winter of 1941-42 in ski training and testing cold weather equipment on Mt. Rainier in Washington. The War Department then decided that this nucleus should be expanded to full division strength by the winter of 1943, and it chose as a training site a narrow, steep-walled basin, crunched like a huge footprint into the Colorado Rockies where they flanked the continental divide.

When work on the camp began in April 1942, Pando was a railroad station, two houses, and an icehouse overlooking a subarctic flat. Nestled in the Eagle River's marshy valley bottom north of Tennessee Pass, it was described in an article published in the *Saturday Evening Post* as "one of those whistle stops that would cause the [train] passengers from behind the car windows to remark, 'Can you imagine anyone *living* there?'"[1] At that time of year, it was knee-deep in slush that froze hard on cold nights, but in winter the average snow depth was about 12 feet, and the temperature sometimes hit 30 degrees below zero. Nearby, the mountain peaks rose to 14,000 feet. Along the edges of the bowl that contained the camp ran U.S. Highway 24 and the main line of the Denver & Rio Grande Railroad. Denver itself was 150 miles away, and it took a good part of a day to reach it by car or train, which greatly reduced a soldier's time on weekend leave. The landscape, though beautiful, was forbidding, the terrain climbing at a sharp angle above the highway and railroad tracks to the Chicago Ridge, a demanding climb often used for training exercises. It was no Shangri-la.

The job of putting together a great military cantonment under immensely

View of Camp Hale from one of the adjacent ridges (courtesy Denver Public Library, Western History Department).

difficult conditions in a swampy river bed nearly 10,000 feet up in the heart of the Colorado high country, was done in a seven-month battle against time and weather. Although it was built to contain as many as 20,000 men, at its peak it never exceeded 15,000.[2] When the camp opened in December 1942, there were two-story, 63-man barracks for the men, corrals for 5,000 mules, and a

200-dog K-9 unit.[3] That the terrain was less than ideal was attested to by a reporter for the *Denver Post* who visited the camp in April 1943. "Its streets are rivers of mud. Its parade ground is a sea of the same.... [It] is not a pretty sight to see these spring days. But its men are. For in no place in this war-torn globe will you find better specimens of physical manhood."[4]

One specimen was still suffering from the shock of his abrupt entry into service. The impact of the sudden loss of freedom and contact with family and friends, coupled with the requirement to accommodate myself to the harsh demands of the military and its many unattractive practices—infantry combat, of course, being the extreme example to come later—were quickly reflected in my letters home.* Many months were to pass before I could even begin to accept the disappointments I was experiencing with some degree of equanimity and live for the moment.

> *Fort Sheridan, Illinois*
> *Thursday, April 8, 1943*
>
> Well here I am. I'm sorry I didn't give you the full explanation but everything happened so fast, I hardly realized what was happening myself.
>
> I got up Tuesday morning to find my orders in the mail saying I should report to Fort Sheridan for active duty on April 1st. It was then the 6th but the orders had arrived too late, having gone to the wrong address. I called the Military Adviser and he said I should leave the next day. So Paul and Pat came down, and we spent Tuesday together. Paul saw me off at the station and I left for Fort Sheridan, arriving last night at 5:30 P.M. Since then I've been going through tests, physical exams, Articles of War, a speech by a chaplain, etc. I got my uniforms today and am getting used to them slowly. I expect to leave here around Sunday if nothing goes wrong, and will go immediately to Camp Hale, Pando, Colo....
>
> Don't worry about me. So far it hasn't been bad, and I'm getting along all right.... It was rough leaving Chicago, Pat, Paul, and all my friends. The two boys who applied with me for the ski troops both failed to go. One backed out and the other received a postcard yesterday saying that the Army was taking no more E.R.C. men into the ski troops. It was a great disappointment to him, and I can't understand why they didn't do it to me. I was the only man called and I guess it is because I joined the ski troops and didn't remain in the unassigned E.R.C.

Two days later I received orders, effective April 12, transferring me from Fort Sheridan, the army reception center, to the "Mountain Training Center" at Camp Hale and authorizing me a travel allowance of $3 per day for food. In my second letter from the service, I reflected the dismay of a new recruit experiencing military anonymity and loss of freedom for the first time.

---

*All these letters, unless otherwise indicated, were addressed to my mother.

Fort Sheridan, Illinois
Sunday, April 11, 1943

Well I haven't left here yet, but I expect to leave tomorrow. This is a completely new existence. It is such a tremendous change that it is difficult to believe that it is real. I almost feel that it is all a dream. I can hardly realize that it is actually me in an olive drab uniform sitting on an army cot. It seems so irrational for me to be here, with no will of my own or freedom of action. It is a great change and hard to get used to.

I am lonely, naturally, and hunger for a familiar face. I called Pat by long distance today, but it only made me feel more uncomfortable and out of place. I'm not homesick exactly. It is just that I hate regimentation and the crushing of individuality. I sleep well and the food is quite good, but I'll certainly be glad when this war is over. Right now I just want to get out of here and get to Colorado.

Dad, you might close up my account with the Mt. Eaton Bank. I only have about $1.41 left there. I think I'll put the money I save into the Army's banking system. I also took out the $10,000 life insurance policy for which I pay $6.50 a month. Almost everyone took one out. Also I am giving $12.50 a month in bonds.

With these first letters, Mother began her practice of sharing them with my brothers and sister, Mother jotting a note at the top of this letter saying: "Margaret—Send this on to Paul. Paul on at once to me again please. It's such a *brave* sweet letter! How hard for Robert this all is. Write to him often."

Paul sympathized greatly with my abduction by the military, but this didn't prevent him from dividing with Edwin what usable civilian clothes I had left behind. I accused the two of them of acting like the sons of Jacob—as described in the Bible—when they stripped their youngest brother Joseph (because they thought their father loved him best) of his "coat of many colors" and sold him into slavery for 20 pieces of silver.

Upon arrival by train at Camp Hale, I quickly discovered what distinguished the camp and the ski troops from all other military facilities and units in the U.S. at the time. These factors included the camp's isolation from all normal human habitation, its extreme altitude, a climate unequaled in severity for snow and cold, the smoke and dust-laden air filling the basin where the camp was located and its impact on our health, its extraordinary physical demands despite the absence of accustomed levels of oxygen, and the high intelligence and education characteristic of its newly arrived volunteers. All the above were described in many letters to come, including the first.

Camp Hale, Colorado
Friday, April 16, 1943

Here I am, finally. The camp is situated in a beautiful valley amongst snow-capped mountains. There are two regiments, the 86th and 87th, totaling about 12,000 troops, and I have been assigned to the 86th regiment.

It's going to be a tough three months of training. The altitude is about 10,000 ft., and you certainly feel it. My nose bled today and everyone here has a cough, some sore throats, etc. The sergeant says you'll probably have a sore throat the whole time you're here. It snows off and on during the day but is very warm at times also. The accommodations are poor. Our beds have no sheets or pillows—only two blankets.

Almost all the men here are college men, and because of the resulting formidable competition, the chance of becoming an officer is pretty slim. The men are almost Herculean in abilities, and need to be. The training is fierce. We drilled almost four hours today in driving wet snow.

It's different from what I expected in many ways. The sergeant says it's every man for himself. If a man falls over beside you because of the altitude and exertion you're not to help him at all. You're not to fall out of rank until you actually fall unconscious. This may sound like an exaggeration, but it's not. Those are our orders. I could say lots more but have no time.

P.S. On Thursday 10 out of 50 men collapsed because of the altitude and exhaustion. It is a grim story.

By the time I arrived at Camp Hale, the National Ski Patrol recruitment activity had attracted enough young men to permit the formation of a second regiment, the 86th, to supplement the 87th, which had trained on Mt. Rainier. And my remarks about the effects of the altitude and the prevalence of coughs and sore throats were not hyperbole. As Frank Harper described it in his book *Night Climb*, "Sung of and cursed at once, Camp Hale was a wild, terrific, terrible place where each year half the men dropped out because of the rigors of climate and exercise."[5] William Johnson, a reporter for *Sports Illustrated*, in a February 1971 article about the division and its training, agreed: "The elevation caused critical problems for many men. Some wobbled about in states of chronic dizziness and nausea; some simply could not catch their breaths."[6]

The coughs, known as the "Pando hack" I soon learned, were mainly caused by smoke from the coal-burning stoves used to heat hundreds of barracks. The smoke blanketed the lower half of the basin where the camp was located, and our only escape was to climb the sides of the mountains (which formed a bowl surrounding the camp) to get above the polluted air. Since the stoves were used almost the entire year around, the Pando hack became our constant companion.

Camp Hale's isolation drew from me the comment in my next letter that "This place is so far from civilization that you get pretty lonely, and feel quite cut off from the world. I don't know when I've felt so far from friends and familiar places. How carefree those hectic college days seem now!" As for the army itself, I added: "I don't know when I've disliked anything so much.... I don't mind the physical discomfort, such as early rising, marching, etc., but I really hate taking orders, and being regimented. I almost like the physical exercise, but the rest is a different story."

I was impressed, however, by the men, whom I described as "top-notch" and being "from all over the world: Switzerland, Austria, Germany, Norway—everywhere." Indeed, before long a battalion was organized at Camp Hale, designated the 99th, which was composed entirely of soldiers of Norwegian

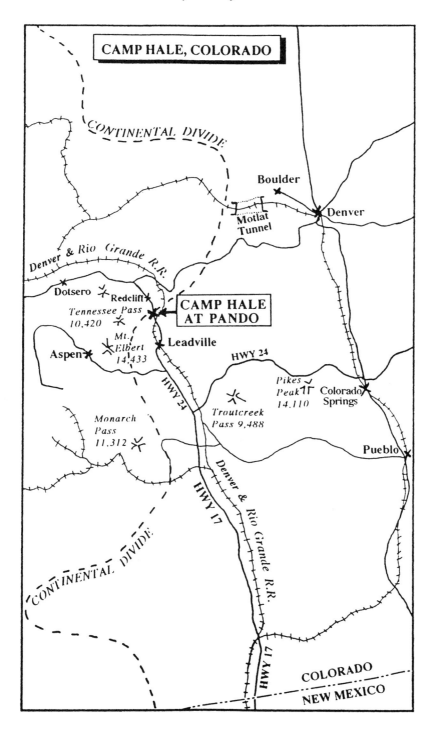

CAMP HALE, COLORADO

CONTINENTAL DIVIDE

Boulder

Denver

Moffat
Tunnel

Denver & Rio Grande R.R.

Dotsero   Redcliff

Tennessee Pass
10,420

CAMP HALE
AT PANDO

Mt.
Elbert
14,433   Leadville

Aspen

HWY 24

Pikes
Peak
14,110   Colorado
Springs

HWY 24

Troutcreek
Pass 9,488

Monarch
Pass
11,312

Pueblo

Denver & Rio Grande R.R.

HWY 17

CONTINENTAL DIVIDE

HWY 17

COLORADO
NEW MEXICO

ancestry. There were other refugees, too, from almost every country in Europe. These included Finns, Swedes, and Danes in great numbers, as well as Czechs, Swiss, Italians, Bulgarians, Rumanians, and Poles. There were also Icelanders, Croats, Turks, and Lithuanians, some Frenchmen, and quite a few Germans.[7] The majority of these—including Torger Tokle, the former Norwegian, who held most world and U.S. ski jumping records—were assigned to the various line companies in the two regiments.

My depressed attitude after the first day or two at Camp Hale was not helped by having to be hospitalized, as I revealed in a letter to my brother, Paul, who shared it with my parents.

US Army Ski Cantonment, Camp Hale, Colorado
Friday, April 23, 1943

Dear Paul,

So far the life here has been Hell. For a few days I thought I'd go AWOL. I got here Thursday night and entered the hospital on Saturday night. I didn't write Mother about my being in the hospital, and I don't think you should tell her. It would just get her worried. I had a temperature of 102° with a bad cough and cold. I got very depressed in the hospital but feel better about my status now, although I'm still in the hospital.

Everyone here has asthma, or rheumatic fever, or colds, etc. Nearly everybody has a perpetual cough. It's quite a life. Actually, I don't know much about the place since I have been sick most of the time.... I may have made a serious mistake by getting into this. There is hardly any chance for advancement, even to a corporal's or sergeant's rank, because the competition is so stiff. The men are nearly all from college, and many are from foreign countries. There is a Norwegian company, and other foreign companies.

The country is beautiful though, with snow capped mountains all around.

Dad and Mother were naturally curious about some of the details of army life at Camp Hale, and Dad was especially concerned about his youngest son being tempted by alcohol and wayward women. Given the isolation of the camp, it was hardly likely that I would find many of the latter running around. Nevertheless, after only one week in camp, I tried to answer their questions and minimize the dangers to my sobriety and virginal state.

Camp Hale, Colorado
Saturday, April 24, 1943

Dear Dad,

To answer Mother's questions, there are around 60 men in my barracks making up my company. We're not allowed out of a certain area for two weeks because of quarantine safety measures, so I haven't seen what the recreation room looks like, but I understand it's pretty nice. We get off after supper, and then we can go to the movies or write letters, etc. We get off Saturday noon until Sunday night. No studying of any sort so far. We get up at 5:45. There is enough reading matter. I don't especially want any food either. We get fed abundantly and well.

Now for your questions, Dad. As for drinking, the Army discourages it tremendously and only .02% beer is allowed in the camp. They are very strict on drunkenness even on leave. One of the first acts when at Fort Sheridan was to give the men information on venereal disease—a movie and a lecture were both required. It was very clear, and the Army is definitely against it. Prostitutes do follow the camps, but few soldiers have either the time or the desire to fool with them.

They have entertainment in the Service Club—billiards, books, etc. I think buying bonds is a good idea. It's a good way to keep myself from wasting too much money.

I am looking into this Army specialized training, but 13 weeks basic training here is required first. My salary is $50 a month. But I won't get paid until May probably.

My reference to army specialized training had to do with a program announced jointly by the secretaries of war and navy on December 17, 1942, under which they would send qualified military personnel for college training in fields needed by the armed services. The army named its activity the "Army Specialized Training Program" (ASTP), with the curricula focusing on medical, dental, veterinary, engineering, and foreign language and area studies. According to Louis Keefer's history of the ASTP, entitled *Scholars in Foxholes* (from which much of the data reported here is taken), the program was strongly opposed by General McNair, commander of the Army Ground Forces. He saw no reason why it would improve a soldier's fighting skills and believed it removed from likely combat units young men most needed there for their intelligence and leadership abilities. Secretary of War Stimson and Army Chief of Staff General Marshall, however, pushed the program vigorously, Marshall going so far as to remind all command elements, in an April 1, 1943, letter, that footdragging in selecting soldiers to participate would not be tolerated. "The number of eligible men recommended for training," he said, "has been disappointing. I desire that every echelon of command support this program and make it a success. I desire further that proper action be taken by you to insure that all in your command are informed of these facts and of the need for wholehearted cooperation."[8]

Camp Hale, Colorado
Thursday, April 29, 1943
This is the first chance that I've had to write for some time. Every muscle in my body is sore from the work I've done during the last three days. I'll give you a short resumé.

Tuesday. Up at 5:30. Breakfast at 5:45. Inspection from 6:30 to 7:00. March over to parade ground and do calisthenics for one-half hour. March back for lecture (1 hour) on military discipline and courtesy. Other lectures on guarding prisoners, etc. Lunch (march over to it) 11:30-1:30. Dig foxholes for practice after a lecture on them. Drill for an hour. Run a mile.

Then supper 5:00. After supper, march two miles and sit on the side of a mountain to observe demonstration of night firing by machine guns (range 1,000 yards) and M-1 rifles, done in the dark with tracer bullets. Really amazing accuracy at a 1,000-yard distance. Also observe a 5-man patrol harass enemy positions with "Molotov cocktails" and submachine guns. Around 9:30, walk back to barracks and take showers to kill the Rocky Mountain spotted fever ticks. Bed at 11:00.

Today we had about the usual morning work but this afternoon we were issued gas masks and instructed on their use. We entered gas chambers, the first time with the masks on. The second time we took them off inside and ran out crying. (It was tear gas.) The third time we went in and put them on inside. The tear gas burns the neck skin and makes you cry, but it was a real learning experience, I assure you. Then we went on a five-mile hike up a mountain and we just got back. My body is really sore.

I certainly do appreciate the letters from everybody. At the end of an exhausting day, it is wonderful to relax with a letter from friends or home and think of the outside again. I'd like them every day if possible. Some days I can't write for they don't give us time, and other days I'm so tired I can't lift a finger so I don't then. So I can't answer everyone's.

Please mail my letters to the others in the family, Mother. I'm so tired right now I can hardly sit up to write this. Sorry about the telephone call. I stood around most of the day, but finally gave up. Better not try to phone me. I'll write later how to do it, if absolutely necessary. I don't know how now.

In addition to testing your ability to put gas masks on when under the stress of gas released in an enclosed chamber, the army would occasionally have someone surreptitiously place an open canister of tear gas in your vicinity when you were outside. The gas was scented to smell like apple blossoms, and I was fooled more than once into happily inhaling and remarking on the delightful aroma before I realized what was happening and hastened to don my gas mask.

Prior to receiving the M-1 Garand rifle, we drilled using birch logs as rifles, stacking them upright in a wooden frame in the barracks at the end of each exercise requiring "weapons." There was always a mad rush when we were ordered to fall out with "rifles" since each man hoped to get the lightest log possible out of the stack. Even after the logs were taken away, some of us, pending the arrival of enough Garands to go around, had to settle for carrying the 30-06 caliber M 1917 rifle (known as the "Enfield" because of its British origin) which had been the standard U.S. infantryman's rifle in World War I. The Enfield, unlike the Garand, which was the first military self-loading rifle to be adopted in more than experimental quantities, required the user to reload the chamber by manually operating the bolt.[9]

A few days after writing that "39 men out of our company of 207 are now in the hospital," I reported that my morale was somewhat improved by the fact that a captain in the Medical Corps had offered me and a few other men with IQ's over 110 and some background in science, the opportunity to enter the medical part of the ski troops. "We finish our regular basic training and then take four months of medical training. He says the chances for becoming officers are good, and that except for the Medics, only one man a month is sent to Officer's Candidate school from this whole camp."

I didn't understand why I had been picked because I had had very little scientific training, but I accepted the offer, provided I was given the option first to enter the ASTP foreign areas and language training program. The possibility of a commission was highly attractive to me and the captain's other naive listeners. Enlisted men in the army who achieved a score of 110 on the Army General Classification Test (AGCT) were supposedly qualified for Officer Candidate School (OCS). My score was 135. Unfortunately, because of the large number of college men at the Mountain Training Center, its members averaged unusually high scores on the test. According to Johnson's article in *Sports Illustrated*, one regiment of the division "had no fewer than 64 percent of its troops ranked at or above the OCS level, and 92 percent ranked above the Army's average score of 91."[10]

The high percentage of company personnel in the hospital was not unusual. Harper wrote that, on the average, approximately half of the men in the line companies were in the hospital, and that as a result, men were typically discharged with a temperature of 100.4 degrees. Respiratory troubles were common, as were illnesses caused by ticks carrying Rocky Mountain spotted fever, numerous cases of high altitude sunburn, and in the summer, injuries caused by lightning strikes hitting troops on high mountain peaks.

Reports of the high rate of sickness and even deaths at the base became public knowledge as early as February 1943, causing a Colorado congressman, Rep. Rockwell, who was concerned about the impact these reports might have on tourism in his state, to query the surgeon general of the U.S. about the matter. This distinguished apologist for the bureaucracy of the day denied there had been any deaths among the troops in training and claimed that there were only the "lesser afflictions" common to a group of men suddenly brought together from various parts of the United States. Echoing this view, Congressman Rockwell told the House of Representatives, "Considering the high altitude and the vigorous exercise necessary to train mountain troops, I think that the health record of no deaths and only minor ailments among the thousands of troops stationed there is remarkable."[11]

Camp Hale, Colorado
Saturday, May 15, 1943
    This has been about the hardest week so far. We've started our series of marches, carrying tremendous packs and rifles. We leave about 2:00 P.M. each day, and get back around 5:00 P.M. We do this three times a week, with each successive march getting a little tougher.
    The other night one of the men had a "respiratory collapse." He had been lying down and I guess didn't get enough oxygen, creating an oxygen debt. He awoke gasping and thrashed around as though in a fit. The

medical officer finally got him quieted down but it was a nervous time for all. We're all a bit on edge and that sort of thing doesn't help. The doctor thoroughly explained why it had happened, and that calmed everyone down. Things like this happen so frequently that we're getting sort of callused to them. For instance a man fell over in ranks the other day—flat on his face. You see or hear of this happening almost every day. Men faint or collapse very suddenly and the hospital is crowded. Fifty-seven men out of our company of 207 are in the hospital right now.

I got my complete ski uniform and all my mountain clothes yesterday. It really looks swell ($850 worth). I am taking pictures of myself and my surroundings, and will send them along soon. I hope they turn out all right. When they are developed, please send them back to me so I can see them. There is no place here to get them developed.

We've been on quarantine since Monday, and are bored stiff by the confinement. I should have written earlier this week, but we've been so busy, and I've been so tired at night, I couldn't do it. You've got to get all the rest you can or you'll be in trouble.

Our training this last week was mainly on rifle marksmanship consisting of the three firing positions, and all the fine points involved in firing this complicated rifle. We won't actually fire the gun for another week, but we study positions and aiming almost three hours a day. Although it's boring after a while, I guess it pays dividends in the end. Frequently we go out about a mile from camp and study field tactics such as arm and hand signals, reaching specified points by compass, methods of attack, uses of camouflage, duties of scouts, etc.

We continue to get our daily calisthenics around 7:00 A. M., rain, snow, or shine. I got a good face burn from the sun when I dug trenches all Wednesday in my light fatigue shirt, while today I almost froze when a heavy snow storm buried us under.

In answer to family questions about my quarters and the camp, at the end of this letter I drew a rough sketch of the camp layout and my barracks "habitat," commenting that we had no sheets, only two blankets (one to cover the mattress), and one comforter. "One room downstairs is used for drying the ski equipment and clothes. The officers sleep in other barracks and eat in a special mess hall. The barracks are wood with 14 windows to a floor and coal-heated.... Denver is five hours away by bus."

Included with the dress uniform, which I later wore on home leave, were ski boots, white gaiters (a cloth covering the ankle and upper part of one's boots, with a strap going around the instep) into which the pants were tucked, olive drab pants, and a light green "mountain jacket" with matching ski cap. The jacket was a very handsome windbreaker featuring four patch pockets, epaulets, and a belt.

The soldier who ran out of oxygen while asleep and then hyperventilated was, like many others unable to adjust to the altitude, transferred to another army unit at a lower elevation. It was generally accepted at the camp that it took about a month to adjust to the altitude before a person could handle any severe physical exertion, but a significant percentage couldn't tolerate even ordinary activities without getting into trouble and had to be reassigned. Why the War Department chose to put a training camp at such a high elevation remains a mystery. Most Alpine passes, as one writer has pointed out, range from 6,000 to 8,000 feet at their highest point.[12]

Calisthenics were conducted on the rocky and barren drill field in the early morning light. It was always a challenge to be ordered to strip to the waist to begin the exercises in those cold dawns, with the temperature usually hovering around freezing and the sun not yet peeking over the mountains. When it rose sufficiently and its rays finally did strike you and provide some warmth to your chilled body, you almost felt human again.

The occasional trains, blowing their mournful salutations on the Denver & Rio Grande Railroad line as they passed by the camp, accentuated the loneliness and feeling of isolation we all felt in our remote site, for they represented one of the rare contacts we experienced with the outside world.

On home leave in dress ski-troop uniform with mountain jacket, gaiters, and ski boots, May 1944.

Thursday, May 20, 1943

Dear "Civilian" Ellises,

I finally fired my rifle today. These two weeks of practicing positions, and today's actual firing of a small bore, light mountain rifle (similar to a 22), have been leading up to firing the Garand on the outdoor range at distances of 200 and 500 yards. If we get a certain score out on the range, we qualify as "expert," and get a medal to hang on our chest. In today's firing of these small-bore rifles I was second high man in the company. The range was 1,000 in. (indoors): 5 shots prone (5 min.), 5 shots sitting (5 min.), 5 shots kneeling (5 min.), 5 shots standing (5 min.), 10 shots rapid fire prone (40 seconds), and 10 shots rapid fire kneeling (40 seconds).

A perfect score is 200; I got 192. I hope I can do as well on the range so I can get a medal.

This afternoon we observed a three-hour demonstration of the different types of demolition methods used by the Army. One land mine blew a jeep body about 400 ft. in the air. It was quite a sight. Although we were about 300 yards away, and were wearing steel helmets, a rock hit one guy on the helmet and really gave him a jolt, denting it way in. The doctor said it would have killed him except for the helmet.

We're going on some night demonstration tonight and probably won't get back until midnight. I don't know what it's about, for you never know about anything in the Army until it actually happens. The rumor is that it's something to do with night patrol action and scouting. I was looking forward to relaxing tonight but I guess that's out....

What about a few more letters from my brothers and sister? Less polishing of the blue star and more writing please.*

P.S. Bob Pastor, the famous boxer, arrived this week for basic training in my regiment.

Bob Pastor, one of the many great athletes who joined the 10th, was a New York native and one of the world's high-ranking heavyweight boxers. He fought Joe Louis twice, the first time managing to go the distance in a ten-round bout, a feat which surprised everyone because Louis had a long string of knockouts in the fights that preceded him. Two fights later Louis defeated Braddock to win the world heavyweight championship. Pastor fought Louis again in 1939, but this time was unable to backpedal effectively enough and was knocked out in the 11th round of a fight scheduled for 20 rounds.[13]

Camp Hale, Colorado
Wednesday, May 26, 1943

I'm in a different Company now—M Co.—and surely miss my friends back in L Co., but so it goes. I'm handling a machine gun now instead of a rifle.

I'm doing everything I can to get out of this new setup. I've applied through the C.O. for the Army Specialized Training Program (ASTP) in languages. I told him I know Syrian, Turkish, and Persian and he said he'd report it to the Post Adjutant. Pray with me that I'll get it for I'm more discouraged now than I've been since I entered the Army. The future looks very black and I hope the dawn breaks pretty soon.

I never appreciated the freedom of civilian life before, but I surely do now. How I long for home and old friends.

ASTP training in foreign areas and languages was aimed at developing trainees for a wide range of assignments with the Ground Forces, the Air Corps, the Military Intelligence Service, the Signal Corps, and the Provost

*It was the custom during World War II for parents with a son (or daughter) in military service to hang a Blue Star, in the form of a standard emblem provided by the government, in a window facing the street. A Gold Star signified the family member had been killed in the service.

General's Department. The last-named department, for example, needed language and area training for officers who would be assigned to duty in the administration and rehabilitation of occupied areas. To qualify for ASTP, a soldier had to score 110 (and near the end of the program, 130) on the Army General Classification Test (AGCT) and for language and area training had to have a "substantial background" in one or more languages.[14] My transfer orders, sending me from Fort Sheridan to Camp Hale, mentioned that my knowledge of foreign languages had been reported to the War Department.

In the letter which followed, I referred again to the .30-caliber machine gun being the weapon to which I was now assigned, and it turned out—much to my sorrow—that its deployment and operation remained my so-called MOS (Military Occupational Specialty) throughout the war.

The transfer, however, introduced me to a new set of friends. One of them, John Horrall, had been a senior at Stanford University, where he had been editor of the *Stanford Daily*, the student newspaper, until his induction into the army a few weeks earlier, and we became inseparable. Other soldiers assigned to the company came from every walk of life imaginable. One was the Swedish technical adviser for Metro-Goldwyn Mayer motion picture studios in Hollywood, another was a skater in an Ice Follies troupe that traveled all over the U.S., while a third was a reporter on a small-town Massachusetts paper.

Although it was now June, I found that summer was not terribly evident at our high altitude camp, and I wore long woolen underwear until the month was well underway. I also found that small cuts for some reason did not heal quickly. I'd had some for three or more weeks.

Camp Hale, Colorado
Thursday, June 10, 1943

There is an undercurrent of excitement here, as the threatened European invasion could mean rapid changes for the mountain troops. We have two main regiments—the 87th and the 86th. The 87th has been here for a long time, and is moving out now. They'll probably go overseas in a few weeks. Several men from my barracks and from M Co. were transferred to the 87th. Luckily, I wasn't among them, so I guess I'll be here for a while.

My hopes have risen again for Army Specialized Training because I know my name is up for consideration. I made sure of that by checking on it again at the Personnel Office, and the clerk said he'd do everything he could for me.

It was quite chilly here this morning; in fact I had to wear my wool mittens. It certainly is strange to hear you talk of such unbearable heat, but even in this cold I stay sunburned because the air is so dry.

I guess I'll get my chance to fire on the range after all, as we go on the range next Monday. I certainly would like to get a marksmanship medal. It helps on your service record.

I got a wonderful picture from Pat yesterday. A large crowd immediately gathered around when I unveiled it. It's a beautiful picture of her.

The 87th Regiment was actually headed for Fort Ord, California, where it underwent weeks of training in amphibious landing assaults preparatory to embarking on one of the most unusual invasions of World War II, the attack on the American-owned island of Kiska in the Aleutian chain, which had been seized by the Japanese in 1942. The Army General Staff estimated that there were probably about 10,000 Japanese dug in there who were well prepared to defend the island to the death, as they had the nearby island of Attu, another remote fragment of American territory they had occupied.[15] There they had taken advantage of the atrocious Aleutian weather, characterized by continued gales, rain, and fog, to wage a bitter and fanatical struggle against the American 7th Division before being finally overcome. (Eight Distinguished Unit Citations were awarded components of this division in recognition of their heroic deeds in recapturing Attu.)[16]

The attack on Kiska was launched on August 15, 1943, two battalions of the 87th making an unopposed landing on the southern end of the island; the following day another battalion hit the northern beaches. As it happened, most of the Japanese had been withdrawn some weeks before and a small holding force was evacuated by submarine the day before the landings. Nevertheless, the impenetrable fog, combined with the planned strategy of having battalions of the regiment attacking from opposite directions in the mountainous and desolate terrain, led to fire fights between these units which resulted in some 28 men being killed and 50 wounded by "friendly fire."[17] It was not a happy introduction to combat for those elements of the mountain troops unlucky enough to experience it. It also led to the composition of a cynical song by those same troops. The chorus, sung to the tune of a well-known GI ballad, went, "No Japs at all, no Japs at all—they gave us an island with no Japs at all!"

After the capture of Kiska, the 87th spent another five months there in training before returning to Camp Hale. The climate was ideal as a testing ground for winter warfare troops, boasting some of the worst weather in the world as well as hilly terrain and impossible mud.

Those of us in the 86th Regiment who remained at Camp Hale continued mountaineering training, which included demanding climbs bearing 90 pounds or so of rucksacks, as well as weapons and other military gear, up the precipitous slopes of the peaks which surrounded us. In one letter, I said: "We hiked all afternoon way up into the mountains. It was a beautiful climb—the mountain sides were lush with spring wildflowers. We climbed through the deep shade and quiet of the dense pine forests on and up over green mountain meadows until we reached the top—10,800 ft. up. It was quite a climb with our tremendous packs. I longed for the camera to record the terrific vistas of long valleys and snow-capped mountains. I'm enclosing some Rocky Mountain mint picked on the way."

One of the favorite 10th Division anecdotes arose out of an incident— possibly apocryphal—which dramatized the extreme physical demands made on its soldiers, not only by the 100 pounds of equipment they had to carry in order to survive and fight in the mountains, but also by the fact that they had to do so at altitudes where Army Air Corps regulations called for pilots to turn on their oxygen. According to the oft-repeated story, a pilot was bringing his bomber into the Pueblo, Colorado, air base after dark. Turning on his transmitter he intoned, "Number 15 to Pueblo. Number 15 to Pueblo. Coming in at 8,000 feet. Coming in at 8,000 feet. Gliding. Gliding. Over."

The pilot flipped the switch to receive, but instead of the dispatcher he picked up the tired and slightly bored voice of a radio operator, with a New England twang, attached to a 10th Division unit in the mountains near Camp Hale. Imitating his intonations, the ski trooper responded, "Sugarloaf Mountain patrol to 10th Division headquarters. Sugarloaf Mountain patrol to 10th Division headquarters. Coming in at 12,000 feet. Coming in at 12,000 feet. Walking. Walking. Roger."

In the latter part of June, after having been in the army for more than two months, I finally got a weekend pass to Colorado Springs. My companions were my Stanford friend, John Horrall; Bill Luth, formerly a Ripon (Wisconsin) College student, who was later killed in Italy; and Tim Tyler who had been attending Williams College in Massachusetts.

Alta Vista Hotel
Colorado Springs, Colorado
Sunday, June 20, 1943
It was absolutely wonderful to get away from camp and its interminable routine for a few days. You get a claustrophobic feeling that it's impossible ever to get out beyond that ring of mountains. But we did it, and I must say we've had the grandest time just laughing and talking and walking in the parks and on the avenues. It's a beautiful resort town and would be a great place to spend a real vacation.

John Horrall, Luth, Tyler and I drove down with another fellow and his wife. They were very nice and we sang fraternity and popular songs all the way down. It was a breathtaking drive, with a huge full moon coming over the Collegiate Range as we drove.

I bought odds and ends I needed—forest green overseas hat with sky blue piping, collar holders, black silk tie, etc. I look fairly classy in my uniform now, with all my insignia on and fittings done. Tomorrow, *at last*, we go on the rifle range. I hope the weather stays good for we'll be on the range all week. We take our food with us and just fire all day. I'll probably get a *real* sunburn this time.

John started payments on an engagement ring here yesterday. His fiancée-to-be just graduated from Stanford, and read the speech John had written to the graduating class. He was Class Historian—she Secretary. He was certainly dying to be there but it was not to be. A great comic and a great fellow, he is one of the finest friends I have ever had. I wish you could meet him. We two are the only boys in the company with split lips from the intense dryness, and for some strange reason, that seems to amuse everyone.

My next letter may have to wait a few days, for the week ahead is going

to be very busy. My turn for KP comes up this week and that really takes
it out of you. You get up at 5:00 and work without a break, except for food,
until 8:30 at night, which is a good long day; some 15 odd hours of hard
dirty work. No sitting down and lazily peeling potatoes as is pictured in
popular magazines. It's scrubbing floors, washing dishes, cleaning, etc.

How John Horrall ended up in the mountain troops was a story that
caused endless hilarity. According to him, when he was at Stanford he had been
accepted for training as an army engineering officer and was traveling by rail
from California to the Officers Candidate School (OCS) at Ft. Belvoir, Virginia, when his orders were somehow lost and he was directed to detrain at
Camp Hale. This turn of events came as a great shock, since John had no great
love for skiing and no interest in any other form of athletic prowess.

Although his story stretched the imagination, there were too many army
"snafus"—to use the GI expression of the time—to dispute its accuracy.* It was
also conceivable that the army might discover its mistake and send orders
transferring John to his proper place of duty. He clearly lived this dream, and
we shared it with him. Whenever a solitary messenger was seen approaching
the company during the ten-minute breaks from training or other activity, John
was convinced the right orders had arrived and invariably predicted that he
would soon be bidding us all a fond farewell. For a time we, too, believed the
impossible might occur, but as the months passed by, the hope faded and in
the end only the joke remained.

Because of his journalism training, John was asked to write articles for
the camp newspaper. One he wrote was about the training activities and men
of our Company M, which included Lt. John Litchfield, one of America's great
skiers, formerly on the staff of the Sun Valley Ski School; Pvt. Clarence Knapp,
who had been a rookie with the Chicago Cubs; Pvt. Jack Kelly, a professional
boxer and former member of the Notre Dame freshman football team; and Pvt.
Anthony Bergsen, who had served as a lieutenant in the Austrian army before
coming to the U.S. Our commanding officer was Lt. Otis Halverson, who was
later killed in action with the 85th Regiment in Italy.

John ended his article with this anecdote: "Following Lts. Halverson,
Dolby and Briggs over one of the more rugged trails in the nearby mountains,
the company found itself back in time one afternoon for retreat. As Sgt. Rogers
called the company to attention, men began falling over like ducks in a shooting gallery; the toll was six red-faced and embarrassed men. But that doesn't
happen any more. Conditioning is doing its work now."

Mother believed in supplying me with food treats, despite the army's
very satisfactory provisions, and one of her packages arrived two days after my
birthday on July 3. "I got your cake last night; it was delicious. John, Bill Luth,
and I snuck it away to our ski room. There with some food of Bill's (it was his

*SNAFU was the army's acronym for "Situation Normal All Fucked Up," while the initials GI,
in World War II parlance and since, are simply an abbreviation for "government issue."

19th birthday yesterday, too) and the cake, we really had a feast. We ate half the cake, and then I took it into the barracks and let the others finish it off. They all said it was *really* good. They sang 'Happy Birthday' to me in great harmony, and we had a lot of laughs."

A few days later I described one of the more unpleasant duties I was about to be given.

Camp Hale, Colorado
Thursday, July 8, 1943
From now until next Thursday is going to be a very interesting, if nerve-wracking, time for me. I've been assigned to guard prisoners for one week. It is really a tough job. If you slip up on anything, allow them to escape, etc., you are subject to court martial. We were instructed all afternoon on how to handle them. Some of us have dogs with us on sentry duty and we were also instructed on how to handle *them*.

We carry double-barreled shotguns or pistols. It's a risky situation, for some of these prisoners are tough, and I'm afraid I'm not used to making anybody toe the line at the point of a gun. It certainly will be no game, in fact about the most serious thing I've ever done. If a prisoner escapes, YOU serve his sentence. If you are careless, lax, ignorant of your orders (and there are plenty), or make any mistake of that sort, you are subject to court martial or company punishment.

It is called "prisoner chasing," and is supposed to be an honor, but it's an honor I'd gladly do without. A week is a long time for that kind of duty, but there's no way to get out of it—it's just a part of Army unpleasantness. Most men do it only once while they're in the Army, so probably I'll never do it again.

Whether the army actually would have made us serve the sentence of a prisoner if he were allowed to escape is questionable, but at the time we all believed it. For this reason we had to convince our charges that we were no pushovers, and yet we quickly learned (as I supposed all prison guards soon do) not to treat them so harshly that they would seek retribution. This was a difficult art form at best. There were a multitude of ways in which they could make trouble for you, and the army was quick to attribute the blame to you, so the stress brought on by the assignment was considerable.

Camp Hale, Colorado
Tuesday, July 12, 1943
I'm beginning to feel like Warden L. E. Lawes of Sing Sing, I've been guarding prisoners so long.

I was a witness at an intensely interesting procedure last night. It was the court-martial of a boy of 17. I was the guard so I got to hear the whole thing. The boy had lied about his age, had joined the Army, and had then gone AWOL for two months. He was very immature and undisciplined, but seemed to come from a nice family. He had studied architecture at the University of Washington.

I felt sorry for the lad, but the Army is short on compassion. I tried to advise him on what to say before he went into the courtroom, and advised him to play up the youth angle for all it was worth. This he did and managed to get off with a lighter sentence than most of the men. He got three months at hard labor and two-thirds of his pay taken away each month. You can see that the Army doesn't fool around. The only thing they're interested in is whether you're guilty—not your own personal problems or reasons for your misdeed.

In July our status was changed by the army to a true division, the 10th Light Infantry Division (Pack, Alpine), consisting of some 13,000 troops, including a third Infantry Regiment, the 85th. "Light" divisions were planned as all-purpose divisions to be employed under any conditions where relatively little equipment would be carried. This would save shipping space and avoid the need for special refitting of standard infantry divisions. Such divisions were designed for mountain, jungle, airborne, or amphibious operations where they could rely on attached pack mules, native bearers, gliders, or landing craft, respectively. In addition to the 10th, another specialized division authorized in June 1943 was a jungle division known as the 71st Light Division (Pack, Jungle). It was built around the 5th and 14th Infantry Regiments, which had already received jungle training in Panama.[18]

To fill gaps in the ranks of the 10th, recruits with no ski training or particular experience in the outdoors were transferred to the division from other army units. In addition, many career noncommissioned officers, who had been stationed (of all places) in Hawaii, were sent to Camp Hale to help complete the cadre of the division. It was a particular shock to these senior-grade sergeants to be required to master the skills of mountain warfare in a climate which would challenge a polar explorer.

I was afraid that the formation of a new regiment might possibly send me to another unit again and wrote, "Transfers are beginning to take place, with 14 men from Co. M leaving for the 85th tomorrow. I'm hoping against hope that John, Bill, Jud Decker and I will stay together but we probably won't. This is the hardest part of Army life—leaving your friends—for they are what keep you sane. When friendships break up you're truly bereft, and there's no alternative but to put up with it." Letters from home, I said, were about "the only tangible thing in all this confusion," and I mentioned that Pat wrote "such good, cheery letters" that "I know her now better than I ever did."

My fears came true, as it turned out. I was transferred to Company F of the 85th, which with a few absences remained my home for the rest of the war, while John was sent to another company in the 86th, and Bill Luth and Jud Decker (another close companion, who had been attending Princeton) were sent to Companies E and A, respectively, in the 85th.

Even at this early date my hopes were that the invasion of Western Europe would come soon. I cheered when British Commonwealth and American troops invaded Sicily on July 10, 1943, and hoped that Italy would give up. Mussolini was in fact overthrown when the Fascist Grand Council turned against him, and he was imprisoned. German paratroopers rescued him in a daring raid, however, and he became head of a puppet government under German protection in northern Italy.

In F Company I asked to be a machine gunner, reasoning that if worst came to worst and I saw action with the company, I'd have a powerful weapon in my hands. I wrote Mother that the company was "really a rifle company but every company has a machine gun (handled by four men), so I'll be going to a machine gun school now for two weeks." Actually, every rifle company had two machine gun squads in their so-called "weapons platoon," which also boasted 60mm mortars. What I failed to recognize was that, while the machine gun could deliver a high rate of fire on the enemy, it impeded one's movement in combat because of its weight and it would also be a preferred target of answering fire from artillery and mortars.

In August my minister brother, Paul, and his new wife, Mary Elizabeth, who were now living in the West, came to see me at the camp and we drove into Denver for the weekend. Paul, like his grandfather, the Rev. Edwin Ellis, had agreed to serve in his first pastoral assignment as a Sunday school home missionary in a primitive area, Paul's headquarters being the village of Claunch in a remote region of New Mexico. This visit from family members, one of only two I experienced while in an army camp, did wonders for my spirits.

Still hoping that I might be accepted into the ASTP, I wrote on August 19 that "I was told to report before the ASTP board tonight, but they postponed it until tomorrow night. Anyway, I was excited for a moment and still am on tenterhooks. I just pray that after this long wait they won't refuse me, which seems likely. So many men here speak so many foreign languages that the chances of my being selected over them seem pretty slim, but we'll see." Parenthetically, I went on to say: "I fire the machine gun for record tomorrow. I hope I do well. It's been a long week. The General watched me fire yesterday, and told me that good machine gun firing is essential to the success of the 10th Division. He seemed like a nice man—very weather beaten and grim though."

As it happened, the next day turned out to be one I would never forget—in fact the happiest one I experienced in training stateside.

Camp Hale, Colorado
Saturday, August 21, 1943

Well I suppose you know the great news from my telegram. It was the luckiest day by far that I've had since Uncle Sam took me over. Thursday night I was told to report with two other men from my company to the ASTP board. Then, in typical Army fashion, they postponed it until Friday. So the next day dawned, and there my story begins.

We were firing the machine gun for record, Friday, so we went out to the range around 6 A.M. As you know I've been in a regimental school for all the machine gunners in the 85th Regiment. We've been training for about three weeks now.

Well, lo and behold, on the range your mild-mannered son fired 237 out of 256, making the highest record score of anyone in the school and, therefore, of the regiment of 4,000 men. The head of the school, Major Koeber, came over and congratulated me warmly, and said that the Colonel (commanding officer of the 85th) would hear about it. He asked me not to destroy my targets, for he wanted to show them to the colonel. All the officers congratulated me on my top score—even the chaplain.

I was quite surprised and very pleased, for 60% of the men didn't even qualify. 180 constituted a grade of "2nd class" gunner; 200 constituted "1st class" gunner; and 218 "expert" gunner (the highest qualification). There were only three men who qualified as "expert" gunners. One man got 220, the other 222, and I was the third with my 237.

One man claimed that the Colonel would probably send me to machine gunner's school at Fort Benning, Georgia, where I would take the officer's candidate course. However, this brings me to the second part of my big news.

Friday night I went for the ASTP interview. It was held in divisional headquarters, and about 30 men were there from all over camp. Our names were called off, and we were interviewed one by one. I was about fifth in line.

First I saw a captain who checked my qualifications regarding college education, age, and credits. Then he marked "O.K." on a slip of paper, and sent me into another room where I was interviewed by another captain. I told him a little about my college studies and about my life in the Army. All the time I was at my military best: my shoes were beautifully polished; I was wearing a borrowed "clean" shirt and my full dress uniform; and I was clean shaven, and had just had a haircut. I saluted smartly, snapped out my answers, and in every way tried to make as good an impression as possible, although I was very nervous. I'd been waiting a long time for that moment.

Well, to go on—this second captain put another O.K. below the first, and sent me on to the lieutenant colonel (the Inspector General of the camp). The man before me was refused by this lieutenant colonel so I was quite tense when I walked in. We discussed—or rather he fired questions at me about—what I hoped to do in future life, why I wanted to study in ASTP, and why I picked "languages and foreign area study." I reeled off a line, for I knew this was the big test. Suddenly he began firing questions in French at me. I managed to keep my wits about me, and was able to answer him in French satisfactorily. I spread it thick about my life in Persia and my one-time knowledge of Russian, Syriac, Persian and Turkish. Finally he said, "Well, Ellis, I'll recommend you for ASTP training, but you must realize that you can fail later on in college." I said, "I realize that, sir." Then he said, "All right, you've qualified." I stood up, saluted, said, "Thank you, sir," and walked out about the happiest soldier in the Army.

I'd waited so long for that moment, that I could hardly believe it had finally arrived. I've never tried so hard for anything in my life, and those final interviews were certainly stressful. I've felt a little sick today—probably just nervous reaction. So ends the story of my lucky day, August 20, 1943.

I don't know when the order to leave camp will actually come through. It might be tomorrow, it might be two or three weeks yet. I'll first go to a "STAR Unit," which is some college where they give you a great many comprehensive tests in every known field.* Those tests and interviews

---

*Because some of the first trainees who were assigned to colleges directly from army camps were found to be unqualified, all trainee selection was shifted to certain colleges designated as Specialized Training and Reassignment (STAR) units, where panels of professors supposedly performed the screening.

will probably last for a week or two. Then I'll be sent to some college or university to study. Where, I don't know. They say you can request a certain school to study in, *but that doesn't necessarily mean that they'll send you to that school.* There is always the chance that I'll be found unqualified at the "STAR Unit," but I think once I'm that far along, they won't drop me.

Hope you got the telegram all right. Pat telegraphed back her congratulations.

P.S. This is the big chance I've been waiting for: the opening into my chosen field. I'll be studying just what I would after the war. It's the ideal setup: my field will be languages and foreign area study. Isn't it perfect in every respect? A free education in the specialty I want to pursue. Thank God for this. You can imagine how pleased I am. Life has a purpose and meaning now, and I'll work like I never have before.

During the weeks which followed, I had little time to contemplate what I hoped would be my early return to the academic life because we were living in the open, practicing field tactics both night and day, and then "crawling exhausted into our tents and sleeping bags at night."

Camp Hale, Colorado
Saturday, September 11, 1943
This is the first chance I've had to write for quite a while. Still no transfer orders. I'm writing this in a tent high up in the mountains. A candle on my helmet furnishes the light. This is certainly the rugged life.

The bivouac was tough, but we all survived. The camping area was quite high up, and it was as cold as I've ever been for any length of time. In the mornings the tent would have a sheet of ice inside due to perspiration plus evaporation from our breathing collecting inside the tent and freezing. It would warm up around 10 o'clock.

There were about 200 of us sleeping in two-man tents. During the day we would have field problems. One problem had a company of our men theoretically pinned down by enemy fire on a ridge in front of us. Our job was to fire over their heads and wipe out the enemy. I actually had a lot of fun firing my machine gun at targets about 700 yards away on the mountainside, but my gun broke down before the problem was over, and I couldn't get it fixed in time to fire any more. I hope that won't happen in real combat.

Another day I volunteered to carry mortar ammunition in order to watch the mortars being fired. Although the ammunition was the heaviest load I've ever carried, the demonstration of mortar fire was very interesting.

I also fired on a combat course with my rifle. As you walk through the forest, suddenly targets shaped like a man spring up. It tests your reaction speed, etc.

I fired a machine gun in a demonstration before the rest of the battalion. It consisted of an attack by some rifle squads on my machine gun position, which was protected by four rifle men and myself. The colonel said afterwards that it was the best demonstration he had ever seen, including those at the Fort Benning Officer's Candidate School.

> We came back down to camp Thursday night, and did it ever feel good
> to sleep in a bed again!

Much effort was expended at Camp Hale and earlier to select the proper
equipment for the ski troops, and much testing of the equipment chosen was
conducted in the field. For the first time, climbing ropes made of nylon were
used, and a number of America's mountaineering techniques were also initiated at Hale.[19]

Advice was sought from many experts in cold weather operations and
polar exploration, including Vilhjalmur Stefansson, who led a number of expeditions to the Canadian and Alaskan Arctic regions between 1913 and 1918,
and Sir Hubert Wilkins, who not only accompanied Stefansson on one of his
expeditions, but also led an Antarctic expedition and was even more famous
for his air explorations in the Arctic and Antarctic. Ome Daiber, a Seattle-
based mountaineer who was a cofounder of organized mountain rescue operations in the U.S., worked on the design of our packs, clothing, mountain tent,
and even a mitten with a trigger finger. Brad Washburn, one of the few men
to have climbed 20,300-foot Mt. McKinley in Alaska, one of the coldest places
on earth, helped in the final testing of equipment. Malcolm Douglass, a dog
team driver and assistant meteorologist in the 1940 Byrd expedition to the
South Pole, enlisted in the 10th and became an instructor in skiing and dog
team operations.

Disputes raged over such items as skis, ski bindings, snow shoes, boots,
waxes, sleeping bags, rucksacks, ultralightweight tents, collapsible camp stoves,
dehydrated food, parkas, mittens, socks and other underclothing, how to build
igloos, and motorized snow vehicles versus dog sleds, to name but a few. A
tracked vehicle we called the "Weasel" was developed for the 10th. A forerunner
of the snowmobile, it was painted white and used as a cargo carrier. Sleeping
bags filled with goose down—consisting of both inner and outer bags—met
severe tests of minus 40-degrees-and-below temperatures, and white felt boots
called "Bunny Boots," if not subjected to wet snow, were a delight for frost-
bitten feet in the arctic temperatures experienced at our high altitude camp
sites.

Since the mountain tent fabric, unlike present day Gore-Tex and similar
materials, would not permit the passage of air and moisture, we soon learned
not to touch the sides on arising in the morning if we were to avoid an ice
shower. We also learned to bring our boots and any clothing into the tents at
night if we expected them to be at all pliable in the cold dawns. Occasionally
a daring soul, who was either genuinely deranged or a superb actor, was willing to violate these rules and undergo the harshest of conditions in trying to
qualify for a discharge under Section 8 of the army regulations. Section 8
authorized separation from the service of the mentally ill, but it took some
doing to convince the authorities of your case.

One private in our company, whether we bivouacked in falling snow and

Igloo-making instruction from Arctic explorer Vilhjalmur Stefansson, Camp Hale, 1943 (courtesy National Archives).

below-zero conditions or in more hospitable weather, would strip naked in the open at bedtime, hang all his clothes carefully from nearby tree limbs, place his boots and socks just outside the opening to his tent, and climb nude into his sleeping bag. In the morning—and we usually arose well before dawn—he had the unenviable task of emerging bareassed and barefoot from his tent and trying to get into icy clothing which had turned stiff as a board during the night. He eventually disappeared from our midst but, to our great disappointment, we never learned whether it had all been an act or not.

Others who I came to believe were equally unhinged, if not certifiably demented, were those who, after climbing impossible slopes all week while carrying the proverbial 90-pound rucksacks as well as weapons, would go hiking up the same mountains on weekends. I could excuse those who invited some of the few WACs stationed at Camp Hale to accompany them because I assumed they might have other diversions in mind besides scaling the nearby peaks. As for the rest, evidently their choice of climbing instead of other alternatives, even a weekend pass, surprised another 10th Division trooper, Francis Sargent, who later rose to become the governor of Massachusetts. As quoted by William Johnson, Sargent said he never could understand why "half of the sonuvaguns in the outfit would rather go climb some rock than go down to town and look for booze and broads. I remember thinking it was the damnedest

A "Weasel," ancestor of the snowmobile (courtesy Denver Public Library, Western History Department).

thing for soldiers to act like that. But, of course, when the 10th got a few drinks under their belts they'd go into their hotel-climbing act, which no other outfit could top.* And there never was anything wrong with the 10th when it came to girls, come to think of it—not once they came down the mountains and got their skis off, anyway."[20]

*He was referring to the habit of some troopers of exiting a window of the hotel where they were staying and either climbing up or rappelling down several stories of the brick exterior.

Mountain tent with vent hole, Camp Hale.

Camp Hale, Colorado
Sunday, September 19, 1943

The war seems to be going pretty well, and we're counting on the Russians to break through. The view here is pretty optimistic, with most people—officers included—thinking it will be over by this time next year. I hope they're right....

We went through divisional battle courses this week that were harder than anything we've done up to now. In an infiltration course, we crawled flat on our bellies for 100 yards through barbwire, shell holes, trenches, mud, and sand, and all the while machine guns were firing live ammunition 18 inches above our heads, and half sticks of dynamite were blowing up all around us. It was quite an experience. You begin to grasp some of the reality of war in a situation like that.

About 300 German prisoners were brought here the other day, and we see them being taken here and there in trucks, closely guarded of course. They look quite healthy and wear the hats of Rommel's Africa Corps.

The German prisoners of war were from the Africa Corps and were not only healthy but were considered incorrigible and eager to escape. They were incarcerated at Camp Hale to make such escapes less likely, but their presence led to one of the more sensational stories of romance and collusion (which amounted to treason) between U.S. soldiers and Nazi war prisoners which occurred during World War II.

In March 1944 the army revealed that five WACS stationed at Camp Hale had been writing secret romantic notes to the prisoners of war, as well as having other friendly exchanges, and that four male American soldiers had been charged with helping two of the prisoners escape in an attempt to reach Mexico. One of two Americans caught with the Germans on the Mexican side of the border was Private First Class Dale Maple of San Diego. Maple holds the dubious distinction of being the only American soldier in the history of this country to have been convicted of the army's equivalent, under the Articles of War, of the civil crime of treason. A 1941 graduate of Harvard, where his academic achievements earned him a *magna cum laude* citation and Phi Beta Kappa membership, he had organized and led the escape effort. What prompted him to undertake such an action in time of war, and how he went about it, was the subject of an absorbing 1950 four-part *New Yorker* profile entitled *Annals of Crime: The Philologist*, by E. J. Kahn, Jr.[21]

Maple had no connection with Germany by birth or heritage, his parents being of English and Irish origin. But at Harvard, where he went on a full scholarship after graduating first in his San Diego high school class, he breezed through his courses, finally concentrating on comparative philology—the study of linguistics—with an emphasis on German. And there he became increasingly identified with the Nazi regime. After being pressured to resign from the university's German Club for offending everyone by singing the Horst Wessel and other songs associated with the Nazi regime at meetings, he was interviewed by the daily *Crimson* and quoted as saying, "Even a bad dictatorship is better than a good democracy." The day the Japanese bombed Pearl Harbor, he even had the audacity to call the German Embassy in Washington asking if he could accompany their diplomatic staff back to Germany if, as seemed likely, the U.S. declared war on Germany. He was told the request was premature.

In February 1942, Maple enlisted in the army. Both the army and FBI, however, had been maintaining files on him, and he was eventually assigned to the 620th Engineer General Service Company. This was one of three segregated units, totaling some 1200-1500 soldiers, who were not allowed to bear arms and were given jobs of a menial and nonsensitive nature such as grading landing areas, making camouflage nets, or digging ditches.

Maple's unit was eventually shipped to Camp Hale. There he managed to contact the German prisoners housed in the stockade near his quarters, and on one occasion, he even went so far as to spend a three-day pass dressed in an Africa Corps uniform inside the German compound. While there, he convinced some prisoners that he could get them out of the camp and on their way home.

The common interests of the prisoners of war and the 620th company soon came to the attention of ski troopers in the 10th Division who, in addition to engaging the American turncoats in acrimonious debate at the service club, also occasionally vented their anger by beating up on some of the same soldiers. This was not surprising because there were many refugees from Nazi aggression who had fled to the U.S. and joined the 10th to help free their homelands. Maple, however, was not deterred, and after purchasing a four-door, 1934 Reo sedan and other provisions for the trip, he helped two of the Germans escape from a work detail. The three eventually managed to get to Mexico, crossing the border some 60 miles west of El Paso, Texas. There they were picked up by a Mexican customs inspector and eventually turned over to the FBI.

Maple soon confessed and was arraigned on the civil charge of treason. The army minimized the publicity given to its blunders, which, in addition to sloppy security, included not having reported the absence of the prisoners of war for more than 24 hours after the escape. (Kahn wrote that "the administration of Camp Hale at that time was not strikingly efficient.") Since Maple was a soldier, the civil authorities had to defer to the army, and the latter took control of the case, initiating a general court-martial composed of what Kahn described as "probably the highest-ranking panel of officers in American history to sit in judgment on an enlisted man."

The panel tried Maple for desertion, which, under the 81st Article of War, is the closest equivalent to the charge of treason. Maple, and later three of his associates from the 620th, were all convicted under the same statute, and Maple was sentenced to be hanged. Two of the other three soldiers involved received life imprisonment, while the third was sentenced to five years. The romantic WACs were subsequently sentenced to serve terms in the guardhouse ranging up to six months.

At that time, no U.S. citizen had ever been sentenced to death for treason, and President Roosevelt commuted Maple's sentence to life imprisonment.* In 1946, the army reduced his sentence to 10 years, and Maple was later released and went into the insurance business in California.

Despite my forthcoming transfer to the ASTP, the army in its infinite wisdom decided at this point to recommend me for noncommissioned officers school training. Since ASTP regulations required that I be broken to private first class when I entered the program, NCO training and its accompanying promotion (assuming I completed the three-week course successfully) made no sense. Accordingly, I asked to be excused from the course but was forced to attend anyway. While the course was very demanding and competitive, I admitted enjoying some of its required exercises, remarking in one letter: "I drilled a company yesterday. At first I was quite nervous but soon felt perfectly at home, shouting commands and seeing the men jump. It was quite a thrill."

I was equally upset by the army's refusal, using the excuse of my forthcoming move to the ASTP, now that it suited its purposes, to grant the furlough due me which I hoped to use to attend my sister Margaret's wedding. She was about to marry a North Carolinian, Bill Moore, who then was the manager of a North Carolina textile mill and later during the war managed the Fairchild Aircraft plant in Hagerstown, Maryland.

*In 1951, Julius and Ethel Rosenberg became the next persons to receive such a sentence. In 1953 they were the first to be actually executed, in their case for supplying Russia with atomic secrets.

As I waited for my orders, winter neared.

Camp Hale, Colorado
Monday, October 11, 1943
   Our first snow started about a half hour ago. It's really pouring down
and must be an inch deep already. Boy, will I be glad to leave this scene,
despite its beauty. Men who have been in the Army 15 to 20 years have
told me that never in their Army experience, in camps all over the States
and in various of our island bases, have they ever been in a worse station.
They say Camp Hale is the worst post they've ever seen, and I believe it.
During the summer it's dust and smoke that fill the valley; in the winter
it's abnormal cold, wet, and still the same smoke. Well enough of that.
   This is my last week of NCO school. I've been recommended for corporal, and believe they'll tell me today or tomorrow.

Pat had now been accepted at Oberlin, a private college of outstanding
reputation in Ohio, and was heading there for her freshman year shortly. I told
Mother I wished she would get to know her better. "She's pretty independent
and has strong ideas, and I admire that," I said. "However," I added, "I'm not
getting serious about marriage or engagement for a good four years at least."

Camp Hale, Colorado
Sunday, October 17 [1943]
   This bivouac was with other members of the non-com school. We
packed mules, and then led them up to our bivouac area. That was a new
experience, getting mules up those mountains. Once those animals get
going, it's all you can do to keep up with them. I just hung on to one of
the belly straps, and let my mule pull me most of the way.
   My tent partner and I fixed up about the best tent spot I've ever slept
in. We had little mountain stoves (one for two men) on which we cooked
our mountain rations. The food we got was this famous dehydrated stuff
like milk, cereal, beans, potatoes, etc.* It's very good—all you do is mix
water with it.
   I'm not officially a corporal yet, but my recommendation is in our
major's office going through channels. It's merely a formality and it ought
to get through the various offices by Thursday. Since I'll be broken to a
PFC before I go to ASTP, I may be a corporal only for the impressive time
of two or three days. Who cares, as long as I'm out of here?
   We had a divisional parade here yesterday. It was the official forming
of the 10th Division with the presentation of the colors, a speech by the
governor of Colorado, and a huge display of might by all the mountain
and ski troops of the U.S. I marched in it with my regiment, and we were
reviewed by our commanding general, Major General Jones, and Major
General Hall, commander of the XI Corps. It was quite a spectacle and
lasted about four hours.

One of the pleasures we experienced at Camp Hale, one which recruit-
ers never spoke about, was the care, feeding, and handling of army mules,

---

*Some mountain warfare experts recommended 6,000 calories a day for an active man, although
10th Mountain rations specified 4,000 to 4,500 calories.

eugenically bred at Fort Reno, Oklahoma, and elsewhere into awesome size (some stood 16 hands high). They were delivered to the 10th to transport artillery and supplies in the mountainous terrain. As noted earlier, Camp Hale had approximately 5,000 of these mules, as well as a 200-dog K-9 Unit. The mules typically carried 100-pound loads on top of saddles which also weighed about 100 pounds, but I always thought that, given their apparent size and strength, their packs were disproportionately light when compared to ours. For this reason my conscience was always clear when, unbeknownst to any officer or non-com nearby, I would try to grab the mule's strap and (staying clear of those dangerous rear legs) let the animal drag me up the steep paths. The mules, of course, did not appreciate pulling this extra weight, and complained mightily, striking out when the opportunity arose.

Even loaded, a mule would climb up a mountain faster than a man, but would descend more slowly, exercising care as to where it would place its feet and trying to lessen the shock of the load by taking short steps. The army field manual on "Mountain Operations" advised us that we should walk beside the animal's head on the downhill side of a slope or along the edge of a cliff because "The mule has an instinctive tendency to walk on the inside edge of the path as far from the downhill side as possible."[22] Clearly, this demonstrated the mule's intelligence in getting the soldier leading it to assume the greater risk, and they could add to your troubles in other ways. For example, if they sensed you were about to tighten the belly straps which held their saddles on, they would immediately expand their stomachs, giving you the impression all was tight and orderly until the loads began slipping off when they later relaxed their extended muscles.

A particularly memorable duty was being assigned to clean out the hooves on the animals' hind legs. To do this, you would face to the mule's rear and attempt to raise his foot between your legs to get access to the underside of the shoe with a pick. The mule, naturally, did not like being forced to stand on three legs, and if you attempted to pick one up, he would simply lean more heavily on that foot. The secret, we learned, was to surprise him by suddenly striking him sideways with your shoulder, thus throwing him off balance, while at the same time lifting his leg. Unfortunately, this technique did not always work, and if he chose to lash out with the leg you grabbed, you could experience a form of free flight you would never forget. Needless to say, when this happened, it caused some outbursts of profanity, even from a missionary's son.

Late in October I was promoted to corporal but, as expected, retained that rank for only one day because my orders sending me to an ASTP STAR (Specialized Training and Reassignment) unit—in my case located at the University of Nebraska in Lincoln—finally arrived. I telegraphed home the good news, indicating that I expected to be there for a few weeks at the most, taking all sorts of classification tests, language exams, personal interviews, etc. If I passed all those hurdles, I would be sent to another college or university for the foreign area and language training.

Unhappily, my hopes for the final training—I even dreamed of the possibility of being returned to the University of Chicago—were never realized. But in the meantime, at Lincoln, I luxuriated in my release from the Arctic atmosphere and extraordinary physical demands of life at the army's Mountain Training Center, especially now that winter had begun to make its presence felt.

3

Off to Heaven and Back to Hale

University of Nebraska to Camp Hale,
October 1943–June 1944

University of Nebraska
Sunday, October 24, 1943

Talk about heaven, compared with Camp Hale this is it. It all seems like a dream these past few days. Leaving the cold barren wastes of Camp Hale and coming to this green college campus is quite a change.

We get a Class "A" pass which means we can go into town every night. Reveille's at 6:15 A.M. instead of 4:30. Just being down here where you can breathe again, and feel a little autumn warmth in your bones after so many months of cold, is best of all.

We arrived Friday night, got settled in some nice dormitory rooms, and began to pick up information about the system. On Saturday we had a tough psychological examination lasting about two hours. I'm by no means in the ASTP even though I'm here, I find. I'll have another exam tomorrow—a language aptitude exam—and following that an exam in French. If I do quite well in these, then I go up before the so-called "STAR Board" composed of a colonel and two majors. They decide whether my language aptitude is high enough, and whether my actual knowledge of French and the Army's needs coincide. Many men are being refused by the STAR Board, and sent back to their former camps. Acceptance won't be easy for me, for most of the men here were born in Europe and really know their languages. Also most of them know two or three, while I only speak one and I'm forgetting that fast. I'm counting on my former knowledge of Turkish to pull me through, and if that fails, then I'm sunk and back to Camp Hale I go. I don't even want to think about that, but guess I should prepare myself.

If I pass, I'll probably be here for four or five weeks waiting for my next transfer orders to the college where I am to train. I ought to know the outcome by next Friday.

Just called Pat; it sure was swell to hear her voice after almost seven months.

My delighted reaction to my change in circumstances from Camp Hale to Lincoln, Nebraska, was shared by others who left infantry units for various colleges. Zaro Calabrese, who later went on to study Italian at Lafayette, where he bunked with Frank Church, a U.S. senator-to-be from Idaho, wrote home the first day from the STAR unit, at what is now Auburn University, to say: "I don't believe it. This place is beautiful. Miracles never cease. I never dreamt army men could enjoy the kind of living that goes on here. It's better than paradise!"[1]

One of the many foreign-born students in the ASTP unit at the University of Nebraska was Godfrey (Jeff) Ettlinger, a fellow of German origin, who spoke good but heavily accented English. Jeff and I shared quarters and became good friends. When I met him again some 50 years after the war ended, he recounted with much good humor the hazing to which I had subjected him. One of his most vivid memories was of my gleefully questioning both his patriotism and understanding of American democracy, telling him early in our relationship, "Ettlinger, you are obviously lacking in American background."[2]

As for the quality of the "STAR Boards" made up of army officers, one ASTP candidate at the Georgia State Teachers College STAR described being tested by "officers who looked like they were drawn from the bottom of the Army's talent bank."[3] Fortunately, those who examined me, if not incompetent, at least were easily misled.

> *University of Nebraska*
> *Wednesday, October 27, 1943*
> The long struggle is over. Six months of effort, aiming for one goal, have finally brought fruit. I passed the exams with high honors, according to the "STAR Board" of officers, and passed their interview also.
> Yesterday afternoon, after *two full days* of nervous waiting in an outer room for my name to be called, I was called up before the Board. It consisted of three lieutenants, one captain, and one lieutenant colonel. They told me that my psychological exam grade had shown high ability, my language aptitude exam grade was very high, and my French exam grade was tops. Next they asked me a little about my life—where I learned Turkish—and then brought into the room a Frenchman to test my speaking ability. To my own amazement, I managed to control my nervousness and converse easily with him. Anyway, he finally turned to the board and said "Why, he's good." What a relief!
> Then they tried to figure out how to test my Turkish ability. It seemed that an Armenian who worked in the bookstore knew Turkish, so they told me to return this morning, when they would continue the interview with the Armenian present. Now I was really nervous, since I had emphasized my Turkish ability more than I could defend, worrying that my French might be too weak to get me through.
> Anyway, the Armenian and I appeared this morning. He asked me some unintelligible question and I sat there dumfounded under the eyes of the whole Board. Suddenly the idea came to me: why not give him some of his own medicine, and at the same time show the Board that I wasn't bluffing. I knew "*bileram* " meant "know," and I knew "*Turki dili*" meant "to speak Turkish," so I said, "See if you can understand this: '*Bilera Turki dili?*'" Luckily he couldn't understand it and I leapt at the chance to

explain to the Board that he spoke the dialect of Turkey, and I spoke that of Persia.

The Armenian and I agreed on the numbers fortunately (*"bir, iki, ouch* [1, 2, 3]," etc.) so that further convinced them that I knew what I was talking about. Then I said to him—forming the line of the familiar song as though it were a question—*"Tabriz dan chukanda ?* [When I left Tabriz]." This naturally stumped him and before long the Board was firmly convinced I knew how to speak Turkish, and that I knew all about the Near Eastern peoples and their problems.

After I'd gone to all this trouble, they informed me that I had passed the board purely on my fluent (?) French, and that the Turkish ability was simply of added importance in determining what I should study. They said that they didn't know what language or field I would finally study, but that my French was so fluent I wouldn't have to take any refresher courses, which is quite unusual. Then the lieutenant colonel said, "Well, three of the officers here want you to work with them in their offices and Lieutenant Cummings has won out." So until my orders arrive sending me to my college for training, I'm going to be working as a clerk and advisor on college credit systems, transfer technicalities, and as a specialist on technical [questions] that arise in the office on relationships with the college men here.

I've never been so amazed in my life to get such a job as this right off the bat. I've certainly had my share of good luck the past few weeks. I ride down town every morning in a command car, am dropped off at the University of Nebraska Museum of Natural History where the offices are located, and am picked up at night. I feel almost like a business man.

My classification is "Advanced Languages and Foreign Area Study," and when my orders arrive I'll study at some college for *9 months*—a free education in my chosen field. What bliss! I have no idea when I'll leave here. It all depends on when the term opens and what courses they want me to take. I don't know where I'll be sent. In the meantime, I'll just work here in this office I guess.

It's certainly a delightful life. A nice college campus with plenty of dates and even my own fraternity on campus, although truthfully, I'd rather get out and start studying. I've been so lucky in getting out of Camp Hale, and even more lucky since I've been here. Of course it's still the Army, but the Army, I find, can be vastly different depending on where you are. I only wish the friends I left at Hale could be here to enjoy all this. They really deserve it.

P.S. The food here is of the best—*wonderful*. I've gained 12 pounds in one week. Can you imagine?

The ASTP interview by the STAR Unit officers and the surprise involvement of an Armenian bookseller to test my Turkish combined to make severe demands on my acting, if not my foreign language, ability. I had forgotten virtually all the Turkish I used to know except for a few swear words I had heard in the streets, the numbers from one to nine, and lines from a few songs we learned as children. If it had not been for the fact that the Azerbaijani form of Turkish, known as "Turki," was a different dialect from that spoken in Turkey, I might well have had my bluff called and been returned to the joys of winter in Pando, Colorado. Instead, I was at least temporarily assigned to a major university campus occupied by thousands of lonely coeds bored to tears by the departure into military service of virtually all males of interest.

> *University of Nebraska*
> *Sunday, October 31, 1943*
> Another week in this heaven of bliss. I still can't get used to it. I work in the office all day long, and keep up the morale of the coeds at night. The girls here are really wonderful to us. They're all pretty lonely, I guess, and they outnumber us at almost every dance. It's quite a change from Camp Hale, I assure you.
> There's really nothing much to say. I work surrounded by hairy mammoths and dinosauri, as the office is in the Natural History Museum. The job is boring but not hard, especially when every night is free and life is civilized—i.e., no sleeping on pine needles high in the Rockies with snow blowing in your face.

My delight over the disproportionate numbers of women versus men on campus was shared by other ASTP trainees. E. James Judd, a student at the University of Wyoming who was later sent as a replacement to the 10th Mountain Division in Italy, said there were some 2,500 women on his campus but only about 260 ASTP men. Charles McCaskill, who ended up at the University of Nebraska, not in the STAR unit but as a basic engineering trainee, agreed with me that the loneliness of the female residents was a situation that had to be corrected. He told Louis Keefer, "The University's male population was at a very low ebb when we arrived, and the ASTP kids moved in to help fill the void. Sororities had tea dances where boys and girls could meet, and many of us ended up with steady girl friends."[4]

When Mother wrote asking whether I was dating different girls or only one, I responded that in the 23 days I had been there, "I've had around 16 dates and I haven't dated the same girl twice.... Also nine of the girls were from different sororities. All of them were nice but ordinary, and I am settling down now to one girl. She rings the bell as far as I'm concerned."

One of the reasons this new love, whose name was Iva Foreman, rang my bell could have been that she owned a brand new, fiery-red, Chevrolet convertible. That aside, she was beautiful, and we had much fun together.

In December when John Horrall, claiming fluency in Spanish, arrived to join me in the ASTP, I got him a date for his first night in Lincoln with one of Iva's sorority sisters, a girl named Joey Huntsinger, who he acknowledged was "a sensational coed." To attract Joey's interest, I told her John had played for Stanford in their 1941 victory over Nebraska in the Rose Bowl. Joey, however, had heard lines like this before, and after introductions at her sorority house, she shocked John by producing a program from that game and remarking, "I don't see your name here. Did you play in that game?" John, while not athletically nimble, deferred to no one in speed of repartee, and responded "I was injured." Joey, who had a forgiving heart as well as a sense of humor which rivaled even John's, refrained from questioning him further. The two hit it off and joined Iva and me in our convertible outings as we began to sample the various delights offered in the capital of Nebraska.

To keep amused and occupied during business hours, when not in class, I began working in the paleontology department of the museum. There I removed the prehistoric bones of horses and other animals from casts and wrote the family that "wearing something like an intern's jacket, ... I look like a specialist in Mesozoic fauna."

Discipline at the STAR unit was nothing like that in the ski troops, but they did expect you to be back in bed by a certain hour, and for a time we had "a maniac of a captain who suddenly decided that we weren't looking soldierly enough" (which was no doubt true), so he permitted no absences from our quarters after duty hours for an indefinite period of time. In a later letter I was pleased to report his departure and told of a narrow escape I'd had.

Author in olive drab uniform at University of Nebraska.

University of Nebraska
Monday, March 6, 1944

Our disliked captain left today for a P.O.E. (Port of Embarkation), and we're all hoping he gets bitten by every mosquito in the South Seas.

I had rather a hectic night Saturday. I went out with three other fellows on a triple date. We got separated, and I just got back in time for lights. They were not in so as the "bed checker" came along with his flashlight I was in their beds. The moment he passed by I jumped out and ran to another's bed, just getting under the covers in time for the bed checker. It was touch and go for the beds were in different rooms, but I managed to get away with it, although I barely got to my own bed in time. It saved their necks, for otherwise they would have had to stay in for seven nights as punishment.

Recent arrivals from Camp Hale said the thermometer was now staying at 15 degrees below zero and the snow was from six to nine feet deep in the valley. Walter Winchell, at the time America's best-known radio newsman, told his listeners in a broadcast, "Mothers and fathers of American soldiers, if you have a son in the Solomons or Camp Hale, don't worry about your son in the Solomons." John Horrall said he had frozen his fingers and his nose before he left, and had no yearnings to return. Unfortunately, his Spanish was not as fluent as he claimed, and to the dismay of both of us, he was sent back to Camp Hale shortly after Christmas.

Over the next three months, the ASTP authorities kept introducing new standards that you had to meet if you were to remain in the program. It all stemmed from the fact that there was a shortage of ground troops in Europe, largely because of the number of occupational deferments granted and the exemption of fathers. Almost five million men had been deferred for occupational reasons, and Congress was under great pressure to save more than 200,000 prewar fathers from the draft. In late January 1944, an Associated Press release stated that the ASTP numbered about 140,000 students and the navy program about 60,000 trainees, so the total number of personnel in both programs appeared to match the number of fathers who might face induction.[5]

One of the first changes made after my arrival was that students had to have at least two years of college, their AGCT score had to be over 120, and they had to speak at least one language "fluently." I qualified on two of the three requirements, but had to do some fast talking to convince the Board that, while I had not finished two years of college, I had amassed as many credits as the average student had at the end of his sophomore year.

In January the standards were raised again: your AGCT score now had to be 130 or higher and your foreign language proficiency had to be virtually native because they had now decided you would get no language training at all—only foreign area study, and that for only three months—at the institution to which you would be sent. Again, I managed to escape being returned to the dreaded American "gulag," Camp Hale, because my AGCT score was 135 and language testing was not to be undertaken until I arrived at my assigned university. To improve my chances, I spent my days studying French grammar, reading French language works in the library, and attending a two-hour French discussion class (where only French was spoken) three times a week.

It was particularly upsetting when some 25 of my fellow students were sent off to my old school, the University of Chicago, to begin engineering studies. I was even told by Pat's brother that ASTP men were being housed in my old fraternity house. Finally, in late January 1944, after months of uncertainty and rumor mongering which kept us continually on edge, we learned that the end was near for those in language and area studies. Jeff Ettlinger, my friend with the German background, told me many years later that he will never forget my words when I first heard the news. "You greeted me, while lounging on the lower bed of the doubledecker bunk, with: 'Ettlinger, we have been shafted!'"[6]

In a letter home I said, "It's obviously an attempt by Congress to get the fathers' vote in the coming election." The decision, I continued, "is so utterly absurd. There are so many fathers in the Army anyway that I don't see why they hesitate. Three out of the seven men in my room are fathers. They'll draft them eventually, of course, but that will be after the election, when ASTP is dead and buried."

I predicted I would be sent back to Hale and was bitter not only because the NCO rating I had earned had been taken away, but my participation in the ASTP would end as well. I wrote, "I'll probably go overseas as a private, which is about as terrible a thing as I can imagine."

I was also concerned that if I were returned to the ski troops, I would not be in the proper physical condition to perform my duties effectively.

> I wouldn't say that I'm fat but I'm not in anything like the condition I was at Hale. The day I got my orders to come here, I hiked back to camp from an all-night problem in the early morning. Since the members of my squad were maimed in one way or another, and since I was feeling particularly rugged that morning due to a feeling that something was about to happen, I carried 115 pounds of pack for the eight miles back to camp. That included my full pack and the entire machine gun. Heaven knows I couldn't come close to doing that now. That really required six months of physical training and acclimatization.

Admittedly, I had a selfish interest in not wanting to go back to Camp Hale, especially in the middle of winter, but the ASTP did have a sensible purpose. Foreign-language training sponsored by the navy, for example, was instrumental (among other accomplishments) in helping to break the Japanese code, a feat which vastly improved our knowledge of their planned military operations in the Pacific. And in contrast to the army, the navy did not curtail its program. Its chief of naval personnel explained: "The urgent need for technically trained young officers continues, and the colleges and universities participating in the V-12 Program are doing a splendid job of producing such officers."

My accusation that congressional politics were largely responsible for the army's decision to end the program was not far off the mark. Congress had heard from many parents whose sons were in combat; these parents believed the ASTP men were rich kids being given preferential treatment. Some student songs joking about the program, including the following one, sung to the tune of "My Bonnie Lies over the Ocean," may have reached congressional ears and would not have helped the ASTP cause:

> *Some mothers have sons in the Army,*
> *Some mothers have sons on the sea,*
> *Take down your service flag, Mother,*
> *Your son's in the ASTP.*[7]

Secretary of War Stimson, in his autobiography published after the war, wrote that the ASTP issue came down to "whether it should be continued at the expense of further drafts of fathers, deferred workers, and other civilians." In the end, he said, the choice lay with Congress, not the War Department, and, as a result, "The Army of early 1944 was forced to cannibalize itself, and the soldiers of the ASTP were among the first victims."[8]

Apart from the impact of the deferment policy, what also lay behind the decision to end much of the ASTP program was that the army's personnel system virtually broke down because of errors in planning. In late 1943 and early 1944, projections of infantry and other ground force replacements made early in the war fell short of what was actually needed. According to military historian Roger Beaumont in his study *Military Elites*, "in a frenzied search for manpower, the Army turned on its *crème de la crème*, those highest scorers on the Army General Classification Test, sent to college for special training." These individuals as well as air cadets and others in whom the army had invested much expensive training, were now to be used as "infantry fillers." Since such replacements typically suffer extremely high casualties, Beaumont described the entire affair as having the flavor of "bureaucratic insanity, à la Franz Kafka and Lewis Carroll, a perversion of the selection process."[9]

My statement that going overseas as a private would be a terrible thing was clearly hyperbole, but also reflected how little I knew about rank and its correlation with injury or death in infantry combat. In the infantry, being a corporal or even a captain offers only the questionable pleasure of commanding the less fortunate—not an increased likelihood of emerging unscathed from battle, as I would learn in due course.

The end of ASTP for most of us came on February 19 with the receipt of a telegram transmitting a message from the secretary of war. The telegram said the program would be reduced by April 1, 1944, to 35,000 trainees consisting mostly of pre-induction students and advanced medical, dental, and engineering groups. The secretary's message went on to say that we had been assigned to the ASTP "because it was felt that the courses of instruction scheduled would materially increase your value to the military service." Now, however, "to break the enemies' defenses and force their unconditional surrender, it is necessary to hit them with the full weight of America's manpower." Because of this "imperative military necessity, most of you will soon be ordered to field service before the completion of your normal course" and assigned to the Army Ground Forces for duty. The secretary, however, tried to comfort us by his assurance that "your intelligence, training and high qualities of leadership are expected to raise the combat efficiency of those units" and that "thousands of ASTP trainees who have already been assigned to field service have set high standards for you to follow."

Put more simply and bluntly, what Secretary Stimson was saying was that except for those of us who might have come from the paratroops or other high priority units such as the ski troops, most would be sent overseas as infantrymen to replace those wounded or killed in battle.*

There was a real manpower crisis in the European theater of operations. General S. L. A. Marshall, the noted combat historian, stated that it was caused by a magnification of the role of the machine in war while minimizing the need for a well-trained infantry reserve. Military policymakers argued that we should concentrate on air power and armor, almost to the exclusion of infantry. As a result, he wrote, it forced us in the European theater of operations "to become the first army in modern history to undertake a continuing and decisive operation without the shadow of an infantry reserve." By August 1944, he said, the situation had gotten so bad that, two months after the invasion of Normandy, there were actually no replacement infantrymen ashore in France and ready to go into battle. This governing condition continued until the end of the year, despite the reassignment of most ASTP personnel to the infantry, and made some of the commanders in the Ardennes fighting in late December hesitate about attempting any counteroffensive against the Germans. The threat of defeat finally impressed higher authorities sufficiently that they retrained some of the surplus manpower assigned to the Air Corps and antiaircraft units as infantry reenforcements.[10]

Robert Dole, who later became a senator from Kansas, Republican majority leader of the Senate, and a candidate for president of the United States, was one of those who arrived overseas as a replacement infantry lieutenant and was sent to the 10th Mountain Division. He was promptly severely wounded in action. Let us hope that he "raised the combat efficiency" of his unit before being struck down and did not serve simply as cannon fodder for the random artillery and mortar barrages that characterize modern war.

Mother, hoping to save her youngest son from just that fate, had dreams of getting me into medical school, or even into the Air Corps if I could overcome my color blindness by taking vitamin A. Similarly, many ASTP students were using whatever family connections they could exploit to end up some place other than the infantry. This I believed was justifiable for, as I wrote, "In the Army it's a case of helping yourself as much as you can, for no one else cares, and they seem to do their best to quench the fire of patriotism you have when you enter."

One of those who managed to escape the fate destined for the rest of us was Gore Vidal, who became one of America's most prolific and popular writers. He, like Henry Kissinger, the future secretary of state who attended Lafayette, was an engineering student. Anticipating that the program would soon end, and not liking engineering anyway, Vidal purposefully flunked out in November 1943. Then, according to his own account, he used his "considerable family influence" to avoid becoming, as he put it, "cannon fodder" and

---

*My friend Ettlinger was sent to the 44th Infantry Division and ended up fighting in France, where he earned a battlefield commission, one of the most respected decorations for valor in combat.

ultimately ended up as first mate on a Transportation Corps vessel working out of the Aleutians.* His original group, he said, "was nicely slaughtered" and, he added, "I never regretted my own ability to survive."

Ed Koch, destined later to serve as the mayor of New York, was less fortunate. He had been a student at Fordham for six months but ended up in infantry combat in Holland with the 104th Infantry Division.[11]

One of the people Mother approached for help was the chancellor of Stanford University, Ray Lyman Wilbur, brother-in-law of the Rev. William Shedd, the missionary who died in Urumia while shepherding refugees fleeing the invading Turks. Chancellor Wilbur had quite a responsible position in the ASTP, serving on the so-called Army Specialized Training Division Advisory Committee along with the heads of nine other major universities.

Chancellor Wilbur responded to Mother's request for help by using some of the sophistry employed by the secretary of war. "It is quite clear that the Army has suddenly found itself in need of leaders and has made the discovery that a large percentage of our young leaders are in the Army Specialized Training Program. It may well be that the success of your son with a machine gun and Garnad [sic] rifle will be considered more important that anything else he can do at the present time." This was not a suggestion that gave comfort to a worried mother.

On March 17 the bad news came at last. I was being sent back to Camp Hale that night. I wrote Mother that I was trying to take the whole thing philosophically but found it rather difficult. "I never really believed that I would end up with a job as a machine gunner in an infantry regiment. But it looks now as though that's going to be the only answer. Thank heavens I took some pains to do the job right when I was there, or I might really be in a tough spot. It's not a very thrilling or important job is it, but I guess I can do it as well as the next man."

Louis Keefer's history of the ASTP found that most displaced participants were dispatched without regard for the preferences of receiving units, with about 70,000 sent to Ground Forces and another 15,000 to Service Forces. Of those sent to divisions making up the former, virtually all assigned the students to their infantry components. The Signal Corps and the ski troops, however, apparently asked to have back all the men they had previously relinquished to ASTP training, and this is what accounted for the order to return me to Camp Hale.

Thus ended my connection with the program and my brief escape from the rigors of mountain troop training. As Secretary of War Stimson said in his postwar book, *On Active Duty in Peace and War* (co-authored with McGeorge Bundy), the final choice was "between specialized training and an adequate combatant force."[13] It was obviously a program with good intentions, but

---

*Vidal's grandfather was a U.S. senator from Oklahoma and his stepfather was also the stepfather of Jacqueline Kennedy.[12]

it was badly mismanaged largely because the War Department (unlike the navy) seemed unable to define the ASTP's real objectives. As the *Washington Post* editorialized shortly after the end of the program was announced, the army should have anticipated the need for combat replacements before the ASTP was launched. "All in all, it would appear much better for the Army never to have launched the program in the first place than thus abruptly to abandon it."[14]

My indignation over the entire affair was shared by most trainees who ended back where they started. As one questioned by Keefer put it: "ASTP left me with a very disillusioned attitude toward the military and the government. Why did we cull out the most intelligent people in the military service and then throw them into the meat grinder where they would sustain the highest casualties? After some 40 years, I still think of some of the brilliant young men I knew who were sacrificed."[15]

That many ex–ASTP soldiers lost their lives or suffered terrible wounds is confirmed by many sources. One, James Warren, director emeritus of the Museum of History and Industry at the University of Washington, tells of five close friends from the Pacific Northwest, all 18 or 19 years of age, who had been taking engineering training at Los Angeles City College and had promised each other to have a postwar reunion. After their unit was disbanded and they were sent to various infantry divisions, he was the only one not killed or wounded. "Clair Cullen from Portland was killed on Okinawa while rescuing a wounded friend.... Ed Webb of Eugene was killed while on a patrol behind German lines. Tony Breidenbach of Seattle stepped on a German mine and lost a leg. Al Fretwell of Bremerton suffered frozen feet in Belgium and spent months in Army hospitals." Warren himself went overseas with the 42nd "Rainbow" Division and was captured by the Germans. He came home 45 pounds lighter, thanks to a starvation prisoner-of-war diet.[16]

As it happened, the army couldn't have chosen a worse time to return me to Camp Hale. During the winter, men of the division had been brought to the peak of physical fitness through countless forced marches, mountain climbs, and ski and rock climbing training. There had been numerous tactical exercises involving companies, battalions, and regiments, and now—a week after my arrival—the division was scheduled to begin five weeks of maneuvers in the open, simulating war conditions in the dead of winter. All my old friends were now staff sergeants, I wrote, and I was greatly concerned about my lack of conditioning. Nevertheless, taking Dad's advice, I said, I simply try to "live from day to day." As a result, I found, "It's amazing how each succeeding disappointment seems a little easier to shake off, until now I feel as though nothing could bother me."

Early on a Sunday morning in the last week of March 1944, with the temperature 30 degrees below zero, some 12,000 men (including the 87th Regiment now back from detached duty in Kiska) left their barracks on skis and snowshoes, with heavily loaded mules, for four weeks in the open on what became known as the "D-Series" maneuvers. Military historians now say this exercise held by the 10th Division was probably the most intensive and demanding set of maneuvers in American military experience.

My introduction to it did not begin all at once. Upon my return to Camp Hale and my old Company F of the 85th Regiment, I was given a variety of unpleasant assignments—the last of which was a week of KP—as punishment for having had the temerity to obtain a transfer to ASTP. As a result I escaped the first week of D-Series, which was fortunate because it provided a little over two weeks for me to try and adjust to the altitude again before being subjected to the usual physical demands of the ski troops, much less the kind of maneuvers now being conducted. On the other hand, the kind of work I was given was not doing much to improve my physical conditioning. When I was finally ordered to join the company in the field and I strapped on the rucksack for the first time since my return, its weight came as a rude shock. This weight on maneuvers included a tent, sleeping bag, rations, extra clothing, felt boots, and a rifle or a machine gun barrel and/or tripod, all of which amounted to some 90 pounds. It was this back-breaking load which earlier had inspired someone to compose one of our favorite satirical ballads, "Ninety Pounds of Rucksack," to the tune of "Bell Bottom Trousers." The song, in its last verse, sung by an embittered barmaid impregnated by a skier, advised:

> Never trust a skier an inch above your knee.
> For I trusted one and now look at me—
> I've got a bastard in the Mountain Infantry.
>
> *Chorus:*
> Singing ninety pounds of rucksack, a pound of grub or two,
> And he'll schuss the mountains like his Daddy used to do.

My next three letters home consisted of hastily scribbled postcards, the first dated April 5, saying I was leaving in one hour for maneuvers but that I was coming back in a few days for my furlough, which would start on April 1. (My brother Paul and his wife, Mary Elizabeth, were going to come up from New Mexico, and we would drive to our parents' home in Ohio together.) In the second card mailed on April 8, I apologized for my mistake and reported that my commanding officer now said that I must stay through the end of maneuvers. In the third, sent four days later and consisting of about five lines, I said I was going through "the toughest thing by far I have ever experienced … no sleep, cold, wet, and just had my first food in 24 hours," but that I was still healthy and that I would try to write a real letter in a few days when we would return briefly to camp. I now predicted that I would come home on furlough "*for sure* around the 28th."

The division maneuvers, as Harper described them in *Night Climb*, confused both the umpires and the commanders.

> As a game of war, it was an utterly confusing spectacle even to the umpires.... Most confused were the commanders. No one really knew the

exact location of company and platoon. Whole battalions got lost for days. The standard radio sets didn't work properly in the mountains. If the regiment didn't know where the battalion was, it couldn't send supplies. Thus, instead of tactics being tested, it was a test of how much hardship a ski trooper could take.[17]

I confirmed that the hardships had indeed been severe when I finally got a chance to describe them.

Camp Hale, Colorado
Saturday, April 15 [1944]
I can say with little hesitation that I have just emerged from the worst physical ordeal of my entire life. It's a long story and I had no chance to write so I'll have to tell the high points now.

As you remember I got here on a Saturday. I was on various details until a week later when the maneuvers began. Not having quite enough equipment, I remained in camp the first week, and was on KP all the time. Our first sergeant got back on the 1st, got together the needed gear for me, and out I was sent into the field. Then began the real horror. The packs were almost unbearably heavy and on top of that I had to carry a pistol, machine gun, and snow shoes. They would have three- or four-day problems during which we would eat only K rations and were on the alert all the time.

Easter weekend was the worst. Saturday night we started on a march on snowshoes and skis through snow that was up to our waists. We hiked until 1:30 A.M., then crawled into our bags and fell asleep exhausted in the snow. We were awoken at 4:00 A.M., and had to pack in a snowstorm. (It snowed every single day we were out.) We then started on a brutal climb to outflank another regiment. To top it off, combined with our lack of sleep, empty stomachs, and extreme cold, the snow became a blizzard. For four hours we climbed in that blizzard. Finally soaked clear through, completely exhausted, and almost frozen, I and another fellow fell out. We hiked back to the temporary base camp after rescuing a fellow who had fainted in the snow and taking him to an aid station. I never thought we could make it; you could hardly see 15 yards ahead. We built ourselves a lean-to and got to bed around 1:00 P.M. Sunday.

We slept until 5:00 A.M. Monday, when we awoke to find the company there! That was a wonderful sight for we thought we would have to go out looking for them, and we had no food. Still exhausted we had to hike 15 miles to our next problem area where the situation was nontactical for one day and two nights. But the hike to this area took all day and I had had no food or water (except snow mouthfuls) for 36 hours and no hot food for four days. Somehow I made it, for I knew we'd get a day's rest at this nontactical period.

My feet were covered with blood from where the snowshoe laces and shoepacs had cut my feet and toes. The medics bandaged me up, and when Wednesday rolled around I was ready again. Everything went all right until Friday when I got dysentery somehow, and was up all Thursday night as well as Friday morning. Feeling terribly weak and nauseated I again left the forced march and was given medical attention at the battalion aid station. I rested for a couple of hours, and then set off to find the company.

I caught up with them about noon, and we hiked on in a regimental

Weapons platoon members horsing around at Camp Hale. "Mother" Eyer, with 60mm mortar in front, was wounded April 14, 1945, while LeGassey, on far right, was wounded on Belvedere.

offensive until 10:00 P.M. We slept until 4:30 A.M., and continued the attack until around noon when the problem ended. They decided the men could no longer stand two more weeks of maneuvers, so the ordeal ended after three weeks. We made the 20 mile trip back to camp, and arrived really tired. Along with other discomforts my back and shoulders broke out with sores, my fingers cracked at the ends, my ears were frozen once, etc. I've been tired many times but never so completely washed out in every way. The never-ending snow and standing for hours in an icy fox hole was almost unbearable.

Well, I'll tell you more about it some day but suffice it to say that I made it, although I'm a far cry from the fellow who went out. I lost 17 pounds and every rib shows. The first sergeant congratulated me this morning on the way I had taken it. Frankly, it took me....

[The furlough] won't be long now. That's what kept me going. I couldn't afford to get sick out there.... The time I'm not at home I want to spend with Pat. I've met plenty of women at Nebraska and Denver, but I want to see the one and only now. No new friends, please. This will probably be my first and last furlough before I go overseas and every moment has to count.

The Easter blizzard during which we climbed an impossibly steep slope turned out to be one of the worst Colorado had experienced in many years. It added some eight feet to the existing snow pack and will remain in the memories of 10th Mountain Division men for the rest of their lives. Despite my not wanting to suffer the disgrace of having to drop out of a forced climb—something I had never done before—I reached a point where I was physically unable because of the combination of my poor conditioning and the extra burdens of machine gun and snowshoes, to proceed further. A medical officer approved the request for me and another man to fall out. The other fellow who had to abandon the climb was another ASTP returnee whose name, ironically, was (Umberto) Milletari.

The worst of the maneuvers were now over, but in another postcard I noted that "when you're snowed on for 16 hours at a stretch it gets very uncomfortable." It would be another 10 days before the D-Series would be called off, but I found some of the ensuing exercises a bit more interesting.

Camp Hale, Colorado
Saturday, April 22, 1944

Maneuvers haven't been so bad this past week. We had a very interesting problem in which we attacked fortified positions (pill boxes). I was a flame thrower in the practice attack, but fired a machine gun during the actual attack. It was quite something. First the 75's (artillery) opened fire. Then 37mm anti-tank guns, mortars and heavy machine guns. We advanced to within 35 yards of the pill box with the fire coming over our heads. Then the artillery stopped while our assault detachment attacked the pill box. I fired the machine gun at the slits while the grenade throwers and flame throwers went into action. That flame thrower is quite a sight in action. Then I let up while the rifle men attacked. All in all it was the most interesting episode yet with shells whining over your head and bursting close by, tearing off trees like tooth picks. Amazingly, no one was hurt. Usually something trips up somewhere.

It snowed every day which made it rather unpleasant. But I have actually only two full days more—Monday and Tuesday—and then I'll be on my way. When I return the regiment will be in garrison, I hope. It will be good to have a little vacation, as I'm all cut up with various cuts and bruises. In fact my face looks like I've been through a knife duel.

I'll be looking forward to that Persian dinner, and to home again. It's been a long wait.

An official army report on the D-Series called it "the most grueling training test ever given to any U.S. Army Division."[18] Major General Lloyd E. Jones, the division commander, when asked by the press how he thought the maneuvers had gone, issued a statement in which he reported that there had been no deaths; minimized the number of casualties from frostbite, avalanches, and miscellaneous other injuries; and expressed obvious contempt for those who failed to complete every part of the exercise for whatever reason.

There is no doubt that these exercises were conducted under difficult conditions. In fact, the opinion has been expressed by high-ranking officers with first-hand knowledge of the hard conditions prevailing in certain combat zones that this is the toughest training in the Army of the United States! Isolation, cold, snow, lack of comfort for several weeks at a time—

Ski troopers climbing a mountain during "D-Series" maneuvers, 1944 (courtesy Denver Public Library, Western History Department).

these call for a fortitude and a strength of character which most men in this outfit have definitely proved they have. In fighting the weather, the altitude, and the dangers of the mountains, they have shown themselves ready for combat.

I am glad to announce that no fatalities occurred from any cause whatsoever during the entire series of problems. Considering the many thousand men in the Division, where only 195 cases of frostbite occurred (most of them light) and 340 injuries (sprains, broken bones, etc.), this is a proud record. These figures give the lie to amazing rumors of many deaths which originated in nearby towns even before the exercises began.

I desire to extend my sympathy to those individuals who through illness were unable to complete the series of problems, as I feel it is their hard luck not to enjoy that sense of personal pride and achievement which rewards those who completed 100% of the series. Of 1,378 cases of sickness, 270 did not even warrant evacuation of the patient to the Station hospital. Among the 1,108 men that were evacuated, about 40% came back to duty before the end of the series. I sincerely hope that these erstwhile invalids will rapidly rise to the 10th Division standards of physical and mental ruggedness and moral fortitude.

From an increase in the AWOL rate immediately prior and during our recent field exercise period, I am forced to deduce that a certain number of individuals just don't have what it takes to perform the arduous job of a soldier of the 10th Division: fighting in the mountains. That the training was getting a little tougher proved enough for them to quit.... What their comrades have a right to be shown is that the "quitters" really mean to redeem themselves; that their daily endeavor is bent upon that purpose. Only thus can they regain their place among us, among the men of the 10th Division who will not fail their mission in combat. [19]

Thus spake the military mind—or one of his staff underlings who was asked to draft the statement—attempting through questionable psychology (and a curious definition of "morality") to shame those whose performances were judged deficient in any way into future deeds of heroism. It is interesting to note that Roger A. Beaumont, in his book *Military Elites,* a study of elite forces (such as the British Commandos, the French Foreign Legion, and Merrill's Marauders) in the twentieth century, states that "the U.S. 10th Mountain Division, the most elite U.S. division in the twentieth century in terms of intelligence scores, fitness and training, suffered five times more casualties preparing for combat than any other American division in the Second World War."[20]

Fortunately, my furlough came through without further cancellations of plans or delays, and I walked in from our bivouac location outside of camp to meet Paul and Mary Liz. They had been waiting most of the day, taking turns watching the front entrance to the guest house as each soldier entered, concerned that they might miss me because of my strange mountain-troop clothing and other equipment, including parka, ski cap, and rucksack. When I finally appeared, late Wednesday afternoon on April 26, we left immediately by car for home. It was now slightly over 12½ months since I had begun military service.

Paul's car, a small two-door Ford coupe, was jammed with suitcases and other gear. As promised, we drove round the clock all the way to Ohio, Mary Liz, in the back seat, getting hardly any sleep because of her concern that either Paul or I would fall asleep while driving. Then, too, she was kept awake by one of the bags repeatedly falling off the rear window ledge on to the back of her neck. She told the family later that whenever she complained, my response was, "You should just ignore it," which hardly made the trip any more pleasurable.

The furlough improved my morale enormously, and upon my return I decided to apply for a transfer to the Office of Strategic Services (OSS), one of the few high-priority military organizations to which the 10th permitted one to move. The OSS, the forerunner of what is now the Central Intelligence Agency, was organized in 1942 under the Joint Chiefs of Staff to conduct overseas espionage operations and to analyze incoming intelligence information of strategic importance. I thought I might have a good chance of being selected because of my overseas background and foreign language ability, and while I was not that crazy about parachuting behind enemy lines and the associated risks of operating as a secret agent, anything seemed better than what I was doing. My application, however, came to nought—either because the OSS had other needs at the time or because the 10th managed to block the move.

In the month which followed, we experienced the usual forced climbs, bivouacs, and periodic snowfalls. We exchanged rumors about where we would be sent next, but were finally informed it would be Texas. For a change, we received instruction in mine detection and rock climbing. I also finally had the opportunity to try my hand at skiing again, something I had not done since joining the mountain troops. The reason was that the prescribed means of movement on snow for a machine gunner like myself was snowshoes because the weight and burden of holding the gun made skiing virtually impossible. I soon realized that I had forgotten much of what I had learned in Switzerland, for I was unable to avoid hitting numerous trees coming down the wooded slope where we were bivouacked. Since the winter ski training which I had missed had now ended, I had no opportunity to improve what few skills I still possessed.

On Saturday, June 3, our much-disliked commander, General Jones, who seemed "to enjoy plaguing us and making us as miserable as possible," ordered that some 20 of us from my company, and a few men from other units as well, spend that afternoon and all day Sunday cleaning up a forest area in the mountains. This cleanup detail was one of the more inexplicable army jobs we were given. We had experienced only too often the order to "police the area"—the army's terminology for picking up trash, including cigarette butts—around our barracks and other areas of the camp, but this was the first time we had ever been asked to "police" the sides of the Rocky Mountains. The rationale behind it was apparently to try and find any debris left as a result of the maneuvers we had conducted, but if there was any litter it was virtually impossible to find, and the small number of people assigned to cover the 50 or so square miles involved rendered the task a bad joke. To add insult to injury, we were asked to do the job in a snowstorm, as I pointed out in a letter to Paul.

Camp Hale, Colorado
Sunday, June 8, 1944

Dear Paul,

First of all, I'd better wish you a happy birthday and many more with that interesting roommate of yours.

We are living a life at the present I wouldn't wish on a dog. We have no nights off, and I've been kept in for two weekends. And guess what we had in this lovely spot today? The snow fell from last night until about 15 minutes ago, and it's now Sunday evening. The ground is so lovely and white I feel like screaming.

Also guess what I wore this morning when I went out to police up a forest area: long wool underwear, two wool sweaters, fatigue shirt, parka, raincoat, and mittens. Lovely for a June day don't you think?

Our shipment to Texas is now only a matter of days. We expect to leave in two weeks, and the camp is Camp Swift, about 30 miles from Austin. Rumors have it that it's a Port of Embarkation from which you can either go east to Europe or west to the Japanese theatre. I think we'll go to Europe, however.

Isn't it swell how well the [Normandy] invasion is going? Frankly, I would rather be there than training some more in Texas. I think it will be over in Europe before the end of autumn.

We were now given three days training in rock climbing by what I called some accomplished foreign-born instructors. "It was fascinating," I said, "learning the intricate techniques, which are far more complicated than I had ever suspected. The ropes we used are made of nylon, so when you want to know if giving up nylon stockings is worth it, picture me and several soldier buddies linked together on a mountain by a nylon rope, with our lives depending on its strength."

I also reported that I was back in my "first gunner's" position.

This means I'm second in command of my squad. A sergeant is head of the squad and I'd be in his shoes if it weren't for the fact that I went to Lincoln. However, it's not so bad for I don't have any responsibility, yet I have complete authority over the firing of the gun, over the second gunner, and over the six ammunition bearers. I imagine I'll still be in that position when we go overseas, unless the sergeant transfers out or is broken to private for poor work of some sort. It's what I want, for I'm best at the machine gun and I've been with it quite a while—ever since I transferred to Co. M, 86th Infantry.

Rock climbing posed certain obvious risks, but our instructors were famed mountain guides and we avoided most serious accidents. A danger associated with mountain climbing in the summer months, which we had not fully appreciated, was the threat of lightning. One particularly arduous all-day climb in which I participated, along with the rest of my company and other troopers, led us at length to the top of a peak. There we collapsed, some lying full length on the ground while others, including myself, sat leaning against our rucksacks and dozing. While we rested, we observed a rain storm moving towards us up the valley nearby and ultimately up the slope of the mountain on which we sat. I thought little of it and was dreaming of home and girl friends far away when a bolt of lightning suddenly struck the peak where we sat, causing such a shock of electricity to my body that I was shaken wide awake, involuntarily yelling "OW!" at the top of my lungs.

In the belief that the lightning had been drawn to the metal frames of our rucksacks and possibly our weapons, we threw everything aside that we believed might attract an electrical current and made a hasty retreat off the top of the mountain. It was a wild scene as we dashed about hurling weapons and running to get below the peak of the mountain. I was not seriously injured, but two men were. Both were unconscious, and one wasn't breathing, but we managed to get his breathing started again by pumping his chest—the artificial respiration technique favored at that time.

The other man had been sitting like me, and the bolt had hit his ruck-sack. It had burned through it near the top, then struck him in one shoulder, and proceeded to travel a path all the way down one side of his trunk and down one leg. He was breathing but appeared to be paralyzed. Both men were carried down the side of the mountain on makeshift stretchers to the nearest road, where they were transported by car to the base hospital. We never heard whether they survived their injuries or, if so, whether they suffered any lasting ill effects.

Since my return from the University of Nebraska, I had become much more cynical about the value of playing the "good soldier." As might be expected, the army's answer was to subject me to various penalties. On one occasion I was put on "company punishment" because the MP's turned in my name for having my blouse unbuttoned while on pass in the nearby town of Leadville. This meant that I had to work after regular hours until 10 at night, as well as all day Saturday and Sunday.

Whatever the penalties, they did not deter me from taking advantage of every opportunity to avoid unpleasant or arduous duty—in short, to "fuck off" as the GIs put it. One of the masters of such skills was my close friend, Jack Kelly, a member of my machine gun squad. He was a natural actor and a great comedian who incessantly dreamed up new ways to get us out of details to which we had been assigned.

Kelly was a boxer and fought professionally in Denver and other towns whenever he could get put on the fight card and get out of camp. He was constantly shadow boxing in the latrine, snorting heavily through his nose as he did so. I and others enjoyed accusing him of getting "punchy" from too many fights. He worried about this, but nevertheless kept up his trade. On one occasion when Joe Louis, the heavyweight champion of the world but now a private in the army, came to Camp Hale to give a boxing exhibition, Kelly served as his corner man, and for some time after, he would ask us to admire the hands that had worked on Louis. During the exhibition Louis was frequently gasping for breath because of the altitude and kept complaining jokingly about it to us.

In determining when to try and escape some assignment, you always had to give careful consideration to the brainpower and attitude of the first sergeant—the senior noncom in the company. As might be expected, the styles and talents of first sergeants varied markedly. Not long after I reported to Camp Hale, we had a first sergeant who had been in vaudeville, and he enjoyed performing the role of the all-knowing career soldier counseling recruits. While he had a good heart and gave us quite a few laughs, we grew to dread his lectures in the mess hall on personal cleanliness. It was particularly upsetting in the midst of a meal to be forced to listen to his detailed description of how and why one should clean one's penis or other intimate parts. He was also fond of denigrating our military acumen and bearing, whether we were at meals, standing in company formation, or elsewhere.

"You really tink you's a soldier? You's no soldier ... you *shit* ! *I'll* tell you when you's a soldier. Don't believe anyone else's bullshit about that."

This particular top-kick was not with us terribly long. He disappeared one day, and we learned later that he had gone AWOL, evidently tiring of the army routine. We never heard anything further about him.

Another first sergeant who was with us for quite a while caused us much grief for entirely different reasons. His educational background duplicated that of President Roosevelt, as he had attended Groton, the college prep school favored by children of the elite, and Harvard University. What caused the troops to fear him in particular was the fact that he had a photographic memory. Somehow he could recall, without reference to any paper work, where everyone of some 200 men in the company was supposed to be at any hour of the day or night. This was disconcerting to say the least. If your assignment, say, was to collect the rocks on the parade ground with some other unfortunates, and you were observed instead cleaning your rifle in the barracks, he would stare at you for a moment, while searching his mental storage system for your name, the time, and your job, and quickly demand to know why you were not at your proper station. Needless to say, I fell victim to his talent for accurate recall and suffered the consequences on more than one occasion.

One of the lessons my friend Kelly taught me, however, was to use the army's own rules against it. One of the best examples of this occurred when we were forced to undertake a demanding, all-day ascent of a nearby mountain with full fieldpacks. Kelly had been grumbling for some hours about the load he was carrying and the precipitous terrain we were attempting to climb, when he discovered a tick on his arm. At the time there was much concern about Rocky Mountain spotted fever, and anyone found with a tick imbedded in the skin was supposed to be released from duty and sent to see a doctor.

Kelly told me about what he had discovered. He said that he would ask to return to camp and (if I had no objection) would request that I accompany him to insure his safe arrival. I agreed, of course, and he immediately showed the tick to the lieutenant leading the climb, adding that he was feeling a little wobbly. To my amazement, the proposition worked like a charm, and in no time we left our struggling comrades and were gaily descending the mountain.

Not to be outdone by Kelly's hands-on association with Joe Louis, I had the occasion one evening at the camp to attend an appearance on stage by Jinx Falkenburg, a famous tennis player and Hollywood actress. To conclude her show on an exciting note, it was announced that she would hit a table tennis ball into the audience of GIs and whoever caught it was invited to a one-on-one rendezvous with Jinx in her dressing room. Since I had not only been sexually deprived for a long time, but fancied myself to be both an accomplished tennis and ping pong player, I was desperately eager to catch the ball. After a heroic leap in which I crashed into numerous other rivals, I did indeed manage to seize the flying piece of celluloid. Whatever Mae West delivered to those who responded to her "Come up and see me sometime," my tête-à-tête with Jinx regrettably yielded nothing that might be described as carnal knowledge. But the mere opportunity to have an intimate exchange with such a beautiful woman managed to refuel my fantasies for sometime thereafter.

4

Poison Ivy and Cockroaches

Camp Swift, Texas, June–December 1944

Our move to Texas in ancient railroad passenger cars boasting three tiers of bunks began the night of June 21, 1944, and, as anticipated, our destination was Camp Swift near Austin. In a letter written en route, I said we pulled out around 9 P.M. with a mixture of feelings.

> No one felt any sadness about leaving Camp Hale, but we also knew that the future may be no brighter. The camp gave us as big a send-off as it has ever mustered. A band played a stirring tune for us as we marched through the twilight to the waiting train. We walked down thru the 21 blocks of camp to Pando, and the soldiers, WACs, and civilians staying behind lined up and down the streets waving goodbye and saying so long to various friends as they passed by in ranks. The feeling was best expressed by three young WACs who stood watching us as we marched along. "Good luck, kids," they called, and everyone felt a little more pride and gratitude for having heard this phrase. Our train pulled out immediately, and soon the group at the station was lost from view and the band music faded away.

I also told my parents I was in trouble again. At a time when I was supposed to be on duty, I and two other friends had gone without permission to the hospital post exchange. It was something I had done numerous times before because we were dying of boredom, not having any training, "just lectures on old familiar stuff to pass the time away until we shipped out."

> However, this time I was sought in the afternoon to testify at a court martial of a fellow that I knew because I had promised to testify in his defense. I testified for him that night at the court martial, and he got three months, being acquitted on two counts (swearing at a non-com and refusal to obey an order). Nevertheless, since I had been absent when I was supposed to be in the company area listening to lectures, I was called up before the CO. He bawled me out, and told me that he couldn't understand why I did it when he knew that I was such a good soldier and an

acting non-com. I had no excuse except a hard luck story about ASTP, other bad breaks in the Army, and that I had little interest in listening to old lectures for the umptieth [sic] time. The result was that he broke me to a private again and took away my weekend pass.

When we arrived at Camp Swift, we found it to be a huge camp, almost six or seven times as big as Hale, and one which "definitely outshines Hale for comfort and civilization." One of the delights en route was "to smell green things growing," but the camp also had much improved barracks and far nicer facilities for recreation, including outdoor swimming pools. Unfortunately, I discovered it had two serious deficiencies. One was the Texas heat, which was the worst I had experienced since Persia, reaching exactly 100 degrees in the shade that first afternoon. The other was the thousands of cockroaches, scorpions, and similar creatures crawling around on the barracks floors, walls, and ceilings.

The shock of Texas summer temperatures and humidity after the Camp Hale climate was indeed severe, and it was exaggerated by my having been assigned the nasty detail of helping unload 75mm howitzers from boxcars the afternoon of our arrival. I have never experienced such heat before or since as we endured that awful day, entering and working in those railroad cars.

One of the rumors passed around after our arrival at Camp Swift was that we would undertake airborne training as glider troops. Another was that we would be sent to the China-Burma-India (CBI) theater—presumably because it was mountainous and required mules. The usual joke was "They will find our bleached bones along the Burma Road." The actual reason for our move to Texas, however, was that the Department of the Army had decided—after all our ski and mountain climbing training, testing of special equipment, and high-stress winter maneuvers—to convert us to a flatland infantry division.

Our specialized training and talents had been offered to various theater commanders, including Generals McArthur and Eisenhower, but no one wanted us except on their terms. These terms did not include our unique equipment such as snowshoes, sleeping bags, and mules. At one point even the designation "Alpine" was removed from the division nomenclature, and we were now about to be subjected to training in river crossings and jungle operations, which included dealing with scorpions, poisonous snakes, and other unpleasant denizens of tropical climates. We were also frequently placed on alert to be prepared to depart for our assigned port of embarkation (POE) from where we would sail for some unhappy battlefield overseas.

The likelihood of our mission being changed because of the demands of the war was not an experience unique to our specialized unit. The U.S. Army Tank Destroyer Corps, formed in 1941 to serve in a tank-killer role against superior German armor, was ultimately used more in the form of assault guns and artillery support. Similarly, as the war continued, the Commandos, Darby's Rangers, Merrill's Marauders, and other elite forces were increasingly pressed to serve as conventional infantry.

The special experience and training of mountain troops in other armies was also largely wasted. Most of the German mountain forces ended up as regular infantry units in the Russian campaign, while the only British mountain division, the 78th, fared no better, being reduced to fighting on the plains of France.[1]

Camp Swift, Texas
Monday, July 3, 1944
    ...I went to Austin this weekend and had quite a bit of fun. I stayed in a tourist home with two other guys, one of whom was in Lincoln with me. We went to a dance Saturday night and I met a University of Texas girl, a sophomore majoring in education. I hope to date her again in the future. Austin is a nice town very similar to Lincoln. It also has wonderful places to swim, which seems uppermost in everyone's mind here. The heat is still terrific but I don't notice it nearly so much as I did the first two or three days.
    Edwin's job sounds pretty interesting. I really think he's safe from being drafted for the rest of the war now that the crisis [the cross-channel invasion of France] is over.

My brother Edwin, who had been in continual danger of being drafted since our entry into the war, was told by his draft board in the spring of 1944 that he could definitely be expected to be drafted that year. As a result, Western Reserve Academy (WRA) decided not to renew his teaching contract because he might have to leave in the middle of the school year. To earn a living and to increase his chances of keeping out of the military by taking a defense-related job, he managed to get hired by a local company that manufactured, among other military products, the twin movie cameras mounted on fighter aircraft which operated when the two machine guns on the wings were fired.

As for my visit to Austin, this was a delightful change after our isolation at Camp Hale, and the weekend pass policy was liberal, so that we were able to visit the city frequently. Taking advantage of my fraternity membership, I contacted the Phi Kappa Psi chapter at the University of Texas in Austin; I slept at their fraternity house on occasion and met some coeds through their good auspices. But I did not have the advantage I had at the University of Nebraska of being one of the few available men on campus or in town, because there were some 15,000 other 10th Division soldiers roaming the streets who were equally hungry for female companionship and associated benefits.

When desperate, which was our normal condition, we would stand on the street corners of Austin and try to entice females driving by to let us join them for a day of fun and frolic. These pickup attempts had about as much chance of success as getting back into the ASTP, because the girls knew our interests were not entirely intellectual. Nevertheless, on two occasions Jack Kelly and I were amazed to see the objects of our lust actually stop. The first time it happened the women, whom we assumed were as hot-blooded as we, turned out to be coeds from the university, and we ended up in their off-campus apartment. There we had dinner, drinks, and much passionate kissing and exploration of whatever additional advances might be permitted, but the ladies steadfastly refused all attempts on our part to achieve the "holy grail."

The other two women who deigned to respond to our waves and calls were wives whose husbands had long since disappeared into the jaws of the military, but they too were not about to grant any extreme favors, evidently seeking only the brief companionship of some lonely young men.

Less than two weeks after arriving at Swift, I entered the hospital with a terrible case of poison ivy picked up during an army exercise which required us to follow a compass course at night through some woods adjacent to the camp. Poison ivy, the bane of my prep school days, when I had been repeatedly hospitalized because of my serious allergic reaction to its oily resin, had finally caught up with me in the army. I had never gotten it at Camp Hale, because it was rarely seen in the Rocky Mountains, but Texas was a different story. Although I was familiar with its three-leaved characteristics and could avoid it in the daytime, if not forced to wade through it, the army's periodic requirement for us to stumble around in the dark, engaging in various nighttime operations, insured that I would brush into it sooner or later. And so I did, to my great discomfiture. The suffering that accompanied it was also greatly magnified by the medical staff's refusal to accept the fact that it was a serious affliction for some. They delayed effective treatment, including hospitalization, until the condition of the patient made the need for such treatment indisputable.

At this time it was also announced that by September 1 we would be on Louisiana maneuvers. The army seemed determined, I said, to give us "the most hellish training of all time: from mountains and intense cold, to this desert heat here, to jungle training in Louisiana." As a result, I went on:

> The men—at least in my battalion—are very disgusted and angered. Over 40 applied for the paratroops the other day from my company (of 200) alone, but the paratroops were closed to us the next day. Considering the fact that the paratroops are the most dangerous outfit in the business, you can see what a mental state we're in. Our morale is definitely low. We're overtrained and when that situation exists, every one tries to get out of as much work as possible, no one caring what the training is any more for we've had it thousands of times already. Everything is repetition and endless, exorbitant physical effort.

In a letter to Paul from the hospital where the temperature in my ward was 103 degrees, I complained some more about our being forced to repeat what appeared to be basic training again and our intense dislike for the "chicken" routines (such as changing the way we laced our leggings) being imposed on us. I also added some comments about my fellow soldiers.

I really don't know about this outfit. The men are tops, there is no doubt about that. I wouldn't be afraid of going into combat with them any day. But our battalion officers are very poor I think, although the regimental colonel is a good man and I think the divisional officers are all right.

The men, as I said, are the ruggedest bunch of guys I've ever seen. My machine gun squad, I swear, is the toughest in the division. The squad leader is a pretty good man; I'm first gunner; then there is my best friend Jack Kelly (Notre Dame) who boxes professionally and is the greatest comedian of all time (second gunner); then a Finnish-American boy, rather thick but has one of the most powerful builds I have ever seen; then a 6-foot, 7-inch, 250-pound giant (biggest man I've seen in the Army), who is also a great comedian and true blue; and one other fellow who is tops. It's really an amazing group of men: one that only the Army could draw together.

I commented that my birthday was no picnic because we were up half the night on a compass problem roaming through the woods. "However, I have left my teens behind. I can hardly believe that I entered the Army at 18 and now I'm 20. I'll be an old man before this is over."

The 6'7" soldier to whom I referred was Wally Krusell, whose hometown was Duluth, Minnesota. Krusell, whom we called "Limber," came from a large family where his father, uncles, and all his brothers were well over 6 feet tall and were frequently involved in brawls with others who chose to challenge their physical prowess. One of Limber's better stories concerned one brother or uncle who got into an argument with an opposing player during a baseball game. Rather than lay hands on his opponent directly, he simply took a baseball bat and quietly broke it in half across his knee to demonstrate what he might do to his challenger if sufficiently provoked.

Limber, too, would often return from weekend passes with his head bloodied from various scrapes in which he had participated. The battles usually began in bars where some drunk would feel emboldened to inform him that, despite Limber's height, he was certain he could punch him out. This invariably led to an ugly row which often ended with Limber being hit on the head by a beer bottle, the most handy weapon available.

All during our many months of training in Colorado and Texas, Limber never lost hope that the army would eventually discover that he exceeded the height limits for army service and that they had made a terrible error in inducting him. Since the height limit was, in fact, 6'6", and he had continuing size problems with army beds, clothing, and other gear, he had valid reasons for expecting an honorable discharge and, in his wilder dreams, an abject apology from the U.S. military. As in the case of John Horrall, however, who was mistakenly sent to the ski troops at Camp Hale rather than to Fort Belvoir, Virginia, where he was supposed to undergo training as an engineering officer, the army never admitted it had made a mistake with Krusell. Limber's problem may have been that he was only 6'6" when inducted, but continued to grow beyond the permissible height. Nevertheless, one would think the army might have anticipated that their 18-year-old recruit might well grow a bit more after his physical exam at the time of entry and exercised more caution before accepting him into the service.

The tedium of our repeating training that we had undergone countless times before even led one of our officers to try to liven things up a bit. During an indoor session one day, he allowed one of the men to demonstrate a considerable fraction of the known positions of sexual intercourse for the edification of the less-experienced. And that was definitely the category to which I belonged. The performance offered us considerable amusement and was accompanied by some of the favorite, if apocryphal, GI stories of the time. One concerned the unhappy wife who wrote her husband in the service complaining about being cooped up in their apartment. "I am so sick of these four walls, I could scream," she said. Her beloved mate responded quickly with the warning, "Honey, when I get home all you're going to see is the ceiling."

The 10th got quite a lot of publicity after it arrived in Texas. One of the local newspaper stories announcing the arrival of the division that I sent home noted, "The 10th moved into Swift from Camp Hale, Colorado, bringing with it a large number of pack mules, a distinct novelty at this Post for all units heretofore have been motorized." Men of the 10th, it continued, "at their two-mile high altitude at Camp Hale, underwent training considered by many authorities as perhaps the toughest to which any fighting unit of the Army has been subjected.... [There] they had learned to live in temperatures as low as 38 degrees below zero, and for the greater part of the winter slept in snow." The story ended with the comment that "Already many soldiers of the 10th Division have visited the surrounding communities, and civilian residents of these towns have remarked on the rugged physique and the uniform military courtesy of these new GI's of Camp Swift."

Another Texas newspaper joked that members of the 10th "have a tendency to mop their brows more frequently than is normal even for visitors from the north" because where we had been, "the breezes are not so balmy and the terrain is so steep that the soldiers count off from bottom to top instead of from right to left." There too, the paper added, "Even without a pack, it's no cinch to hike and climb in the rarefied air of the Rockies' timberline regions, but the mountain fighter has to do it the hard way—carrying a rucksack that's just about twice as heavy as the standard flatland infantry pack."

At the end of July, I reported that "The barracks got so bad with bedbugs, cockroaches, etc. that they finally sealed it up and filled it with cyanide gas, which is frequently done around here. Anyway, there are no more bugs. Everyone seems to have a rash of some kind here so I don't feel too out of place. The heat causes boils on some, heat rashes, impetigo, etc. and a few are getting discharges because of it." At the time I was free of any trouble, but I suspected that a two-week bivouac coming up would produce something.

Apart from the bugs whose bodies literally covered the floors of the barracks after these cyanide poisonings, one of the most unpleasant experiences at Camp Swift was a 30-minute run every morning before breakfast. This was the only relatively cool time of the day, but the order (from whatever command level responsible) insured that when the run was over, our fatigues were soaking wet from perspiration as we proceeded on to breakfast and the rest of our daily routine.

The way I adjusted to this trial was to lope along, making what I thought was the minimal effort needed to avoid severe criticism from the accompanying authorities. On one occasion, however, I overlooked a young corporal who had been given temporary command of another squad whose sergeant was on leave, and he let his newly acquired rank go to his head.

"Ellis," he yelled, "get your ass moving and start running."

"Corporal, why don't you go fuck yourself?" I replied, and continued my unhurried pace.

The corporal evidently thought he had suffered some loss of face, and, to my surprise—given his lowly rank and the anticipated negative reaction to his conduct by his fellow GI's—reported the incident to our company commander. I was soon called before the latter to answer the charge of having disobeyed a direct order from a superior officer, an offense which could be construed as cause for a court-martial.

The company commander was a reasonable sort, and I doubted he would really want to have me court-martialed over the affair, but I also knew he was imprisoned by army regulations and would need some formal, even if barely plausible, explanation for my conduct.

"Sir," I said, "the corporal is only an acting squad leader and is not even in my platoon. I did not believe he had the right to order me around as he did, and so I ignored his command. If that was incorrect, I apologize."

The CO refrained from reminding me of my many months of army service (not forgetting NCO School at Camp Hale), which might have caused a less tolerant commander to react to my explanation with hysterical laughter, and happily accepted this explanation. He forcefully corrected my understanding of the pertinent army regulations before he let me go, however.

The middle of August saw us continuing our unpleasant exercises in the Texas heat. One weekend we had to complete a 9-mile march with full packs in 1 hour and 45 minutes, followed by a 25-mile all-night march. Because of the rapid pace set, comments were always being made about how we must be chasing a rabbit. As it happened, on one such march, after an hour of extremely fast movement, we came upon a dead rabbit lying in the road. Its demise, we joked, had been caused by our excessive speed.

As the months of arduous and mind-deadening duty passed by, Jack Kelly and I grew increasingly intolerant of the army routine and sought every opportunity to evade our assigned training or work details. By this time I was performing well only when my pride was at stake—for example, achieving the best time of any soldier in the regiment when running the obstacle course—or when the reputation of our machine gun squad was on the line in some military demonstration.

Sometimes our avoidance of duty led us into unanticipated situations. We were hiding one day, barely having managed to squeeze under a barracks on the post, while the rest of the company was in the adjacent field nearby listening to a lecture. Suddenly, I noticed that the underside of the barracks floor, only a few inches above our heads, was infested with black widow spiders who might be prompted to drop on our faces or elsewhere on our bodies if they thought their habitat was threatened. I pointed out the danger to Jack, but we had no choice but to remain frozen where we were because any movement would have revealed our presence to the company outside.

On another occasion we were well concealed and resting happily in the attic of a lecture hall when, to our horror, the company filed into the room below, where they were subjected to a film on malaria and its carrier, the Anopheles mosquito. All might have gone well except that there was no floor and few joists to support our weight, and Jack accidentally stepped through the ceiling under our feet while trying to move to a more secure location. Since there was no escaping our fate, we jokingly explained our descent to the assembled troops as the Anopheles mosquito they had been warned about and luckily received only company punishment rather than any more serious penalty.

Jack, who was far more imaginative and reckless than I, at one point dreamed up a means of avoiding some upcoming forced marches by laboriously scraping down the heels and soles of his GI boots to the point where they were rendered unsuitable for such demanding use. Since only he and I knew how his shoes, which were of an unusual size, had reached this state and since you could escape from such physical stress if you did not have the proper equipment, he was excused from marches for some time until replacement shoes could be found by the supply sergeant.

Jack's most outrageous escapade occurred when he violated a company order restricting him to camp because of some infraction of regulations. Instead of accepting his punishment and making do with whatever amusements the camp had to offer, he took off without benefit of any pass for Galveston, no doubt to see the nurses of whom he was enamored. Regrettably, he was picked up by the military police in Houston, some 200 miles from camp, for having his blouse unbuttoned or being technically "out of uniform" in some other way. When he returned to camp and told me about the incident, I asked him how he could possibly beat this rap since the MPs would report him to the camp authorities and the charge of being AWOL would be added to his other violations.

That question was a big mistake.

"I am going to deny I ever left camp," he said.

"But how can you get away with that?" I asked. "They'll have the MP report, and they'll testify against you."

Jack's answer, to which he had obviously given much thought, was decep-tively simple. "Yes, they'll have the report, but I don't think the MPs will come all this way just to identify me as the soldier they picked up for a simple vio-lation of the dress code. I know it's a gamble, but I think I can get away with it. I would also appreciate it if you'd tell the company commander that you saw me Saturday night drinking beer in the canteen."

His proposition posed some risk, but because he didn't ask that I do more than say that I thought I saw him that night, without actually conversing with him or sharing a drink, I agreed to do what he requested. To my amazement, his gamble worked; the MPs never showed up and my testimony as to his pres-ence in camp was accepted.

By August 20, I was back in the hospital again, this time with poison oak acquired on the banks of the Colorado River while practicing river crossings in assault boats. The same doctor I had seen before on sick call, when I had ultimately been hospitalized, again dismissed the seriousness of my affliction, telling me to go to bed in the barracks and treat it myself for a couple of days. By nightfall a medical enlisted man deemed my case critical enough to be called an emergency and sent me off in an ambulance without any medical officer's authority.

Because it was different, we rather enjoyed the river operation even though some men almost drowned, and I kept tumbling down banks, stumbling because of the 31-pound machine gun I was carrying. We were not to have a similar river experience until facing a far greater challenge in combat under much more frightening circumstances.

Our planned maneuvers in Louisiana were finally canceled because of General Patton's hurried call for the tank units with which we were supposed to engage in war games. This was followed by more rumors, the strongest one being that the division (the only light division left in the U.S.) would be all broken up and the men sent to other units, both at home and overseas. Con-tradicting this was a talk given a few days later by our General Jones who had just returned from Washington, D.C.; he told us we were going to be a heavy-fire-powered division instead of a light division.

Through it all, having by this time experienced many disappointments in the army, I was reasonably accepting of the fact that whatever change came would probably be bad. What kept me going, as I wrote Dad, was "my phi-losophy of day-to-day living—one thing you and the Army have taught me—and I find that, certainly for this sort of a life, it's tops. Compared to how I felt last year at this time, the life I lead now is wonderful. Back in July of '43 I didn't see how I could stand the Army another month. I hated it like noth-ing I have ever undergone before, but I guess I've changed or hardened to it, for it bothers me very little now. Whether I work until 3 A.M. or whether they let me off at 5:30 P.M., it makes little difference. I seem to be numb to it all."

To my surprise, I was now sent to school for a brief indoctrination on how to educate my fellow soldiers on what the war was all about, our allies and their problems, intelligent citizenship, and the like. High officials in Washington had suddenly concluded that if the average soldier were more knowledgeable about vital issues, he would be a better fighter. I and the other trainees would be used to give orientation lectures to our respective companies and provide written materials for everyone's edification.

Shortly after that, I even came close to getting a relatively safe, full-time assignment in divisional headquarters when I was called for an interview by a captain in the division's Office of Orientation and Education. He wanted me to write news stories "in a manner interesting to the common soldier," and after a lengthy interview, he promised me that if he were unable to get another candidate transferred, I would have the job. Unfortunately, the other lucky soldier managed to get approval for the move, and I remained where I was.

The possibility of my obtaining a transfer from machine gunner in a front-line rifle company to a rear echelon job as a kind of briefing officer on world affairs must have been enormously appealing to Mother and Dad. My failure to get the assignment undoubtedly gave them many sleepless nights. Given their personal experience in Persia with the reality of war in all its ugliness, they must have found little comfort in my expressed willingness to go overseas in the occupational specialty I had chosen and my naive expectation that all would be well. Nevertheless, while they encouraged me to seek the headquarters assignment or any other job which might challenge the mind a bit more, they never dismissed the importance of my assigned responsibilities in a weapons platoon or minimized their value.

John Horrall's fortunes, in contrast to mine, took a drastic turn for the better. He obtained a job, also at divisional headquarters, working as a clerk. Since his previous post, following his dismissal from the ASTP, had been as a scout for his company—a specialty fraught with risk in combat, requiring one to head out in advance of one's unit to locate enemy positions—we viewed his accomplishment as a major coup. Now that he had achieved the impossible, it was my fervent hope that he could somehow wangle a place for me too in that rarified divisional atmosphere, but it was not to be.

> *Camp Swift, Texas*
> *Thursday, October 19, 1944*
> We were placed on alert status a few minutes ago, which means we must be ready to move overseas in 24 hours. Don't get too alarmed though; it doesn't necessarily mean I'll leave tomorrow.
> I'm in a big hurry so I'll sign off. I just wanted you to have the news the minute I had a spare moment to write.

After warning Pat, as well as Mother, of our alert status, I also proposed that I use some code words in a future letter which would reveal to her, without the censor cutting the words out, whether the 10th Division was being sent to Europe or the Far East. If I began the letter with the salutation "Dearest darling," it meant we were heading across the Atlantic; if I wrote "Dearest pen-mate," it meant we were destined for the Pacific theater of operations.

Pat hailed the news of my orientation assignment but had some problems with my other ideas.

Chicago 37, Illinois
October 21, 1944

Darling,

What a wonderful day today: *two* letters from you! ... Yesterday, when I got your letter telling about the wonderful new program you're helping in, I was so darned pleased! It is something to awaken new spirit and interest in you, isn't it? I've often wondered why our army didn't take some pains to teach the soldier what we're really fighting for. I should think they'd make better fighters if they could see the whole picture. And certainly they'll make more just peacemakers....

Your two plans—for going overseas (so I'll know where) and for thinking of each other at noon are swell. But could we make it some time other than 12, because when I get to school I'll be taking last minute notes in class, the bell will ring, I'll be putting on my coat and leaving at 12. What about 10:30 at night—or are you asleep or busy then? And let's make it five minutes and not just three.

I saw a war movie short in which they told of the way in which the ene-mies can piece together little bits of information about a soldier's where-abouts, troop movements, etc. and really damage them, so I don't want to know in any more detail than just Europe or Asia where you're going until it's legal to know. I'll be hoping for a letter beginning "Dearest darling" if I have to get one. Now don't go and write "Dearest penmate" without thinking sometime, you clown, or you'll scare me to death.

Love,
Pat

Late in October, General Lear, head of the Army Ground Forces visited us, necessitating countless inspections and the cancellation of all weekend passes and furloughs. In addition, the entire division had been restricted because at a boxing tournament our own Major General Jones was booed when he got up to award the trophy. As I wrote home, "You can imagine what the mental state of this unit is when they start booing their own commander, and hate with a fierce hatred every officer above the rank of captain."

General Jones, of course, was the less-than-beloved commander who at the end of our famous D-Series maneuvers had criticized those whom he thought "just don't have what it takes to perform the arduous job of a soldier of the 10th Division." William Johnson described him in his *Sports Illustrated* article as "a rather frail officer whom Minnie Dole remembered as 'always sit-ting on a radiator; he could never seem to get warm.'"[2] Unquestionably, he had long been responsible for the pedantic emphasis on the regulatory minutiae affecting our daily lives, or what the GI's called in more blunt language the "chicken shit," at Camps Hale and Swift. General Lear's visit may well have been prompted by reports reaching Washington of the poor state of morale in the 10th and the need for a change in command, which, as it happened, soon followed. He warned us before departing that we would be going overseas soon and also told us how much he'd heard about us in Washington.

The entire division then moved out on November 5 for a month in the field on maneuvers. I had managed to get myself excused from participating by having obtained a signed excuse from a major in the medical corps attesting to my severe susceptibility to poison ivy. As a result I experienced the incomparable joy of seeing my beloved comrades march by me in the heat and dust, trudging off for many unhappy days in the Texas countryside.

"Ellis, you bastard," one called, "you are one lucky son-of-a-bitch."

Their obscene gestures and reflections on my parentage made the occasion even more worthwhile, for I knew they would have given anything to be taking my place. When all had disappeared, I retired to the orderly room and to my arduous paper work and other heavy responsibilities, including dreaming up "make-work" details for the new recruits who remained.

Unfortunately, as on all other occasions of good fortune I had experienced in the army, my joy was short-lived. Three days later the troops marched back to camp, the maneuvers having been abruptly canceled because of the news that we were being shipped overseas. We were told we would be leaving for a port of embarkation (POE) around the middle of December and to wind up our personal affairs, which included sending our wives home and selling our cars. Each of us was also required to make out a last will and testament although, in my case, I didn't know why, for, as I wrote my parents, "I certainly have very little to leave."

We were also officially told at this time that we would henceforth be known as the "10th Mountain Division." This decision came as a great surprise but restored our pride in our unique qualifications, acquired through considerable sacrifice over some three years of arduous training. While we had continued to wear the distinctive shoulder patch featuring crossed bayonets (representing the Roman numeral 10) on a blue powder-keg background since it was given us at Hale in February 1944, we had no assurance, especially after our flatland training in Texas, that the army would ever make use of our particular skills. Another experimental division, the 71st Light Division (Pack, Jungle), which had been trained to fight in jungle conditions, had been converted to a standard infantry division and rushed to France as emergency reinforcements for the troops there. The reason the 10th was officially changed into a full-fledged mountain division was apparently because of its high proportion of mountaineers and skiers, as well as to prevent the waste of valuable training and other assets.[3] Along with our new name, like other U.S. corps d'elite units such as the Airborne and Rangers, we were also given a curved patch bearing the word *Mountain* to sew above the crossed-bayonets symbol. Now we had some hope that something more to our liking was about to happen, and we had not long to wait.

Mother suggested that I give Pat an engagement ring before I shipped out. I demurred, pointing out that, even if I wanted to, I wouldn't be able to get home to do it. But I expressed my thanks to her for keeping in touch with Pat and for inviting her down from Oberlin on holidays. I added, "When you get the news that I'm on my way, I wish you'd call her up and talk a little with her. And keep in close contact with her when I'm overseas. Besides, sometimes she'll have news from me that you won't know about, and vice-versa."

Late in November I wrote that we had been given a new company commander by the name of Lieutenant King, "who seemed to be a fairly nice egg," and that he promised to do his best to fulfill his responsibility to us. The more significant news, however, was that General Jones had been replaced and we now had a new commanding general.

> His name is Major General Hays, and he has just returned from the Normandy front .... He was in on "D" day, fought in Italy, and in the last World War. He also gave a speech today, saying that there is no doubt we'll soon be fighting, and that he'd never command a division in combat that wasn't a good one. Also what amazed us was that he said he'd heard a lot about us over in France, and the story was we're a crack outfit. He also stressed that all we need is to learn to work as a team. Then he said that the days of our taking a beating from fuss-penny generals and other officers were over. He said he'd give us as good a time as possible, for a happy soldier, he said, is mentally fit to be a fighting soldier.
> So all-in-all I'm pretty well pleased with our 10th Mountain's new commander. Here's hoping we live up to our reputation as the most expert mountain fighters in the world.

Our new leader, Major General George P. Hays, seemed to be a refreshing change from the past, if we could believe his promises. Reputed to be a young, aggressive tactician, his credentials were impressive and unique for a general. Born in China, he was, like me, the son of missionary parents. During World War I, he had won the Congressional Medal of Honor for his action in the second battle of the Marne when, as a first lieutenant in the artillery, he had had seven horses shot from under him while going to and from other commands and two French artillery batteries to insure accurate supporting fire. On his twelfth sortie, he was severely wounded, but after recuperating, he fought in the Argonne, where he was decorated with the Silver Star, one of two such medals he held.[4]

In World War II, prior to his assignment to the 10th Mountain Division, General Hays fought in Italy, where he had commanded the artillery at the battle of Cassino and then commanded the artillery of the 2d Infantry Division, which landed at Omaha Beach in Normandy on D-day plus one. He participated in the battle for that beachhead, the battle of St. Lo, and later in the siege of Brest, where his division artillery blasted out the 40,000 Germans who were entrenched around the city.[5]

As reported by Richard Thruelsen in the *Saturday Evening Post*, and as my letter indicated, we mountain troopers were more than a little impressed when he addressed us for the first time. "You men are going into combat. You will have some very tough fighting. But it is not all tough overseas. You will have fun too. When you are not fighting, I want you to relax and have a good time. I want you to be as comfortable as possible. You will have bad times, but you will have good times too."[6]

Regrettably, we did not give sufficient heed to his warning about the bad times.

I now informed Mother that when I thought I'd be writing my last letter to her and Dad before shipping out, I would pen a large star by her name. That would warn her she would not get any mail from me for some time to come. The towns around the camp, I said, were now jammed with wives spending their last few weeks close to their soldier husbands in the 10th Division. It was a pretty trying time for all, I went on. The 86th Regiment had already left by December 9, and I thought it would be quite a relief to finally board the train.

> *Camp Swift, Texas*
> *December 17, 1944*
>
> Dear Ed,
>
> This will be my last letter to you from the States. I hope I'll have plenty of chances to write over there. The war seems to be in a very tough stage at the moment.* An awful lot of American boys must be getting killed in that slow costly attack, and there aren't many replacements left. Our division is supposedly the last fully trained one left in the United States.
>
> Life is really a funny thing. This is the last place I expected to be when I left W.R.A. It's strange, too, how some men face it rather laughingly, and others try every means of getting out. You people hear so little of what actually happens. For instance, we have had at least eight or nine men shoot themselves in various parts of their bodies to keep from being sent across. In fact, a man from my company shot himself in the foot three days ago. Many, I think, are mental misfits, but the line you can draw between that and cowardice is pretty thin. Of course, the vast majority are ready and eager, and great things are expected of this outfit. I expect I'll have quite an experience in the coming year.
>
> Best of luck to you and Georgia. I hope everything works out well at the school, and in fixing up the home. I'll be thinking of you all Christmas morning, and missing you very much.

An incident which I didn't mention occurred when our company was first placed on alert for departure to the port of embarkation. A member of our company suddenly presented himself to the company commander and announced that he had lied about his age when inducted. He now claimed that he was only 16 years old and therefore underage for military service, and he requested

The period of the Battle of the Bulge in France.

that he be given an honorable discharge. The captain passed the problem up the line. We never found out whether the boy got his discharge, but he disappeared from our ranks and we never saw him again.

My experience with poison ivy in Texas suggested that one way of possibly avoiding combat, if I chose to use it, might be to take some bottled form of the ivy resin with me into whatever war zone was to be our assignment, and when appropriate, apply it in such a way as to require my hospitalization. Dad, I thought, could easily supply the drug and its effects would be far less painful and drastic than shooting oneself in the foot. Of course, if the battlefield lacked poison ivy, my falling victim to its ravages might arouse some suspicion, but it was unlikely the army medics would be sophisticated enough not to attribute it to some other local allergy. This would clearly be the case if we were sent to some jungle area in the Pacific where skin ailments were common.

I never gave any serious consideration to the idea, however, having been conditioned otherwise by parental example and training. Moreover, like most soldiers who had yet to experience infantry combat, I was naive enough to think I was indestructible and might even come home a hero.

The letter which followed carried the star symbol, drawn above the salutation, which I had warned Mother and Dad would mean it was the last letter they would receive before we left Camp Swift for parts unknown. *When* they received it, I don't know, because it was reviewed by a censor, and though nothing was deleted, for some reason it had a postal stamp applied at the head of the letter reading "NEW YORK, N.Y., MAR 23, 1945."

Camp Swift, Texas
Tuesday, December 19, 1944

Dear Mother, ✱

    Life has been pretty interesting here lately. Gen. Hays gave an excellent speech today as the 85th Regiment paraded in review. He spoke quietly and plainly with no oratory or profuseness. Our division, he said, is the Army's favorite. We've had more specialized training than any other unit in Army history. He said we're considered the best division ever to go across under the American flag, and that we have a great responsibility. The fight for us, he said, will be long, hard, and bloody. We must be in the proper frame of mind for a very tough fight....

    Well, Mother and Dad, I guess, as the General says, "We're entering upon the greatest adventure of our lives." I hope it won't be too long before I can step off that train in Wooster for good and hug you all close again. Be brave, trust in the Holy Spirit that watches close over me, and we'll all long for the day together.

On December 21, two days after I posted this letter, we departed by rail in very old passenger cars. Our destination was Camp Patrick Henry, the army base nearest our port of embarkation (POE), which was Newport News, Virginia. It was an exceedingly slow trip, the train taking three days to reach the camp in Virginia. There were no sleeping facilities on the train, at least for the common soldier, and we slept sitting up on the ancient, uncomfortable passenger seats. While asleep one night on this train, I experienced the only advance by a gay soldier that I ever encountered during my army service. I was awoken by his fondling me and, in my dreamlike state, was thoroughly enjoying it until I became conscious enough to realize that it was a fellow GI, rather than my imagined girlfriend, who was my benefactor. I proceeded then to push my seatmate off, but I did not make a big issue of the incident and he was not ostracized by others in the company. One reason for the moderate reaction was probably the fact that in those days of our youth, we were all so sexually preoccupied that we tended to excuse any kind of sexual behavior, if not pushed to extremes, as something to be expected.

More surprising was the desertion of at least one member of the regiment while we were en route to Virginia. The train moved so slowly at times that it was not difficult to leap off without serious injury, and at least one comrade who was not enamored of the idea of going into combat overseas, chose to say farewell somewhere in one of the southern states we passed through. Such an action, of course, when headed for a POE, was taken very seriously by the army. It could incur the death penalty if the offender were caught, but we never learned what happened in this case.

My attendance at a communion service Christmas night at our new post prompted a chaplain to send the following form letter to Dad and a slightly altered one to "Rev. Ellis" (my brother Paul).

CHAPEL IN THE WOODS
U. S. ARMY

Dear Dr. Ellis:

It will please you to know that your son, Robert, took an active interest in religious services while at our camp. He partook of Holy Communion and joined with others in singing the hymns of all churches.

We were pleased to have him with us, and sincerely believe his participation in our service deepened his religious convictions. I am certain he will be a good soldier—a soldier of whom you'll be proud.

Write cheerful, encouraging letters and write often. Your prayers and hopeful attitude will go a long way to prepare and strengthen him for whatever lies ahead.

May the Lord bless you and your household.

Sincerely yours,
Chaplain G. E. Mullins

I mailed my last letter from the United States following some very unpleasant work assignments at the camp, including one which occupied me all Christmas Day. My comrades and I also shared the unusual experience in the mess hall chow line at Patrick Henry of being served by German prisoners of war whose duties included doling out the helpings of food. This had the potential for creating some nasty conflicts because of the combination of circumstances that were present: soldiers under stress, about to be sent to some unknown battlefield; the natural dislike of combatants on one side for the enemy who had caused all the troubles they were in; and the usual tension which accompanied the serving of food. Eating was one of the few pleasures one experienced in the military, and if the serving appeared to be less than one deserved or was placed improperly on the serving tray, for example canned peaches too close to one's mashed potatoes, it was easy to feel angry.

Inevitably, one GI kept demanding that one of the German kitchen helpers give him a larger helping of beef, which the server refused, presumably because he was under orders to make all helpings the same. In frustration, the GI finally threw all of his food off his steel tray, stretched out over the counter, and tried to smash the tray down on the server's head and shoulders. While he was eventually restrained, it provided some degree of contentment for all of us who had suffered many similar abuses from unfeeling kitchen staff over the years, but had never dared to take such drastic action.

[Camp Patrick Henry, Virginia]
December 31, 1944
Sunday, New Years eve
   It was good to talk to you and Dad again. I certainly did appreciate all your Christmas letters. [A couple of lines are censored (scissored) out.]
   Well, tomorrow brings the start of a New Year. I hope it will be a victorious one.
   Got a nice Christmas card from the Millars: a family picture card.
   By the way, I have some rather startling news. I don't know exactly how you'll take it. Pat and I have just about come to a parting of the ways, at least as far as I'm concerned. I think it will be easier on her while I'm overseas. For a young girl to attach herself in any way to a far-away remembrance, when the beauty of friends and youth are all about her, seems unduly hard. So I wrote her saying I was calling it quits. I hope she doesn't see through it and realize how much I think of her and remember.
   Keep your spirits high. "Though I walk through the valley of the shadow, I fear not, for Thou art with me."

5

See Naples and Die

Welcome to Italy's Gothic Line, January–February 1945

> You have heard the saying,
> "See Naples and die,"
> Well ... you've seen Naples.
> — *German propaganda leaflet greeting*
> *10th Mt. troops*

General Hays' warning that we could expect a fight that would be "long, hard, and bloody" and that it would be "the greatest adventure of our lives" prompted me, before boarding the troop ship for parts unknown, to consider obtaining a diary in which I could record the events that were about to transpire. While I had written Mother and Dad in one of my last letters from the port of embarkation that I had no fear of the future, this was false bravado. I was not so naive that I did not recognize that service as a combat infantryman, if practiced any length of time, would surely lead to injury or death. By keeping a diary, I hoped to leave the family at least some record of what I experienced in the event that I did not survive the war, and if I did come back, it would be an invaluable record of all that had happened. While army regulations forbade keeping such a diary for the obvious reason that it could prove useful to the enemy if you were captured or killed, this was one of many military orders I didn't hesitate to disobey.

The leather-covered diary I obtained had "1945 Diary" imprinted on the cover and was small enough (measuring only 2¾" by 5⅜") to be kept in my shirt pocket. It contained preprinted day and date entries for each day, as well as maps and other information that might prove useful, but provided only four lines for each day. For this reason, many of my entries were not tied to specific dates, and when I was actively involved in a ground attack or otherwise occupied in trying to stay alive, I did not make any entries until a few days had passed and the situation had eased. Then I would summarize, in the form of penned entries written in a very fine hand (almost microscopic), recent or current events, beginning with the day when we set sail across the Atlantic. These diary notes, interspersed with my letters from various battle areas and comments on both, appear in the pages that follow.

(Diary)

January 4—Sailed today from Newport News, Virginia, on USS *West Point* (America), largest ship in U. S. Band played "Over There" and "Notre Dame Victory March" for Kelly. WAC's, USO people, and Air Corps aboard besides us and the 87th Infantry. We have guard duty and staterooms.

Wrote to Pat to call the romance off, not wanting to tie her down. Kind of hope she doesn't agree. Jud [Decker] in love. John [Horrall] playing the field and not on this ship.

Learned that Naples is our destination. Heavy sea. Fire drill again. Food is poor. WAC's are seasick. Men getting restless. Guard from 12 to 4 A.M. We've not been convoyed because of our great speed apparently. Class distinction is terrific. Women wild.

January 7—Very heavy sea. Many sick. Feel fine despite congestion and lack of air. Everyone in great spirits—gagging it up.

January 8—Trouble on guard duty. Two of our men jumped (George and Davis). Doubled guards.

War news is terrible. Stalemate in Italy and almost one on Western Front.

J. Decker is sick. Have been reading a lot. Poem I liked is *"I Have a Rendezvous with Death."*

Concerned about what fate might befall me in the battles to come, I was receptive to the poem by Alan Seeger (1888–1916), an American who joined the French Foreign Legion and was killed in the First World War. Seeger's poem was representative of the literature of fear that emerged during both world wars:

I Have a Rendezvous with Death

I have a rendezvous with Death
At some disputed barricade,
When Spring comes back with rustling shade
And apple-blossoms fill the air—
I have a rendezvous with Death
When Spring brings back blue days and fair.

It may be he shall take my hand
And lead me into his dark land
And close my eyes and quench my breath—
It may be I shall pass him still.
I have a rendezvous with Death
On some scarred slope of battered hill,
When Spring comes round again this year
And the first meadow-flowers appear.

> God knows 'twere better to be deep
> Pillowed in silk and scented down,
> Where Love throbs out in blissful sleep,
> Pulse nigh to pulse, and breath to breath,
> Where hushed awakenings are dear …
> But I've a rendezvous with Death
> At midnight in some flaming town,
> When Spring trips north again this year,
> And I to my pledged word am true,
> I shall not fail that rendezvous.[1]

Conditions on the ship were, of course, hardly comparable to what I had experienced in previous trips across the Atlantic, going to and from Persia with my family during peacetime. While my company had the advantage of being assigned staterooms because of military police duty aboard ship, most of us were required to sleep one above the other in hammocks five tiers high. Since it was midwinter, we spent most of our time below and much of that time in endless lineups in narrow passageways waiting for chow. We soon learned that you virtually had to get in line for the next meal right after finishing the preceding one if you were not to miss a meal.

Because of the overcrowding with thousands of troops on board, the air was foul, and the rough seas also encouraged seasickness. I had never been bothered by the latter misfortune in past trips by ocean liner, and fortunately my appetite was unaffected even by this most severe of tests.

Morale was very high, perhaps because any change was welcomed after the years of mind-deadening training. Many sexual encounters appeared to be taking place on board, mostly involving officers arranging liaisons with WACs, nurses, and other women, and we had our hands full defending the (assumed) virginity of those ladies not wanting to participate. Crap games, whose stakes exceeded any I had ever observed before (as the following diary note indicates), were held on stair landings and attracted huge crowds, not only for lack of other amusements but because of the amount of money being bet.

(Diary)

January 10—Got a misplaced letter from Paul. No baby yet.

Passed through Gibraltar this morning, escorted by four destroyers. Plenty of PBY's.* Beginning to realize that this is no dry run. Food still terrible. Thank God for my cast iron stomach. See plenty of freighters now.

January 12—Getting punchy from guard. Protecting females aboard from the wolves.

January 13—Passed the Isle of Capri today and some other isle on our right. The former had great high cliffs and a town lay over the saddle. Very picturesque. Saw the first British plane: a Halifax bomber. Expect to land at 3 P.M.

---

*The Convair PBY-5 and PBY-6 Catalina were military flying boats which had blister gun ports aft of the wings and a Plexiglas gun turret in the nose (or "bow").[2]

Eitel [a member of my company] won $1,000 at craps.

Pulled into Naples. Many sunken ships. Beautiful harbor. *Empress of Aus.*[tralia?] docked beside us. Vesuvius in all its glory. Tremendous mountain ranges seen.

On Saturday, January 13, nine days after sailing, the USS *West Point* (the former luxury liner the SS *America*) docked in Naples harbor, Italy, at approximately 4 P.M. amid a series of unpleasant rain squalls.[3] The 86th Mountain Infantry Regiment had arrived almost a month earlier and was attached to the IVth Corps of the American 5th Army. It relieved the 434th and 900th Antiaircraft Battalions (both of whose troops had been converted to infantry because of the shortage of manpower), and the British 39th Light Antiaircraft Regiment, in the division-sized Task Force 45's sector northwest of Pistoia.[4] General Robinson E. Duff, the assistant division commander, who had led an advance party to Italy arriving on November 17, was named commanding general of Task Force 45 until the arrival of General Hays.

In Quarcianella, Italy, the 86th suffered the first casualties the division experienced when an S-mine exploded near the rail line running along the border of the 86th's training area. It was followed by subsequent detonations immediately thereafter. In addition to seven enlisted men being killed and four wounded, a Catholic chaplain was also killed by a mine explosion while going to perform last rites for the men killed.

(Diary)

January 14—We disembarked at 4 A.M. and marched three miles to 16 waiting LCI's [Landing Craft Infantry]. City waterfront devastated. Old castle in ruins. Many beggars. Streets clean. "See Naples and Die." Rumored that 86th [Regiment] chaplain and eight GI's killed by mines (confirmed). Men nonchalant.

Sailed for 30 hours up coast to Leghorn [Livorno]. Very rough . Slept on floor of ship. Beautiful coastline. Saw Elba [island where Napoleon was exiled]. K and C rations. Unbelievable. Wondered if family could guess. Prout and I exchange death letter promises.

January 15—Arrived 6 P.M. and boarded trucks for Pisa. Leghorn wrecked. Barrage balloons, cruisers, PT boats and Ack-Ack [anti-aircraft artillery].

January 16—Bivouacked in field outside Pisa (staging area). Many friendly planes. Good food. Many ragged children begging. Cold. Lined tents most of day. Spoke French to an Italian. No mail going out.

January 17—Decker and I rode a jeep into Pisa and really saw the town. The Leaning Tower and cathedrals unharmed. People very poor and hungry. Town mostly in ruins. Drank some wine and visited the Red Cross. Very cold, wet and miserable. No equipment. Very disgusted.

Our landing in Naples, the Allies' principal supply port in Italy whose harbor facilities had been heavily bombed by the Luftwaffe in the spring of 1944, and the evident desperate poverty of the Italian people, brought the war home to us very quickly. The division was also greeted by German propaganda leaflets welcoming us to the Italian war zone and asking whether we were familiar with the Italian proverb, "See Naples and die (*Vedi Napoli, e poi muori*)." We were advised, "Well, you've seen Naples."

The trip up the coast was unescorted but otherwise uneventful, although the sleeping accommodations on the steel floor of the ship were hardly pleasant. The bivouac area to which we were taken on arrival in Leghorn was located three kilometers west of Pisa and in peacetime served as the hunting grounds of King Victor Emmanuel III.[5] There we were supposed to be supplied with vehicles, additional clothing and equipment, and ammunition, but none of the specialized cold weather clothing and other winter gear we had tested and left behind in Colorado was forthcoming.

My first letter home from Italy was a V-Mail letter sent from this tented bivouac area.

(Letter)
"Somewhere in Italy"
January 17, 1945   V-Mail
    We had a comparatively pleasant voyage over except for a couple of days of very rough weather. I felt fine all the way across despite the fact that it was a far cry from the old days. I was on guard duty all the way over—maintaining "light discipline," keeping order during "abandon ship" alerts, etc. It wasn't too hard and we got better living quarters because of it. We passed Gibraltar around the [censored] and landed in Italy on the [censored]. I'm afraid we'll see action [censored]. I can't say where we are, but we've seen a lot of mined cities and ports. The food and clothing situation over here for the Italians is very acute. Little ragged children beg food from us when we finish eating, and we scrape it out of our mess gears into little cans they carry. Then they carry it over to their ma's and pa's standing nearby. The U.S. soldiers of course are very touched and astonished at the scenes of suffering all around. Old medieval castles in ruins and the waterfronts are especially ruined. The bombing seems not to have been haphazard.
    It's pretty cold where we are, but no rain as yet. All of my old friends are here: J. Decker, J. Horrall, etc. Jack Kelly and I are sleeping together, and exchange humorous anecdotes continually. I'm feeling very well so don't worry on that score.

(Diary)
    January 21—Moved up to the front in trucks for 75 miles. F Co. first into the line. High in the Apennines in the little town of Gavinana. Sleeping in a Catholic school. People very friendly and kind. Picking up Italian.
    Priest speaks French and I'm interpreter for everyone. Visited him at his home and drank excellent port. Looks like Bing Crosby. We discussed Communism and the state of Italy. He blessed Kelly's medal.
    Little boys work for us. Germans five miles away. Got a woman to do my washing. Italian barbered me. No letters yet. Wonder when we'll attack.
    86th men captured two Nazis and killed two. Expect to be sent on patrol soon.

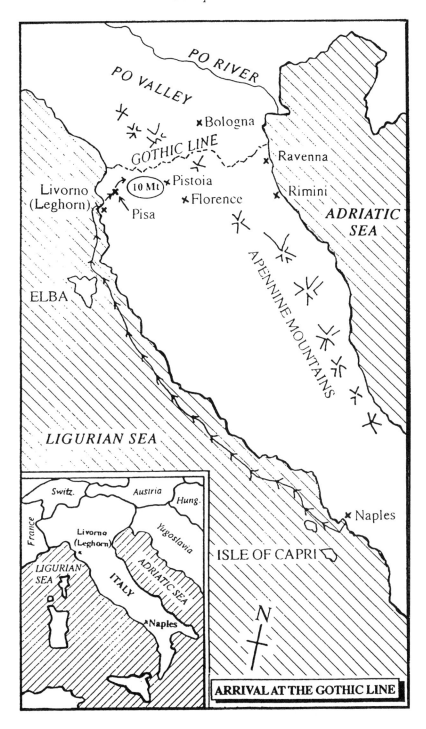

ARRIVAL AT THE GOTHIC LINE

SS troops used to be here and took men to Germany as slave labor. Very cruel to the people here. Two Americans were hidden for a year here by the priest.

My French is coming in very handy. Miss Pat and the family very much. Wonder if I'll ever see home again.

The main body of our 85th Mountain Regiment cleared the Pisa staging area on January 20, 1945, and we traveled by truck to positions in the front lines, where we joined the 86th and 87th Regiments under Task Force 45. Our 2d Battalion, under the command of a West Point graduate, Lieutenant Colonel Francis Roche, which included Company F to which I was assigned, was headquartered in Gavinana, a mountain village high in the Apennines.* Our official mission was to occupy, patrol, and be prepared to defend all of our assigned Task Force 45 area. The Apennines in this area are the most rugged mountains south of the Alps, rising to considerable heights, and during the winter months they are covered with several feet of snow. Fortunately, our sector, and indeed the entire Italian front, had been relatively quiet thus far during the winter, with both the German and the Allied armies resting and regrouping their divisions in preparation for spring offensives.

The Allied armies, including the American 5th and the British 8th, were a melange of troops: Belgians, Brazilians, Canadians, Cypriots, French (including mountain troops from Algeria and Morocco), Palestinian Jews, Indians, Italians (who had joined the Allied cause after Italy's surrender on September 8, 1943), Nepalese, New Zealanders, Poles, South Africans, Syro-Lebanese, and Yugoslavians. In addition to our unit, which was the U.S. Army's only specialized mountain division, the American combatants included one of the last two segregated black divisions, the 92d Infantry Division, and the 442d Infantry, composed of Americans of Japanese descent. The latter was to become one of the army's most decorated regimental combat teams. With our arrival, the IVth Corps' front was held from left to right, beginning on the Ligurian Sea on the west coast of Italy, by the 92d Division, then by Task Force 45, which included the 10th Mountain Division, and finally the division-sized Brazilian Expeditionary Force, with the 8th Indian Division constituting a reserve.

This winter line had been named the *Gotenstellung*, or Gothic Line, by the German theater commander, Field Marshal Albert Kesselring.† It was along this line that he hoped to make another stand, as he had in the winter of 1943 along the Rapido River and before Cassino. Thus far he had been quite successful, having fended off four attempts by the American 5th Army to break through its area of responsibility (the high ground of the Apennine

---

*Until a few decades ago, Gavinana was simply a name in history books, having been the site of the famous battle of 1530 which marked the Medicis' return to power. Today it is a summer and winter vacation resort, with ski lifts, hotels, and other tourist attractions.[6]

†It was the German idea that this name would recall the presence of the Gothic kingdoms established by Germanic tribes in Italy in the 6th century A.D.[7]

Mountains), as well as repeated efforts by the British 8th Army to advance through German defensive positions in the lowland along the Adriatic flank. As a result, the Allied effort to reach Bologna and wrest control of the Po Valley before winter set in had been frustrated since the end of October 1944.

Our arrival in Gavinana was greeted with great joy by the village inhabitants, who had suffered severely under the German occupation. Under the leadership of the village priest, they had hidden two American flyers who had been shot down in the area. I met frequently with the priest in the evenings to play cards and enjoyed being able to converse with him in French. In appearance the priest looked remarkably like the singer and actor Bing Crosby, who coincidentally starred as a Catholic priest in *Going My Way*, a very popular movie of the time.

From the good father, I learned that German SS troops had occupied the village, but when the American army approached, they had withdrawn, taking all available food with them, including the priest's pigs. In an added touch of cruelty, the SS officer who had shared the priest's quarters next to the village cathedral smashed all the priest's glassware before departing. Since the Americans did not physically occupy the village until a week or two after the Germans left, its residents were literally starving before we arrived. We helped replenish their food supply, but couldn't fully resolve the situation. A serious food shortage existed throughout the Allied-occupied regions of Italy because of deficiencies in the grain import program resulting from the lack of sufficient merchant ships to carry the grain and the higher priority given to troop and weapon shipments.

My weapons platoon, consisting of two machine gun and three mortar squads, was quartered in what had been a girls' school near the center of the village. There we slept on the concrete floor. Some of the local children picked up our laundry for their mothers to wash and were helpful in other ways. In turn, we gave them food, candy, cigarettes, and leftover food. We had few facilities for washing our own clothes and were delighted to unload that burden on the local women, but we were deeply affected by the solemnly patient little ones waiting with their tin buckets for whatever food was uneaten or could be spared by our cooks or other kitchen help. Such close relationships developed with the villagers that many 10th Mountain soldiers were treated as members of the family.

In the evenings, if we weren't on guard or otherwise on duty, we often visited one of the village taverns, where we swilled watered-down vino and the potent, colorless Italian brandy called *grappa*. The latter brought out the worst in some soldiers, whose personalities seemed to change completely "under the influence." One GI often sat uncomfortably near me while he vented his anger about army life, and any other ills he thought of, by driving his bayonet repeatedly into a helmet liner resting on the bar. Somehow this detracted from the pleasure of the "happy hour."

(Diary)
January 23—A few fascists in this town. Their attitude at times is provoking, to say the least. One stole my overcoat.

Celebrated Wally's [Krusell] birthday by a (pseudo) spaghetti dinner. Life goes on.

Warren Lucas' fingers shot off by his bazooka exploding. Many men killed in the 86th—mostly on patrols. Skinner, in the 3rd. Battalion, was shot today and killed for not knowing the password.

Norton, Lt. Hanks, Parker, Perry, George, and others are on the ski patrol. They left Sunday for a long patrol. They're good men. I hope everything turns out all right.

Played rummy with the padre. Danced with a cute Italian and was asked to a dance by my wash woman. Played hard to get.

Our initial weeks on the front lines were devoted to further training and patrol actions, the latter designed not only to indoctrinate us in the realities of fighting the enemy, but also to capture prisoners for interrogation, to ferret out paths through mine fields, and to test the strength of the enemy outposts. These patrols, some employing skis, somehow lacked the swift, clean thrill of skiing into "battle" we had felt in Colorado; instead they often resulted in sharp clashes with the enemy, with soldiers being killed and wounded on both sides.

One raid—deemed highly successful because it resulted in the capture of six Italian prisoners of war and one dead Italian lieutenant—involved a long climb by our troops over hard-crusted snow on such steep terrain that it required the tedious cutting of steps in the snow. A less successful 22-man patrol from the 3d Battalion of the 85th was also sent to attack enemy positions and bring back prisoners. German automatic weapons fire, including light artillery, split the patrol, with the result that four of its members were wounded and, along with five other men, were captured. The following day when nine of our medical corpsmen, wearing Red Cross helmets and arm bands, went out in search of the wounded men, they were fired upon and had to withdraw. Thus we learned how little the enemy cared about abiding by the Geneva Convention.

Soldiers new to combat are often prone to shoot without much reflection, as our 87th Regiment learned on Kiska when all the casualties that occurred were attributable to friendly troops firing on each other through the dense fog. Thus Skinner's loss, reportedly because he did not remember the password, was not that unusual. On January 28 another mountain trooper, Private First Class Donald Schneider, was shot by a friendly outpost while he was passing through our lines with a patrol and died of his wounds in an aid station.

As for my concern about those sent out on the ski patrol, some were of more than a little interest to me because one, Staff Sergeant George Norton, commanded the section comprising our two machine gun squads, while another, Lieutenant Charles Hanks, was the officer heading the weapons (mortar and machine gun) platoon in which our section was located.

A few of the villagers in Gavinana regretted the departure of the Germans and were not above stealing a warm GI overcoat if given the opportunity. Most, however, regarded us with great affection and arranged social events where we could talk to, as well as "swing and sway" with, some of the local girls under proper chaperonage. I had been so thoroughly indoctrinated by countless army showings of movies about venereal disease and the likelihood of contracting it from women of questionable purity that I was leery of what was surely an innocuous invitation from my washerwoman. As for other young ladies of unquestioned innocence and virginity, their parents wisely gave us little opportunity for unchaperoned, lustful explorations.

(Letter)
Gavinana
Jan 25th, 1945   V-Mail
I'm writing you now from the front lines high in the Apennine mountains of Italy. I've really been using my French for all its worth, and it helps a lot when I try to speak and understand Italian. I've picked up a lot of Italian, and have a standing challenge that given five minutes, I can make any Italian understand whatever phrase or idea I want to convey. And I haven't been stopped. It's amazing how comparable it is to French.

Yesterday, the 24th, I received your V-mail letter of the 11th telling of the birth of Paul and Mary Liz's baby girl. That certainly is wonderful. Give them my congratulations, and I'm eagerly awaiting more news on it. And, by the way, V-mail is much faster than air mail, apparently.

There is so little I can say without it being censored that about all I can write is that I'm all right and feeling quite healthy. Since I've been over here I've received letters and V-mail from you and Dad, Paul, Margaret , and Pat. I've never seen hide nor hair of the camera or radio. I sent 40 dollars home the other day and my monthly pay deductions in bonds will start at the end of February.

I wish you'd collect all the writings of Thomas Wolfe that you can for my library.

I'd like a picture of you and Dad together. Pictures are always swell to get and I only have one of you and Peggy.

I hope this great Russian offensive keeps up. In fact all of us here are watching it with eager anticipation. Everyone here is in high spirits and one high-ranking Allied officer told us we were the finest troops he has ever seen. He said: "They don't want to stop—they want to keep on chasing 'Jerry.'"

My diary entries and letters used different nicknames to refer to the Germans. In the First World War, the Germans were almost always referred to as the "Huns," but that name was rarely used in the Second World War. In the beginning it was usually "Jerry," the name I used above, but we also used the terms "Kraut," "Nazi," "Heine," and the Italian word for Germans, "Tedeschi." The last-named expression (in which the "ch" is hard like the "ch" in "chorus") became most popular near the end of the war in Italy when the Italian inhabitants of the villages we transited would call out to us that they believed the "Tedeschi" were giving up.

The two German phrases I made sure I learned before we went into combat were "*Hände hoch*" ("Hands up") and "*Ich ergebe mich*" ("I surrender"). I
decided those would cover the most critical situations and didn't want to risk
forgetting them by trying to get too fancy with others.

> *(Diary)*
> January 28—Third Battalion moved up to the front. Third Platoon is
> still up ahead on outpost duty on the front lines. Perry almost shot today
> because of password. I never can seem to remember them.
> Paul and Mary Liz's baby arrived the 10th. Her name is Judith Frances.
> Broderick killed in ambush and Lt. Traynor. 20 man patrol lost. Rus-
> sians 90 miles from Berlin. Fired the bazooka. Company ski patrol
> returned safely.
> Got high on Battalion Guard and forgot the password. Rather embar-
> rassing.
> Sent 90 dollars home. Fired our M.G. for about 2,000 rounds. Worked
> fine. 6 degrees below zero.

Since we arrived in Italy more than two weeks earlier, our bathing facilities had consisted of water collected in a steel helmet, and we all were more
than a little rank. About this time, arrangements were made to truck us all to
an unheated building a short distance from Gavinana which had some very
slow-running shower heads emitting cold water only. The cold concrete floor,
the wind whistling through the shower room, the maddeningly slow trickle of
icy water, and temperatures hovering around zero degrees Fahrenheit made it
a bathing experience never to be forgotten.

I sent two picture postcards at this time from Gavinana, one to Mother
and the other to Margaret. The cards displayed slightly different photos of the
village, but the name of the town had been cut off by the censor, Lieutenant
Wayne Mackin of Company F, so neither Mother or Margaret could determine where we were. The card to Mother tried to calm her fears about my
safety, and because I had not yet seen any real combat, I could be honest about
that.

> *(Letter)*
> *Gavinana*
> *Jan. 28, 1945   V-Mail*
> This is your roving reporter reporting that all's well on the Italian front
> as far as I'm concerned. I've been receiving your V-mails pretty regularly
> now and I hope you're getting mine. I'm really in very little danger so don't
> let your imagination play tricks with you. I certainly could do with some
> cans of food though. I'm half-starved most of the time.

The letter to Margaret was equally uninformative, but erroneously
assumed she would know from the card where we were located.

(Letter)
"Front Lines—Italy"
January 28th, 1945   *V-Mail*

Dear Margaret,

By this time you must have found out from the family where I am. If not the above [referring to the name Gavinana, which had been censored out] will tell you. It's rather serious work over here—even my humor is a little dampened. This postcard may lead you to think I'm on Cook's tour, but I assure you it's far from that, even though the transport did take us by Gibraltar, Capri, etc. Frankly, Italy is in one hell of a mess and even their wine is watered. However, we struggle on in this seemingly thankless effort to get it over with and ourselves back home in good condition.

(Letter)
Gavinana
February 3, 1945   *V-Mail*

Life goes on—we watch the Russian offensive and stir up a little trouble ourselves now and then. I'm afraid a lot more of my friends and comrades will die so that others may live freely before this is over. I doubt if they'll ever launch a full scale attack here in Italy, however, as long as we can tie up German divisions this way. Of course they'll have to retreat eventually.

It's no use my trying to contact other soldiers I know in Italy for I'm well tied down and about the only people I have contact with are the other members of my machine gun platoon. I haven't seen Jud Decker or John Horrall since I left the transport and have no idea just where they are. Jack [Kelly] and I of course practically shave each other, we're so close all the time, and along that line I am the possessor of a full moustache at the moment. Perhaps by the time I see you all again I'll look like a red-bearded Uncle Fred.

Hope Dad doesn't work too hard. I want him to give me some competition at golf when this war is over.

Upon letting my moustache grow, I was surprised to discover it came out red rather than brown like the rest of my hair. As for the "Uncle Fred" I referred to, he was a retired missionary from Persia who had a magnificent full white beard. He had been taken in by Mother and Dad when his own relatives had abandoned him in his old age, and he stayed with my parents until his death.

My comment to Mother about the difficulty of communicating with other people in our war zone was in response to a letter she sent suggesting that I contact a lieutenant colonel she knew who was attached to some Allied commission in Italy and might be able to get me transferred to a less dangerous assignment. I dutifully entered his name and address into my battle diary, but expressed doubt that I'd get the opportunity to see him.

I was also fairly confident at the time that we would not be a part of a major offensive with its accompanying heavy loss of life. My opinion—which reflected American, if not British, strategy—was that by harassing the Germans

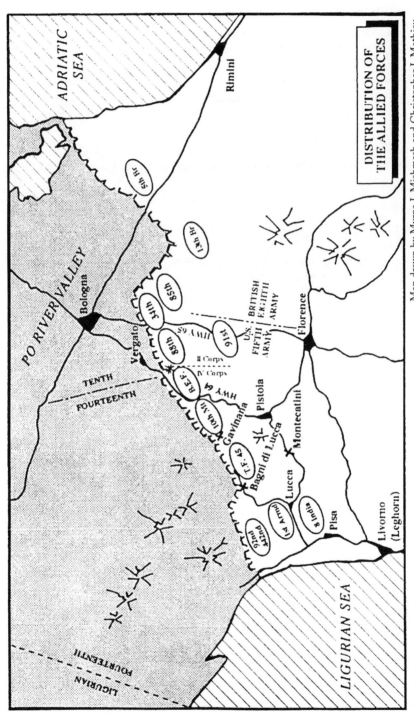

DISTRIBUTION OF
THE ALLIED FORCES

Map drawn by Myrna J. Mishmash and Christopher J. Mathieu.

sufficiently along the Gothic Line, we could keep their army in Italy occupied, preventing reinforcement of their forces on the Western Front and permitting Eisenhower and the Allied forces there to advance into Germany proper. The diversion of enemy strength from the Russian front and Western Europe had been the basic goal of Allied strategy in the Mediterranean since the invasion of Sicily. As stated in the U.S. Army history of the Mediterranean theater of operations, *Cassino to the Alps* : "The American view reflected a longheld conviction that the Allies should concentrate on driving along the most direct route into the heart of the Third Reich rather than on nibbling away at enemy forces with a series of peripheral operations of indeterminate length that could deflect Allied strength from the main thrust."[8]

The British, on the other hand, and Churchill in particular, not only wanted to advance at least to the Po River in northern Italy, but following the stalemate in the northern Apennines, to launch a trans-Adriatic amphibious operation into the Balkans. The latter would be designed to outflank Kesselring and at the same time prevent Russian forces from establishing an uncontested sphere of influence in that region. Roosevelt's and Stalin's opposition, for differing reasons, forced Churchill to abandon this idea, but there remained excellent strategic arguments for the Allies to stay put in the northern Apennines. As noted by the author of *Cassino to the Alps* in his concluding assessment of the Italian campaign, staying there constituted the Allies' last opportunity to halt while still containing large numbers of enemy divisions in Italy with relatively few Allied divisions. Once beyond the Apennines, the country opens up and also beyond the Apennines lay the Po River and finally the Alps. The latter offered naturally strong positions which the Germans could themselves have held quite economically, so that it would have been the Germans who would have contained the Allies along that line. In short, the assessment argued, it made no strategic sense to drive the Germans from the Apennines and into the Alps unless the Allies had sufficient strength to break through the Alpine defense line and into the mid-Danube basin and southern Germany proper.[9]

(Diary)

January 31—Got paid and sent $90 home. Received word that we're moving up as a reinforcement to the 3rd. Platoon. [N—] drunk.

February 3—Moved out Friday morning in trucks along a shelled road. Mission seemed very dangerous and everyone was nervous. Hiked up steep road on ice for seven hours in rain and snow. Quarters are lonely house above a small town near Catigliano. Germans visible on the opposite ridge. Climbed to the summit and dug machine gun positions all day (pill boxes). "Died like a mule" (favorite gag). Limber [Krusell] said, "If Pat could see you now, carrying that load, she would either think you the greatest man in the world or a fool for killing yourself."

Climbed to the outpost again. Olsen saw a German observing us. Couldn't catch him.

Got a terrific scare at 7 P.M. Shrapnel through the trees and noises all around. "Custer's last stand." Kelly and I back-to-back in the trench. Unearthly sound of the telephone sending for help. Artillery all around.

This patrol for the purpose of reconnaissance and contact with enemy positions was the first really demanding physical requirement made of my platoon and one which involved incoming artillery fire. While the northern face of the Apennines is friendly, sloping gradually and invitingly toward the valley of the Po, the southern face which we had to assault repeatedly is hostile. It drops sharply and is marked by broken ridges, spurs, and deep, pocket-shaped valleys providing a series of excellent defensive positions. The range's summits have an average crest elevation of 3,000 to 3,600 feet, while some exceed 4,000 feet and in the western part of the range, 6,000 feet.

To reach the top of the ridge which was our objective, we had to climb what was virtually a 45-degree slope, carrying all our heavy weapons (mortars and machine guns) and required ammunition on our backs without benefit of mules or tracked vehicles. The lack of pack animals required us to serve as beasts of burden and prompted the bitter joke that our obituaries would honor us for having died like mules. Constant joking was the prime GI attribute that made our soldier's life bearable. During the climb, since I was feeling particularly healthy and energetic on this occasion, I bore a greater burden than usual. In addition to carrying the 30-caliber, air-cooled machine gun—which was my duty as first gunner in the squad, and which alone weighed some 31 pounds—I also carried a pistol, a pack, some ammunition for the machine gun, and other equipment amounting to some 90 pounds in all.[10] This is what led my companion, Wally Krusell, the so-called second gunner, whose job was to carry the machine gun tripod (weighing 14 pounds) and other gear, to comment on my load.

At the time, we thought the incoming artillery shells meant an attack by German infantry would follow, but for some reason the assault failed to materialize.

(Letter)
Bagni di Lucca
Feb. 8th, 1945   V-Mail
    This is the first chance I've had to write for some time. We've really been busy. Four days ago we moved further forward than anyone into what most of us thought would be a very dangerous position. It was killing hard work and the weather was really miserable.
    For four days and nights we stood guard on positions, but save for some artillery and sniping, and a couple of bad scares when we thought we were in for a real fight, we came out ok. But I've never been through such a physical strain. My whole platoon is pretty well exhausted and half sick with dysentery, colds, fever, etc. I'm half dead myself.
    [Censored lines]
    We can't keep this pace up much more.
    If anyone tells you this is a stagnant front, don't believe them. It's really miserable in these mountains and keeping these 25 German divisions tied down is plenty of work.

I've never been so dirty, unshaven and tired. I've had one bath since I left the States and the rest of the time I use my helmet as a pseudo bath tub. Kelly is sicker than a dog at the moment, and everyone is lying around talking of home. I hope the Russians and Americans can finish it off soon. We're cut off from most of the up-to-date news, and get only meager reports such as "40 miles from Berlin," etc.

Mail from home is about the only relief we get, and we have to read that on the run usually. I'm sending $90 home. I hope the money order arrives safely. I miss you all so much, and dream of that day when I can return. Deep love to you all.

P.S. I haven't time to write to every one in the family but I certainly appreciate your and Paul's letters.

[Diary]

February 7—Lucas (Andy) killed two Jerries with an L.M.G. [Light Machine Gun]. Many wounded in K Co. attack.

Returned to Gavinana as the 87th relieved us. Terribly tired (Kelly sick, and others). Told we're to be a "raider company" with H Company in support. Washed in my helmet. Slept on the floor.

February 8—Moved out for Bagni di Lucca on our new mission. (Plenty of dead I expect this time in the Company.) Quartered in something like the Broadmoor.* No heat.

February 9—Had first hot shower since leaving the transport (against orders of course). "Seems fair enough" standing gag response to all bad events. Everyone has had dysentery for days. The usual competent medical service of course.

Met Jud Decker. Spent the afternoon over vino catching up on each other's experiences. He's been on four raids. Says our 50's [50-caliber machine guns] are damned dangerous but useful. Saved a girl from rape (he says). Told story of girl who turned around to the ribbing GI's and said "I lived three years in Pennsylvania."

February 12—Tremendous spring baths here. Went to a dance with Tim [Prout] and Jud. Looked like a hockey rink or the Met. Pushed a couple of babes around. Italian band played "I Love to Ride the Ferry."

Guy milked a goat during an "88" [German 88mm artillery] bombardment.

February 16—Jack Kelly was evacuated to a hospital because of dysentery. Got 50 caliber M.G.'s for an expected raid but it never came off. Moved back by night in trucks to Gavinana. Got in a sulphur springs bath and a suit of British underwear. Spent today resting in the warm sun.

Big Three Conference news is wonderful.† Looks like we're on the road to lasting peace. I feel as though if I'm killed I've at least died for something worthwhile. A great price has been paid but the gains seem great.

The Broadmoor, a historic hotel, one of only eight in America currently awarded Mobil's five-star rating, is located in Colorado Springs, Colorado. I had visited it occasionally while on weekend passes from Camp Hale.

†*This so-called "Yalta Conference" in February 1945 was attended by Roosevelt, Churchill, and Stalin at Yalta, a famous resort in the USSR. They mapped the final assault on Germany and the postwar occupation of that country. They also made provision for a meeting in San Francisco to lay the foundations of the peacetime United Nations organization.*

The K Company attack I referred to concerned a raid this unit conducted as a reinforced rifle company to destroy German emplacements and capture prisoners of war. While they took command of some ridges and advanced to within 600 yards of their final objective, heavy enemy fire eventually forced them to withdraw without any prisoners. Their casualties included two dead— one private killed by fragments of an 88mm shell and the other by a direct mortar hit—and six wounded, including a lieutenant, the first officer casualty in the 85th Regiment.

Bagni di Lucca (Baths of Light), an Italian resort town boasting warm mineral waters, had been popularized as a spa by Elisa Baciocchi, Napoleon's sister. Its waters had been consumed and used to treat arthritis and similar ailments for many centuries, and we found it a delightful change from our mountain village of Gavinana.[11] While we had supposedly been sent there to participate in a combat patrol, the plans were later canceled, and we were able to take advantage of the local baths, trade some of our gear for long underwear from British troops sharing our quarters in a local hotel, and see friends in other units from whom we had been separated for some time.

Wally Krusell's 6'7" frame caused a considerable stir in the Italian villages and towns, particularly among the women, when we wandered the streets. It was evident, even from what limited knowledge of Italian I possessed, that their comments to each other, which were invariably accompanied by raised eyebrows, long glances up and down his unusual height, and suggestive giggles, included speculation about his sexual equipment and prowess. Doing my best to share in the adulation, I made it clear we were inseparable and implied I was equally well endowed, but their only interest in me appeared to be whether I would part with any cigarettes or chocolate.

Our brief stay in Bagni di Lucca increased our resentment of those army decisions and orders which were not only unduly harsh, but lacked both common sense and concern for fair play. For example, initially we were denied permission to take hot showers in our Bagni di Lucca quarters. Similarly, despite the amoebic dysentery which was ravaging our entire company, we were given virtually no medical attention and almost no drugs to treat the condition. Such incidents led to the standard wry response of "Seems fair enough!" to all inexplicable orders.

Jack Kelly, my closest companion and friend, both in training and now overseas, was finally carried off on a stretcher when his dysentery became so severe that he could no longer stand or perform even the simplest duty. His long-standing reputation as a consummate actor and "fuck-off" caused many (even including me) to wonder whether his illness was genuine, in spite of the fact that most of us were suffering from the same disease. If it was feigned, he did not share his secret with me, so it was generally accepted that he was truly sicker than the rest of us. In any event it resulted in his transport to the 5th Army's Evacuation Hospital No. 16 behind the lines.[12]

Kelly's departure hurt me a lot. He was a superb soldier when he chose to be—intelligent, strong, and aggressive—and he was a great companion with an unmatched sense of humor and a talent for bringing ridicule to the pompous. As such, he was a bright spot on a black canvas, and I felt his loss deeply.

My reunion with old friend Jud Decker, who was now assigned to a rifle company in the 1st Battalion, 85th, our relish in exchanging experiences, and the fun he, Tim Prout, and I had at a local dance together helped me adjust to Jack's absence. I especially enjoyed Jud's story about what happened when he and others from his company encountered a voluptuous Italian girl who was washing clothes in a stream. One of his buddies exclaimed: "I think I've fallen in love. That woman has a better body than Betty Grable."

Another observed: "I'd give my right arm to spend three minutes in the sack with her."

Suddenly the object of their desire turned towards the admirers favoring her with these and other ribald remarks, and to their shock and astonishment said in perfect English: "Perhaps it would interest you to know that I lived three years in Pennsylvania."

A few days after arriving in Bagni di Lucca I was clearly depressed with the existing state of affairs and said so in the following letter to Mother and Dad. The next letter, written four days later after our return to Gavinana, was the last before we were thrown into our first major battle. Little did I realize at the time how comparatively peaceful and undemanding our lives to date had been.

(Letter)
Gavinana
February 12, 1945 `V-Mail`
   I'm sorry to hear the work is so heavy still for Dad and you. Dysentery, rain, cold, snow, etc. combine to make my life miserable. However, you eventually acquire a certain apathy toward everything—the uncertainty, the hazards, and all the suffering and pain. All one can do is dream and pray for that glimmering day in the future when this insane life is over.
   I hope you're getting my letters comparatively regularly. I doubt if I'll ever get a chance to see any of your friends who are here in Italy. In fact I've not even seen John Horrall since I left the States, and when you consider that we're both in the same outfit and such good friends, you can see how tied down we are. In fact, I see only my immediate platoon members most of the time.
   Hope all are well—do you contact Pat often?

(Letter)
Gavinana
Feb. 16th, 1945 *V-Mail*
   At the moment I'm sitting in the warm sun with little Italian "bambini" playing around me. It seems very unlike war at the moment. Every once in a while we get more or less of a restful day such as this one.
   Today I received quite a batch of V-mail from you, the date of the latest one was February 3d. Keep scanning the *N. Y. Times* communiques,

and one of these days you'll recognize us in the dispatches. I've been writing Pat rather steadily so she should be getting almost an equal number of letters as you.

I got in a wonderful hot sulphur spring bath the other day and felt as though in another world. Then the British gave me a change of long wool underwear so I feel like a new man. I'm feeling quite well today. Kelly was taken behind the lines yesterday to an evacuation hospital. He contracted some sort of amoebic dysentery.

The news of the Big 3 Power Conference and their agreements is certainly something to be praised. I read about it this morning in the *Stars and Stripes*.

Best to Ed, Margie and Paul. Why doesn't Ed write?

6

The Bastards Blew My Arm Off

Scaling Riva Ridge and Mt. Belvedere
February–March 1945

> You smug-faced crowds with kindling eye
> Who cheer when soldier lads march by,
> Sneak home and pray you'll never know
> The hell where youth and laughter go.
> —Siegfried Sassoon, *Suicide in the Trenches*

With the failure of various winter offensives and the diminished possibility of capturing the strategic city of Bologna in the Po Valley—the focus of earlier 5th Army planning—Allied commanders shifted their thinking from the idea of a deliberate thrust into the valley to wide-sweeping movements by both the 5th and 8th Armies aimed not only at encircling Bologna but the entire German armies. In order to accomplish this, they had to win better positions for starting the spring offensive.

General Crittenberger, commander of the IVth Corps under the 5th Army, decided to use the 10th Mountain Division, his only fresh and untested division, for the principal role in this limited operation. As noted earlier, commanders in other theaters, including Generals Eisenhower and McArthur, who had been offered our division, had declined our services on logistical grounds.[1] No theater commander—other than General Mark Clark—had wanted the light 75mm artillery we employed, versus the 105mm and 155mm howitzers used by a standard infantry division, and they were not attracted by the need to supply us with mules, skis, ice axes, or other peculiar equipment. But it was our specialized training and experience in terrain similar to the Apennines that enhanced our attractiveness to an army engaged in mountain warfare.*

Following the end of the war, the supreme Allied commander in Italy, British Field Marshal Alexander, addressing some assembled 10th Mountain men, said, "Sending your division to Italy was one of the best turns General Marshall ever did me."[2]

Planning was initiated at the 5th Army level for our attack, code-named Operation Encore, with the objective being to capture a series of mountain peaks and ridges dominating a 10-mile section of Highway 64, one of the two main routes leading from Pistoia through the northern Apennines to Bologna. As long as the enemy held these peaks, he protected all routes of approach to Highway 64, his vital supply and communication line. If the Americans could seize this terrain, we could observe German activity almost all the way to the Po Valley, some 40 miles away.[3]

The scene for the 10th's introduction to combat, as described in the postwar *Saturday Evening Post* story about the division, was "a stage set for a debacle."[4] Dominating the region were two ridges whose highest peaks rose between 3,000 and 5,000 feet. One (Pizzo di Campiano–Monte Mancinello) became known to American troops as Riva Ridge.* It overlooked the division's left flank and dominated routes of approach to the second ridge: the Monte Belvedere–Monte Gorgolesco–Monte della Torraccia Ridge. The side of Riva Ridge facing the division was a cliff rising some 1,500 feet above the valley floor.

Three efforts had been made by the Allies in the fall and winter of 1944 to capture Belvedere and the adjacent ridge leading east to Gorgolesco and della Torraccia. On one occasion the summit of Belvedere had been reached and held for three days, but then abandoned after a German counterattack. The German defenses had been further enlarged because Field Marshal Kesselring, the German commander in chief in Italy, was more concerned about this sector of the front than any other. As he explained in his *Memoirs* after the war:

> ...if the front south of Bologna could not be held then all our positions in the Po plain east of Bologna were automatically gone—in which event they must be evacuated in good time so as at least to save the troops and material. Therefore all our strongest divisions must be fed to this part of the Apennines.[5]

The German success before our arrival in stopping what Kesselring called the Allies' "magnificent fighters" led him to boast, "The battle of the Apennines can really be described as a famous page of German military history."[6]

Indeed, these heights appeared to be an impregnable fortress, and it appeared doubtful that any force large enough in size to overwhelm the enemy could be brought together for the assault without being seen. Since the Germans had an excellent view of the entire area from their commanding heights, and there was little cover for troops crossing the snow-covered ground other than scattered clumps of shell-ravaged trees, German artillery and automatic weapons would make a killing ground of any attempt to advance up these

---

A name later given a horse which won the Kentucky Derby in 1972. Its owner, a member of the Mellon family, married an alumnus of the 10th Mountain Division.

A view of Riva Ridge, which was captured at night by rope-climbing mountain troopers, February 1945 (courtesy Denver Public Library, Western History Department).

slopes. Nevertheless, the 10th, as its first major combat mission, was given the job of breaking the line.

Faced with the reality that Riva Ridge would have to be cleared before the main attack could advance up Monte Belvedere and along the ridge towards Monte della Torraccia, the plan devised by the division was for the mountain troops to scale the 1,500-foot cliff and surprise the Germans on the summit, who would not be expecting an attack up the cliff face.

Intelligence, helped by Italian partisans as well as our aggressive patrol actions, which included the capture of prisoners, had given us a fairly good understanding of the enemy dispositions. Three German regiments (the 1043d, 1044th, and 1045th) belonging to the Wehrmacht's 232d Infantry Division were in line across an 18-mile front, with a fusilier battalion and elements of a mountain battalion in reserve. More than 80 German artillery pieces covered the approaches to their positions. In addition, all the roads and many of the open areas on the mountain sides were heavily mined.[7]

The plan of attack on a regimental basis, as described in the *Combat History of the 10th Mountain Division, 1944-45*, placed "the main brunt upon the shoulders of the 85th Mountain Infantry"—my regiment—as "the spearhead of the Corps effort." The 1st Battalion of the 86th, together with Company F of its 2d Battalion, was assigned the unenviable task of scaling the rock face and capturing Riva Ridge, thereby allowing the other elements in the assault

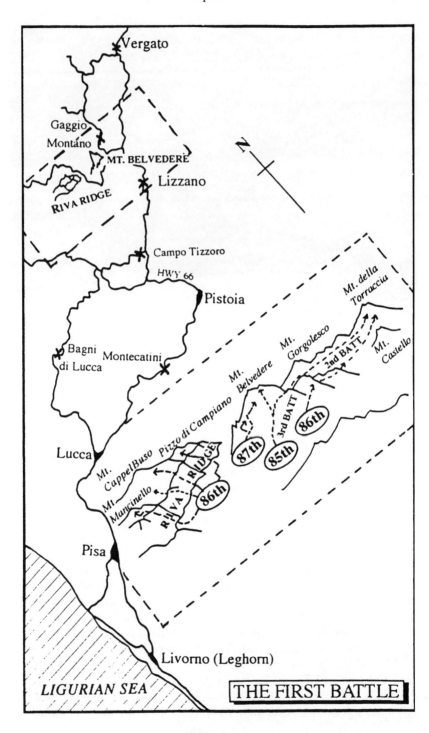

to accomplish their objectives. The attack on Monte Belvedere itself was to be made by the 3d Battalion of the 85th, while the 1st Battalion to the east attacked Monte Gorgolesco. My battalion, the 2d, was to follow and pass through the 1st Battalion and go on to capture the final objective, Monte della Torraccia. The 87th was to move parallel to the 85th on its left flank and take a ridge running northwest from Belvedere.[8]

To conceal preparations for the attack, the entire division moved under cover of darkness the night of February 18-19 to assembly areas at the base of Monte Belvedere and Monte Gorgolesco. My Company F of the 85th's 2d Battalion, consisting of six officers, three medical aid men, one Italian partisan, and 200 enlisted men assigned to three rifle and one weapons (machine gun and mortar) platoon, left Gavinana by truck at 8 P.M. the night of February 18 to a detrucking point near the foot of Belvedere.[9] We then proceeded on foot over mountain trails to our front line location. There, with the small shovels we habitually carried, we hastily dug foxholes in the rocky ground to protect ourselves from enemy fire if our presence were discovered. Even though we and other units were directly under the observation of the Germans, concealment was so effective (we later learned from captured prisoners) that the 10th's presence was not detected, and as a result, the attack which followed came as a complete surprise.

While the major elements of our attacking force were engaged in the darkness and bitter cold below Monte Belvedere, teams of picked rock climbers of the 1st Battalion of the 86th were assembling coils of ropes over their shoulders and clusters of pitons and other rock-climbing gear on their belts. All the years of alpine training on Mount Rainier and Camp Hale, so publicized in newsreels and Hollywood movies, were now about to be tested. In fact, what developed was to be the only significant action in which the 10th had to use this most specialized kind of training. Nevertheless, no one in the War Department or in the 10th could later deny that this single exploit on Riva Ridge justified all the demanding training that had gone before.

A dusting of new snow covered the rock face and upper slopes of the mountains. The valley floor was a quagmire of freezing mud. Searchlights behind the combat area scanned the low-hanging wall of clouds and reflected a scattered, shadowy light over the terrain below. But the valley itself and the ridges were dark. Climbing in the dead of night, members of the teams hammered steel pitons into the cracks in the rock, attached snap links to them, and then fastened ropes to the links which, hanging down, offered lines which those who followed could use to pull themselves up the vertical face of the ridge.

When the advance teams reached the top at approximately midnight, they signaled to the 1st Battalion units below that they could begin the ascent in force. These units advanced in a column of companies toward the foot of Riva Ridge and then split up, each taking a different route up the face of the cliff. Fortunately, the haze which hung over the lower elevations of the ridge continued to help conceal the attacking mountaineers. With a biting and wet wind whipping them about, the climbers clambered cautiously up the wet rocks with the aid of the preset ropes, fearful that any dislodged rock that clattered down the cliff face would be followed by bursts of enemy machine guns and grenades.

Inevitably some rocks did fall, causing the climbers to halt in dread anticipation of the hail of death to follow. "Perfect fear casteth out love," joked the Briton Cyril Connolly in his travesty of I John 4:18, and members of the 10th came to fully appreciate that remark in this introduction to combat.

By 4 A.M. on February 20, all three companies of the 1st Battalion, 86th, and Co. F of the 2d had reached their separate objectives on top of the ridge unseen and had charged the holding units of the German 1044th Infantry Regiment with rifles and grenades. Surprise was complete.

"I don't see how you did it," one German defender stated. "We thought it was impossible for anyone to climb that cliff."[10]

With the coming of daylight, the Germans began to launch the expected counterattack after counterattack, accompanied by heavy artillery fire on the ridge. When accurate counterartillery bursts repulsed one attack, the Germans came back with their hands up, feigning surrender. After nearing the 1st Battalion positions, they dropped and began firing again, but were finally driven off with heavy casualties. One platoon alone, with the help of our supporting artillery, accounted for 26 Germans killed, 7 captured, and countless wounded.

Before the division's left flank was finally secured on Riva Ridge, the acid test of battle for the 85th Mountain Infantry began when the 1st and 3d Battalions crossed our designated "line of departure" (LD) at one hour before midnight on the nineteenth, and began moving in complete silence up the slopes infested with mines and booby traps in a frontal assault on Monte Gorgolesco and Monte Belvedere, respectively. At the same time, the 87th Infantry was proceeding toward a trio of villages lying between Belvedere and Riva Ridge to try and outflank the defenses on the crest of Belvedere. In the effort to achieve surprise, both attacks dispensed with any artillery barrage in advance of their attack.

This method of approach evidently paid off, for many of the units were virtually atop the enemy's outposts before they met resistance. By 6:10 A.M. on the twentieth, word was received that the 1st Battalion had seized Monte Gorgolesco, and by 6:15 A.M. all members of the 3d Battalion were atop Monte Belvedere.

Nevertheless, the cost to company commanders as well as ordinary GIs was already high. One of the four company commanders in the 3d Battalion was killed by a sniper's bullet in the forehead and another was wounded, while Captain Charles Smith, commander of the 1st Battalion's Company C, had both legs shattered by a mine explosion while moving up the slope. In Company L, all but two men in the machine gun platoon had been casualties in

10th men moving up with Monte Belvedere in background (courtesy National Archives).

this assault.[11] All together, before that day was over, the 1st Battalion would lose 27 killed and 68 wounded assaulting Gorgolesco, while the 3d Battalion suffered 26 killed and 88 wounded capturing Monte Belvedere.

At 9:15 A.M. on the twentieth, General Hays ordered that the 3d Battalion, dug in on Monte Belvedere, prepare for the defense of the mountain, and at the same time, my 2d Battalion, which had been following the advance, was directed to move on through the 1st Battalion lines. Our mission was to take the final divisional objective, Monte della Torraccia, at night.[12] Finally, I was to experience the reality of ground combat, up close and personal.

As my platoon proceeded in single file up the slope of Belvedere, the first shock we encountered was when we met a line of six small Italian mules coming down the mountain towards us carrying dead GIs lashed across their backs. They were lying belly-down across the packsaddles, their heads hanging down on one side and their stiffened legs sticking out awkwardly on the other. As they approached us on the rough terrain, their bodies pitched and rolled, and no attempt was made to conceal their wounds or disfigurement under a blanket or in the mattress covers used for burial by the Army's Graves Registration Service. (A similar scene was accurately depicted not long afterwards in *The Story of GI Joe,* a powerful and remarkably frank Hollywood movie about infantry combat in the Italian campaign.)

Walking wounded and a litter squad head for an aid station on Belvedere (courtesy National Archives).

The effects of artillery shells and other killing weapons were all around us, with wounded infantrymen waiting by the side of the trail for evacuation to a medical aid station and some dead GIs lying where they had been killed. We were particularly unsettled when we came upon a dead German sitting with his back against a large rock, appearing relatively unscathed, but with a half-burned cigarette, which also had expired, still in his mouth.

As we passed through the 1st Battalion lines to relieve their attacking elements, I met my old friend, Jud Decker, returning down the trail with others in his company. With some trepidation, I greeted him, but we only had time for a brief exchange.

"How has it been?" I asked.

"Boy, am I glad to see you!" Jud answered. "In fact I'm glad to be able to say, 'I'm glad to see you.' It's been pure hell, and I'm afraid you'll find it just as bad."

By late afternoon we had passed through the 1st Battalion lines and after moving along a ridge through other troops digging in furiously, we reached our intermediate objective in relatively dense woods. The Apennines in this region have many beech, pine, and chestnut trees. The chestnuts in particular in these woods were tall, with wide-spreading branches which covered the terrain.

Throughout the attack, our regiment had encountered enemy mines and booby traps which had caused many casualties. Men from the Regimental Service Company were required to assume duties as litter bearers to evacuate the dead and wounded, as well as to accompany enemy prisoners to the rear. At about 7 P.M. that evening, our battalion was told that if we could seize the high ground northeast of one of our immediate objectives, we were authorized to wait until daylight to continue the attack. The battalion succeeded in reaching the objective in the dark, capturing it at 9 P.M.

We were then subjected to heavy mortar and artillery fire. The Germans also launched a strong counterattack which Company G managed to beat off. (The attacking enemy was identified as three companies of the German 1044th Regiment's 4th Mountain Battalion.) Rounds from the artillery were timed to explode in the tops of the trees, raining deadly fragments on our foxholes below.[13] This was my first real experience with incoming shells landing that close. I and another member of my machine gun squad, George Olsen, had dug a foxhole in the trees on the edge of the ridge, and we now crouched there with fear awaiting a projectile or shards that might find a mark in our hole.

Among the exploding rounds coming our way were rockets which we learned troops in veteran Allied divisions called the "*Screaming Meemies*," but to us they became known as the "*Moaning Minnies*." The German term for the launcher which fired them was the "*Nebelwerfer*," which literally means "smoke thrower." It consisted of a six-barreled launcher which fired the rockets electrically, one after another, at a rate of 6 rounds every 90 seconds. It had a range of up to 7,700 yards.[14]

The firing did not make a great roar, and the projectiles swished forward at a relatively low velocity, but they were accompanied by a sound of unparalleled viciousness and power, making an unearthly grinding and moaning noise in a descending pitch as they returned to earth in your vicinity. The noise was frightful enough when the shells were coming directly at you, but even when they were directed at an angle some distance away, their long, drawn-out groaning sound was bloodcurdling.

More deadly, even if not accompanied by such a fearful noise, were the incoming shells from the German 88mm Flak-41 artillery piece, perhaps the most effective and feared weapon of its kind in World War II. General Omar Bradley, often called "the GI's general," described it as the nemesis of infantrymen and tankers.[15] A multipurpose, flat-trajectory gun, it was designed not only as an antiaircraft weapon, in which capacity it was the backbone of German air defense throughout the war,[16] but as a component of the squat 63-ton German "Tiger" tank, where, as Bradley put it, "it could both outgun and outduel any Allied tank in the field."[17] Regrettably for us, it could also be deflected for direct fire on advancing infantry.*

*Another authority, Paul Fussell, writing on the murderous requirements of "conventional war," describes it as "the single greatest weapon of the war, the atomic bomb excepted."[18]

Unlike the Moaning Minnie, the 88's shells came at the astounding speed of 3,280 feet (1,000 meters) per second, much faster than a rifle bullet,* with the result that essentially all you heard was a "whish-bang," both sounds being heard in a fraction of a second. Moreover, it could fire its shells, which weighed about 21 pounds, at a rate of some 20 rounds per minute for a distance of over 12 miles.[19]

The events of that day and night were experiences one could never forget. My companion, Olsen, who seemed old to me although he was probably only in his upper thirties, kept warning me during the night that he was dying.

"Bob, I'm having a heart attack."

"No, I don't think so, George, it's probably just the cold and the explosions coming so close."

But I could not be sure, and the combination of the shells blasting the trees all around us, the awful moaning of the incoming rounds, the night and the possibility of Germans with bayonets and grenades assaulting our positions, and all the wounded and dismembered bodies I had seen that day had a traumatic effect unequaled in my brief experience. Evidently, my companions were similarly affected. My platoon sergeant, Jim Orwig, says his battle notes about that night reported: "Last night vicious counter-attack and almost steady 88 pounding.... Like giant scythes in the tall pines.... Shudder in fox hole....Wish it were a cave."[20]

Since sleep was impossible, I gave a lot of thought to whether war—given its nightmarish reality—could ever be justified, however cruel and inhuman the enemy. To be sure, my knowledge of the Third Reich and Hitler's regime was entirely intellectual, having been derived from the written media and photographic sources, so I had never suffered personally from any evil actions initiated by their supporters (other than my forced service in the military). And at the time I was not aware of Buchenwald, *The Story of Anne Frank*, and other atrocities of the Nazi regime. Nevertheless, I knew what had happened at Pearl Harbor, the rape of Nanking, the effects of German dive-bombing on innocent civilians in Europe's most populous cities, and the incredible slaughter the German invasion had inflicted on the USSR. Yet, despite all, I remained uncertain whether the horror I had experienced this first day, given its effect on those who had lost their lives or suffered such terrible wounds, justified a continuation of the insanity we had encountered. One thing I did promise myself: I would never let time soften or falsify the experience. Real war was tragic and grisly, and its reality, for all intents and purposes, beyond the power of any literary or philosophic analysis to suggest.

Despite the experience of the previous one day and night of battle—a day which the army would describe as resulting in relatively low casualties, in that

---

*Bullets from the M-1 (Garand) rifle used by the U.S. infantry in World War II had a muzzle velocity of 2,838 feet (865 meters) per second, only about 86 percent that of an 88mm shell.[21]

we lost only two men killed and eight wounded in our company of some two hundred men—Olsen and I survived to greet the dawn and prepared for the action to come. It was now February 21, and we were greeted at 6 A.M. by the order to climb out of our holes and advance forward with the rest of our company in a renewed attack to try and capture della Torraccia. This day, and the one which followed, it turned out, would be the bloodiest days of the war for my squad and platoon.

The advance began with the commander of the heavy weapons company (Company H) in our 2d Battalion, Captain Ernest Bennett, and Lieutenant William Young, commanding his mortar platoon, moving to an observation post in order to assess the situation. While thus occupied, Captain Bennett was killed instantly by an 88mm tree burst, and Lieutenant Young died a short time later at the battalion command post from shrapnel wounds. Company H also suffered heavily in the loss of other leaders, at this point having only one officer who had not been killed or wounded.[22]

Advancing in a column of companies with Company G leading and E and F in the rear, at 7 A.M. we fought off a heavy counterattack in which the executive officer of Company G was killed by shrapnel from an artillery barrage while he was checking one of his rifle platoons whose commanding officer and platoon sergeant had just been killed. These and other casualties necessitated some reorganization of units and shifts in officers and noncoms in command in order to continue the attack. At 7:45 A.M., Lieutenant Colonel Roche, commanding our 2d Battalion, reported to his superiors that we had broken up five German counterattacks during the night and that the enemy was only 25 yards in front of us, the most forward unit in the division attack.[23]

Our route took us in single file, with the men widely spread out, along a well-used foot trail through relatively open terrain along the side of a ridge. Up ahead we could see our path traversing the very steep sides of a higher peak. The Germans evidently knew exactly where the trail was, and fully anticipated our movement along it, since high explosive shells from their 88mm and other guns were falling irregularly but with great accuracy along the trail as we proceeded forward. It was a classic demonstration of the fact that in infantry combat, as practiced in modern war, your training, brainpower, battle experience, and physical ability often have little to do with whether you will survive an engagement or not.

Simply put, we had been ordered to cross a given stretch of ground in order to advance towards the divisional objective, and it was strictly a matter of luck rather than skill, whether you would be hit in the process or not. You could not predict when or where the unseen enemy artillery would drop the next shell, so, at least in this instance, it was impossible to time one's movement across the killing ground to try and escape death.

As I plodded along with the machine gun on my back, seeing people going down ahead of me, I could not understand why we were walking along this trail of tears instead of running for the relative safety of the steep incline on the peak ahead. Finally I lost all patience and yelled, "Why aren't we running?" At the same time I started jogging as best I could with the gun, and others began doing the same. Orwig's notes describe this feverish scuttling as an "Escape... an animal maneuver lashed into a self-preserving panic of wild flight by the pressure of adrenalin."[24]

After running forward some 100 yards, I saw a formidable barrier confronting us composed of a hedgerow, or thicket, some eight to ten feet deep and five feet high which ran all the way down the side of the ridge. To get through this rampart, we had to find a break somewhere but none was apparent. The shells were hurling their jagged fragments all around us and we could not find an opening.

Suddenly I saw my platoon leader, Lieutenant Charles Hanks, heading for a particular section of the hedge as though he knew what he was doing. I raced after him and found, to my great relief, that he had discovered a semblance of a way to get through and I followed him. After getting through to the other side, I and others from our platoon who had followed, dashed up the steep slope to a point near the top of the peak and collapsed exhausted on the ground. We then turned to see what was happening to the remainder of our platoon and company who had yet to reach the hedge and pass through. What we observed was a scene of terrible carnage.

Men were running up and down the mountain side in a frantic search for a way through the hedgerow. Our yells through the roar of exploding artillery helped little. While we watched, the squad leader of the other machine gun squad, Sergeant Leonard Pierce, was killed instantly by exploding shell fragments, while my 6'7" second gunner, Wally Krusell, was knocked unconscious. One of the ammunition carriers in my squad, Warren Steiner, a tall, handsome young man with a beautiful wife, did not escape the steel deluge, suffering what proved to be a lethal hit in the spinal column which left him helpless where he fell. Unable to do anything other than to watch what transpired, we sat there aghast over what we were forced to witness.

When we finally reassembled, only half of the men in my 1st machine gun squad of six, and about a third of the thirty-two men in our platoon, were left to carry on the attack. Both machine gun squad leaders were casualties, including my own sergeant, John Nevada. Two out of the three mortar squad leaders (Sergeants LeGassey and Everett) were gone, and also the mortar staff sergeant (Carney) commanding all three squads. Among those wounded in my own squad was Swedish-born Sven Modin, who had been in the merchant marine in peacetime. He had received such a slight scalp laceration from a mortar shell fragment that he asked me to check his head to see if anything were amiss. When I confirmed that he had been wounded, his reaction in heavily Swedish-accented English was, *"Holy sheeet, I've been heeet!"*—a rhyming couplet that became a favorite line of the squad henceforth.

At 10:10 A.M. our battalion commander, Lieutenant Colonel Roche, radioed his regimental and divisional commanders that he was out of ammunition, food, and water, and had sustained many casualties; he asked for the relief of the battalion or at least additional men to carry on the attack. General Hays arranged for a pack train to be fitted out with supplies and ammunition for the battalion and sent the lieutenant colonel heading his G-4 (Logistics and Supply) staff to look into the supply situation at 85th Regimental headquarters. The pack train itself was led up the mountain the night of the twenty-first by the regimental executive officer. At the same time, General Hays ordered Colonel Roche to have the 2d Battalion drive on, unassisted, to seize and hold the final objective, Monte della Torraccia, whatever the cost to his battalion.

As directed, and of course unaware of the messages being exchanged between our commanders, the remnants of our Company F moved forward, along with the other three companies in the battalion. By late afternoon another major divisional objective had been captured by our sister Company E, commanded by Captain Robert Neilson, who was seriously wounded in the attack. At 6 P.M. the battalion was ordered to halt its advance at dark and set up a close-in, all-around defense for the night.[25] As darkness fell, I was digging as best I could with the small folding shovel the army called an "entrenching tool" to get some kind of a foxhole below ground where the incoming artillery rounds would be less likely to tear me apart. With Krusell and Sergeant Pierce gone, my foxhole companion on this occasion was a Private Turman Oldham, and we were having a terrible time penetrating the rocky ground which was located on the crest of a ridge.

After some hours of Herculean effort in the icy cold, in the course of which I cut my wrist rather severely on the frame of my shovel, we decided we had gone as far as we could and crawled into the cavity we had managed to eke out. Shortly thereafter we heard a tremendous explosion only a few yards away, which did not sound like an incoming artillery round. Upon investigating, we discovered that Colonel Roche, who was spending the night in our vicinity, had ordered a foxhole dynamited on his behalf into which he promptly disappeared once the hole had been emptied of what loose soil remained. Regrettably, such technology was not available to his subordinates, and the incident, in the heat of battle, did not endear our colonel to us.

When darkness fell, our Platoon Sergeant Orwig returned to the ghastly scene where many of the platoon still lay dead or dying and found Steiner. His battle notes described what transpired.

> That night one of the finest men I have ever known [Steiner] died in my arms, late, in the darkness, with shell sounds crisscrossing their whisperings high over head, muttering and flashing beyond. Life had retreated to a small section by the time I found him. Morphine had dissolved the frame of his reason. But that brief pocket of life strove so piteously and valiantly against the cruelly encroaching frigidity of death that already had claimed his limbs. His features spoke dismay and stayed locked that way as I laid his head back in the snow. The world had lost an excellent man. And the words again flamed in my mind's eye: *This must never happen again!*[26]

Sketch by F/85th's artist-soldier Paul Williams of our machine gun sergeant Leonard Pierce shortly before he was killed in action on Belvedere (courtesy Denver Public Library, Western History Department).

At about 7:30 P.M., the battalion reported that we were under heavy machine gun and artillery fire and requested permission for us to withdraw behind the ridge for the night. Permission was denied, and we were ordered to dig in, hold our positions, and send in shell reports for counterartillery fire. At the time we were just below Monte della Torraccia in defensive formation and an hour later Colonel Roche informed General Duff, General Hays' deputy, that elements of our battalion had taken Torraccia. By 4:30 A.M. the following morning, however, we were seen to be some 400 yards short. Roche corrected his statement and added that we were without artillery support because of the lack of communications.[27]

As might be expected, the actions of the 10th Mountain on the twentieth and twenty-first in capturing Monte Belvedere and Monte Gorgolesco attracted Generals Mark Clark, Lucian Truscott, and Willis Crittenberger, commanding the Allied armies in Italy, the American 5th Army, and the IVth Corps, respectively, to come to the 10th's area of activity to view the ongoing operation. They expressed their delight with the developments thus far and also emphasized the threat to the enemy posed by the breakthrough.[28] Casualties on the first two days of the attack had been heavy, with nearly 75 percent of the second day's losses being suffered by the 2d Battalion. On that day alone the battalion had 24 killed and 76 wounded out of the total for the regiment of 27 killed and 109 wounded. Clearly, it had been a bad day for the 2d Battalion.

When the sun came up on the twenty-second, we were ordered to leave the ridge overlooking della Torraccia, attack the southern slopes of the mountain, and, once having reached the summit, consolidate our defenses and hold the crest against counterattacks. By 10:20 A.M. my Company F, commanded by Captain Charles King, was on a ridge to the right of the summit, Company G was on a hill just beyond della Torraccia, while Company E was in the center and near the top of the mountain. In fact they had actually reached the top but were ordered to fall back in order to help enforce the defense of the battalion against counterattacks. Because of our manpower losses and exposed situation as the most advanced elements of the division, Company G was also recalled from its forward position and put in reserve in the rear of the battalion.[29]

Enemy shelling as we advanced was even more demoralizing than it had been the previous day, and German machine gun bullets were flying all about us. One member of our weapons platoon, Harlan Jensen, was struck and killed only 30 feet from me as we climbed the ridge, but one of our rifle platoons captured three Germans in the course of the attack. The intense fire forced us to dig in on the crest of the ridge, and we did so with great haste, fearing the German 88mm and mortar shells which were landing all about.

There was light snow on the ground, and here too the ground was filled with rocks, so that I had great difficulty making any kind of hole in it. What I finally managed to dig went down at about a 45-degree angle in order to avoid various immovable boulders, but I could not get it deep enough to get my entire body below ground. I then faced the terrible question of whether to leave my head exposed or to protect my lower extremities, particularly my sexual equipment, which I also valued. The thought of being upside down in this narrow tube was not appealing, especially if the Germans launched a counterattack, so I did not often elect to enter the hole head first. But when the shelling became particularly intense, I did expose my legs and rear end, hoping, if worst came to worst, I'd lose nothing more serious than a toe or two.

In this connection it should be stressed that for infantry fighting on the ground, artillery and mortar fire are the most terrifying enemy weapons, in part because of the deafening and frightful noise which accompanies the bursts, but also because of what one soon observes about the damage they can do to the body. The prospect of being hit by rifle or machine gun bullets struck one as being almost surgical in comparison, even though we tried to avoid those injuries as well.

Ernest Hemingway, who was seriously wounded while serving as an infantryman with the Italian army in World War I, wrote in an introduction to his anthology, *Men at War: The Best War Stories of All Time*, that "Cowardice [in battle] is almost always simply a lack of ability to suspend the functioning of the imagination. Learning to suspend your imagination and live completely in the very second of the present with no before and no after is the greatest gift a soldier can acquire."[30] This was easier said than done, especially after one became aware that the bodily damage that could result from exploding

10th men leading Italian mules carrying rations in Belvedere area (courtesy Denver Public Library, Western History Department).

shells could range from total obliteration to partial dismemberment or to compartmentation into tiny body parts which could be flung about in all directions. The thought of what the jagged steel fragments might do to you was almost worse than the impact itself.

Artillery shells bursting on a loose rock surface could also cause shards of rock to be thrown for many yards. In one battalion in Italy, it was found that 15 percent of the casualties were from flying rocks,[31] and in Italy the hills rose to high ridges of almost solid rock. We could not go around them because the Germans were up there looking down on us, so we had to go up and over. A mere platoon of Germans, well dug in, could hold out for a long time against tremendous onslaughts.

By 5 P.M. on the twenty-second, the 2d Battalion's casualties had been so heavy that Colonel Roche reported that he had only 400 men left and needed replacements, ammunition, machine guns, radios, and water. Over 80 percent of the regiment's losses on that day had been suffered by the 2d Battalion, which had 12 killed and 25 wounded. And during the night, the Germans counterattacked again. Nevertheless, the response the colonel received was to hold what he had to the last man, and supplies would be sent up to him.[32]

During the night one of my old friends, Albert Weidorn, serving with one of the companies which took the brunt of the attack, was largely responsible for turning it back by standing up (*à la* John Wayne, we were told), while cradling a 30-caliber machine gun in his arms, and cutting down the advancing infantry. For this action he received the Silver Star. I was particularly delighted to hear what he had done because he had earned the reputation, in training at Camp Hale, of not meeting the soldierly standards of the U.S. Army because of his general attitude, slovenly appearance, and insolence.

One of Weidorn's demotions had come as the result of an incident that occurred during an exhausting all-day climb up a steep Rocky Mountain peak. Weidorn, who was only about 5'6" tall, had chosen for a moment to rest his 85-pound pack and himself on the nearly vertical path leading up the mountain when a pompous major, who was deputy to the battalion commander and greatly disliked, appeared.

"Soldier, move yourself and your gear off the trail," ordered the major.

"Major, I just sat down, and if Jesus Christ himself came up the path, I'd tell him to go around," Weidorn is reported to have said.

Not surprisingly, the major took offense at this response and Weidorn soon found himself once again undergoing company punishment and reduced to buck private.

In his book, *Men Against Fire,* in which he reported on exhaustive interviews with thousands of World War II combat soldiers immediately after their battle experiences, General S. L. A. Marshall reported that no company commander has any way of knowing, prior to combat, which man will carry the fight to the enemy and which will simply go along for the ride. "Discipline," he said, "is not the key. Perfection in drill is not the key.... Some of the most gallant single-handed fighters I encountered in World War II had spent most of their time in the guardhouse." In studies of company after company, he continued, "we found in our work that there were men who had been consistently bad actors in the training period, marked by the faults of laziness, unruliness, and disorderliness, who just as consistently became lions on the battlefield.... They could fight like hell but they couldn't soldier."[33]

Weidorn was obviously one of these. All his deficiencies were forgiven once he displayed in combat the same resolution and fearless determination he had exposed to the major. In this acid test of the ultimate purpose of military service, he had few equals.

No doubt because of his heroic action and that of his comrades, I managed to get some sleep that night even though the night was cold and we carried only one blanket to cover us. (None of our Camp Hale winter warfare clothing and supplies, of course, had been provided.) But when morning came on the twenty-third, the sky was bright and clear, and the sun was shining directly on our foxholes. At 9 A.M., rifle platoons from our Company F attacked and advanced some 200 yards, with what remained of our two machine gun squads firing in their support over their heads. This was the first time I actually saw my machine gun bullets strike any enemy soldiers, killing one German defending the summit of della Torraccia. The machine gun fire also caused a number of Germans to surrender to our advancing riflemen, so for once I was able to observe that our machine gun operations actually had an impact on the enemy.

An hour later another heavy German counterattack was launched between our company and Company E, with the greatest pressure against the left flank of our company. All battalion reserves were committed to stop this advance, and the attack was thrown back.[34] Two of our F Company rifle platoons again attempted to move forward to capture the final objective, della Torraccia, but 88mm and mortar fire decimated them, killing three of our most senior army sergeants who had come to the 10th from Hawaii as NCO cadre. The same shelling wounded a number of staff sergeants and one buck sergeant. The F-Company "Morning Report" for that day, prepared by First Sergeant Ballek, gives one a sampling of the intimate, if abbreviated, daily record (where known) of who got hit, where, and by what:

Company F	144 duty
85th Mountain Infantry	4 sick
Morning Report, 23 February 1945	15 missing
Gaggio Montano, Italy	163 total

Pursell, Clifford   Staff Sergeant
   Light wound in action (LWA) from mortar fragment penetrating thigh.
Dallmeier, Joseph A.   Private
   Wounded in action (WIA), nature unknown.
Toth, William   Private First Class
   Light injury in action (LIA), concussion.
Attick, Nicholas L.   Private First Class
   Severe wound in action (SWA) from 88mm fragments penetrating right
   shoulder and left hand.
Miller, Walter S.   Private First Class
   SWA from 88mm fragment penetrating right leg.
Murry, George W.   Private First Class
   LWA, perforating left cheek.
Orr, Louis Y.   Staff Sergeant
   LIA, sprain of interior colsteral [*sic*] ligament.
Luken, Edward T.   Staff Sergeant
   LWA from shell fragment perforating thigh.
Staebell, Laverne R.   Private First Class
   LWA, penetrating arm; moderate wound penetrating right hand.
Zimmerman, Bertram T.   Private First Class
   LWA, from shell fragment penetrating left thigh.
Facemyre, Hubert F.   Private First Class
   SWA, penetrating right wrist, left arm, and right hip.
Giddix, Leonard R.   Sergeant
   SWA, penetrating leg, left eye, and left hand.
Wallis, George W.   Private First Class
   LWA, penetrating left leg.
Pliscek, Michael S.   Tech Sergeant
   Status undetermined (SUD)

Stepnowski, Edward L. SUD	Staff Sergeant
Carson, Lorin J. SUD	Staff Sergeant
Brown, William O. SUD	Private First Class

The last four listed as "status undetermined" were later identified, in the "Morning Report" dated March 1, as killed in action (KIA). Invariably the indicator SUD was followed a few days later by the KIA designator after positive confirmation was received. Similarly, many of the initial references to the type and severity of wounds received were in error because they were based on incomplete information. Staebell's wounds, for example, were quite severe, rendering him unable ever to use his right hand again because of injuries to his right arm and hand. The "Morning Report" also revealed that the company had only 144 men for duty on February 23rd versus the 201 available four days earlier.[35]

Two other unfortunate incidents which occurred this day included the capture of our 2d Battalion surgeon by German soldiers and injuries to some of our troops caused by shell fire from our own guns. The surgeon, Captain Morton Levitan, left his aid station in the early afternoon to treat a badly wounded soldier up on the ridge. Not knowing the exact location of the front line, he stumbled into German-held territory and was seized. Levitan was Jewish but, as we learned later, was not harmed while in captivity. The trauma inflicted on us by our own high caliber weapons was something that would occur more than once, and we learned to fear it greatly because of the volume and severity of the incoming steel. This time it came from one of our tank destroyers in the rear and hit Company K. Eleven men were wounded when a shell burst in the area of the company command post.

After the last abortive attack of our riflemen on the twenty-third, we were informed that because of the heavy casualties to our 2d Battalion, we would be relieved by the 3d Battalion of the 86th Regiment during the night of February 23-24. In the meantime we had to worry about fending off additional German counterattacks and avoiding death from flying shrapnel.

At one point during the day, I decided to move my machine gun position to another foxhole to get a better field of fire against the enemy, and two members of the other machine gun squad in our platoon, Privates First Class Laverne Staebell and Barr V. Neilson, took over my old hole. Less than 15 minutes later a mortar round landed in a tree overlooking my old foxhole and badly injured Staebell and a Sergeant Leonard Giddix, the one remaining mortar sergeant left in our platoon, who was standing beside the hole trying to direct fire for the mortar squads. A limb from the same tree hit by the shell also fell on Orwig, but he was not seriously hurt and he later noted:

Giddix' self control when hit yesterday was remarkable. Left hand smashed to an unrecognizable mass, flapping from the wrist by a tendon or two, and not a sound from him of pain or fear. He had a shrapnel hole as big as a billiard ball in his buttocks and another in his thigh. And they lugged him down calmly smoking.[36]

Sergeant Orwig had Larry Boyajian and three other men carry Giddix on a litter back to an aid station. En route they were pinned down a number of times by enemy fire, but they delivered their cargo and then returned to the front lines where our platoon was dug in.[37] (Giddix' binoculars were also hit by the shrapnel, which smashed the left unit along with his left hand. Orwig kept the field glasses as a souvenir, the right eyepiece having been undamaged.)

Staebell wrote me 43 years later—when I heard from him again for the first time—"I was very happy to hear from a guy who was about 50 feet away on that ridge in Italy when I got hit. The last I saw of you, you were standing by your hole saying, 'I'm a busy man, I don't have time for this shit!' Then the shelling started and…"[38]

Staebell's account of what transpired follows.

Giddix came up beside us on the right—between us and our gun…. He had his glasses up to his eyes in his left hand. About then I suggested that he move a bit further from our hole. I was firing a rifle I had picked up from a wounded man the night before. That .45 Colt was no good unless you all were in a phone booth. About the time I asked Giddix to move, we were both hit.

It had to be a mortar because no direct fire could have got to us…. The blast got me in the right arm and shoulder as I was on the right side of the hole firing. It took Giddix' left hand about clean off. I saw him later in the hospital just before he left for home. At that time I wished my arm had been gone so I could head that way. We agreed that it was a mortar that nailed us both.

I remember dragging my right arm back into the hole and telling Neilson that "the bastards blew my arm off." He told me they hadn't, and spent the next ten minutes giving me hell for getting up in the hole. I don't recall how Giddix got out of there but assume it was the same way I did—by walking down the hill.

There was a lot of shelling going on at the time and we just waited for over an hour for a letup. When Neilson finally got me out of the hole, Giddix was gone.

At this point I'm going to tell you something that you may not believe or understand. The moment I was hit, the very moment I realized what had happened, that was when the greatest feeling of RELIEF I have ever known took over. Prior to this, especially that morning, I was scared. In fact the reason I got up to fire that rifle was to try and dispel that feeling.

You can't believe the calm that took over. It was amazing. How do you explain it? I guess we all wondered which one had our name on it. I had collected mine—no more wondering. Still what a feeling. I don't know how to explain it.

I can remember dropping the rifle in the dirt. What a good feeling that was too! No more cleaning that thing. O'Brien was a ways down the slope and offered his hole. We finally sat down by Lieutenant Hanks and asked the best way out. He was changing SOCKS—if you can imagine that. The shelling started up again and Neilson got two stretcher bearers to come over and things get fuzzy here. He told me much later after the war that I wouldn't lie down and they had to strap me on the damned thing. I do recall the medics had to drop me twice on the way out due to shells. All I saw was the smoke and dirt, but I will tell you that an awful lot of praying was going on. BELIEVE IT!...

The real heroes [were] the field medics. Those were the guys who went back time and again for guys like me. They were the real heroes, if any one was. I hope those two made it. I told them they had more guts than anyone else up there. I don't believe I could have done their job, I really don't....

Neilson stayed with me until the aid station and then went back up. The first thing I got there—after instant care—was three fingers of FINE whiskey. Believe it. It was good. That same day we were taken by jeep down to a bigger evacuation center. I can remember the driver of the jeep kept apologizing for the rough ride.

Hey man, I'm going home. Who cares!...

When we were coming down that hill, Tech Sergeant Taylor was walking towards the top. He was killed later too. That's the last time I ever saw anyone from the 10th Mountain over there.[39]

Albert Meinke, M.D., a former battalion surgeon in the 10th Mountain Division, has said that every army medical unit was authorized a monthly quota of whiskey "in spite of the fact that the medical indications for its use were at best nebulous." The battalion aid station's quota was four 32-ounce quarts per month. "It was classified as a medicine, ... was ordered using its Latin name, *Spiritus Fruimenti*, ... [and] all of it was used up every month."[40] Apparently, Staebell felt this particular prescription for the injuries he had suffered was hardly "nebulous" and thoroughly enjoyed the treatment.

Needless to say, the effects of the shell fire on my companions close by and the occasional pieces of shrapnel which fell on me, also caused *me* to do a lot of praying and reading of the New Testament which I carried in one of my pockets. Tim Prout, one of my oldest and closest friends who was a sergeant in charge of a mortar squad near me, was knocked unconscious briefly by one of these rounds, but came to in time to enjoy more of what the German artillery chose to send over. Like Staebell, all of us would have welcomed a nice clean wound that would have removed us from the horror around us.

One of the worst effects of sitting there in our defensive positions was that we had long since run out of water in our canteens, and the colonel's plea for water—not to mention ammunition and other supplies—had not been answered for our platoon and, no doubt, for the rest of the company. The lack of water and the continued effects of the sun beating down on the unshaded site began to drive us to near desperation.

It happened that there was a small trickle of water forming a shallow pool some 50 feet from our positions, but to run to it, lay your canteen on its side and let it fill with the water, and then run back to the relative safety of your hole again was a fearful gamble. Finally, when one of us could stand his thirst no longer and decided to chance it, others near him would beseech him to fill their canteens as well. This obviously increased the risk since the longer you stayed out in the open, the greater the likelihood of your getting hit. At the same time, it was difficult to refuse the requests of your closest comrades, so such pleas were rarely rejected.

The sun finally set, darkness fell, and those of us who had survived these first four days of combat waited all night for the units of the 86th Regiment which were to relieve us. They finally got to our positions at about 5 A.M. on the twenty-fourth, and we began our evacuation, heading for the mountain village of Gaggio Montano a short distance behind the lines. We were followed by 88mm fire much of the way, but at 7 A.M. the 3d Battalion, 86th, which relieved us, jumped off to attack Monte della Torraccia while the other two battalions of the 85th held on to their defensive positions. Within half an hour, the 86th had reached the top of della Torraccia, although, according to one participant, with the loss of 70 percent of the men in his company.[41] After capturing this division objective, they pushed on to secure the ridges immediately north and northeast of the mountain. By midnight on the twenty-fourth all counterattacks had been thrown back and the final objective had been secured and successfully defended.[42]

Cassino to the Alps, the last volume in the Mediterranean theater of operations series on the history of the U.S. Army in World War II, describes the Monte Belvedere-della Torraccia operation. After noting that the 10th "had fought with courage and determination ... at a cost of just over 900 casualties, of which 203 were killed," it concludes that, "However deplorable any losses at all, that was hardly an alarming figure for a first engagement."[43] This view has been disputed by other authorities. Beaumont, for one, in *Military Elites*, states that, "When they were committed to action in Italy against German mountain troops, the 10th suffered the heaviest casualties relative to time in combat of any U.S. division in the Italian campaign."[44] It is also of interest that our ratio of wounded to dead exceeded what S. L. A. Marshall says is "the usual battle ratio of four men wounded for every one mortally hit."[45]

According to the statistics compiled by our First Sergeant Ballek, out of the total of 201 in our company who went into combat, we lost 17 killed in action, 46 wounded, and one missing in the four days from February 20 to February 24.[46] During the same period, the 85th Regiment lost a total of 110 killed, 350 wounded, and one missing in action.[47] The division history acknowledges that "the main effort had fallen to the lot of the 85th Mountain Infantry,"[48] while the regimental account notes that, in fighting its way to della Torraccia, the 2d Battalion had experienced the heaviest casualties "and had paved the way for the final assault [when it] destroyed the enemy capacity for strong resistance."[49]

We spent one day in the village of Gaggio Montano, a short distance from

A typical aid station in Belvedere area with small tent and tired litter bearers (courtesy National Archives).

the front, billeting that night in a shelled-out house. The next day we were transported by truck a few miles farther to a rest camp in a factory settlement called Campo Tizzoro, where we were to clean up, get fresh clothes, hot food, and some rest. On the twenty-sixth also came the first public notification in the press that the 10th Mountain Division had arrived in Italy and was responsible for the capture of Monte Belvedere and the adjacent ridges.[50] From this point on, we were no longer referred to as "specially trained Fifth Army forces" or as "trained mountain climbers," to use the language of the *New York Times*, but as "troops of the 10th Mountain Division." The Germans, of course, had long been aware of our arrival, and, as indicated, their propaganda leaflets had been warning us for some time that death awaited if we tried to break through their mountain battlements.

Our return to the rest area and reunion with others in the company after these initial days of battle was an emotional experience that could hardly be equaled. There was much weeping by all concerned, including our company commander (Captain King), the chaplain, and my close friends Wally Krusell, Larry Boyajian, and Tim Prout as we greeted each other and exchanged stories of what we had been through. The shock of losing so many friends was, of course, hard to bear, and it was equally difficult to believe that we had escaped the holocaust.

It seemed beyond comprehension that we had so many killed and wounded after only four days of combat. As Orwig recorded in his battle diary, "[We] swung out Tuesday morning like a happy band of vagabonds, fired by the achievements of forward units. But when the four mules clopped by going down the mountain each with a dead man lashed across its back like a log of wood—a man wearing the same clothing as you, [a man] who must have walked up that same trail earlier—something rose like a chilling, hideously sobering specter inside, and every atom of conscience seemed to shout in one desperate, pleading entreaty [that] this was wrong. *It must not happen again.*"[51]

It took no great stretch of the imagination to realize that it was only a matter of time before we, too, would be dead or maimed. There was no way out of this losing game—in which all the odds were stacked against you—until the enemy surrendered, or you were injured, killed in action, or broke down mentally. A wound would not excuse you from having to return to combat once the injury had healed, unless the injury was so severe that it reduced your military effectiveness. Not much time was to pass before many of our wounded showed up in our ranks again, sometimes after only a few weeks in a hospital. To no one's surprise, they were not as optimistic as they had been before about their chances of escaping with their lives.

In this respect, infantry practice had not changed that much since World War I. In his bitter account of that war, *All Quiet on the Western Front,* called by many the greatest war novel ever written, German author Erich Maria Remarque, himself wounded five times and returned to duty after four of those times, described in his fictional (but no doubt accurate) account how army medical officers assisted in the process. If a leg wound did not require amputation, a staff surgeon might well say: "What, one leg a bit short? If you have any pluck you don't need to run at the front. The man is A-1. Dismissed!"[52]

This is the kind of order—although never experienced with quite that degree of cruelty—that during our time in combat gave birth to such black humor as the standard comment, "Seems fair enough." According to Remarque, a story circulated throughout the German army about a staff surgeon who pronounced a fellow with a wooden leg as A-1 and fit to return to duty, adding, "We need soldiers up there." To this the soldier responded: "I already have a wooden leg, but when I go back again and they shoot off my head, then I will get a wooden head made and become a staff surgeon."[53]

The army solved the problem of our diminished numbers by hurriedly assigning soldiers from what we called "Repple-Depples" (officially, "Replacement Depots") to fill our vacancies and by promoting some of the lower ranks to replace killed or injured NCOs and commissioned officers. On February 28, the day after we arrived in Campo Tizzoro, we received 38 enlisted men (including six NCOs) from the 8th Replacement Depot in Italy and two second lieutenants from other units in the 85th. Some of these replacements were former airmen and antiaircraft artillerymen who had been hastily converted to infantry because the German Luftwaffe, virtually gone from the skies, was no longer a threat. They were not too happy with this career change, having never bargained for service as "dogfaces," the common expression at the time for foot soldiers.

On the same day, ten of our privates first class were promoted to sergeant to head squads, seven sergeants were advanced to the rank of staff sergeant to head sections, and one staff sergeant was jumped to tech sergeant to head a platoon. Since our platoon had lost all five of its squad leaders as well as its mortar section sergeant, all had to be replaced.

I was one of the pfc's promoted that day to sergeant to replace my wounded machine gun squad leader, John Nevada, and other gaps in my squad were filled by some of the new men sent to our rest camp. I changed my battle dress to the extent that I now covered my steel helmet with some burlap sacking to help lessen its reflection and camouflage it from the enemy. I decided not wear my new stripes into combat because many of us assumed that the Jerries, given a choice, would make a special effort to shoot officers and noncoms in order to disrupt the chain of command. Second lieutenants, in particular, usually took care to remove the strips of brass from their collars or shoulders when on the front lines. It was always amusing to see those who took great pride in their symbols of rank dispense with these emblems when the situation so dictated.

The other machine gun squad in my platoon also received some of the new recruits, and one of its members, Private First Class Tustin Ellison, who, like me, had survived the Belvedere-Torraccia battle, was promoted to sergeant to command his squad. Our platoon leader, the indomitable First Lieutenant Hanks, whom I'd had the sense to follow en route to della Torraccia, when he found a way through that impenetrable hedge as the shellfire came raining down, was reassigned as commanding officer of E Company.[54] He replaced their Captain Neilson, who had been wounded in the attack on della Torraccia. Since no lieutenant was immediately available for our platoon, Jim Orwig served for a brief time as both acting platoon leader and platoon sergeant.

To be assigned as a replacement to a line infantry company was one of the most traumatic blows the army could deal. Since no one knew you, there was no shared bond acquired from training or other common experiences with your fellow soldiers and, simply put, little likelihood they would care, until they grew to know you better, whether you lived or died. As we soon learned, the newcomer was often wounded or killed before anyone even knew his name, especially when he had to join a unit that was entrenched in foxholes on the front line. There he might arrive at night and be told what hole to occupy, but otherwise was given little attention. If an attack was launched shortly thereafter in which he became a casualty, his departure would be noted as a statistic but, if the truth be told, he would not be greatly missed.

The combat life of a lieutenant in a rifle company was even shorter than that of an enlisted man. In six weeks of fighting in Normandy, the 90th Infantry Division had to replace almost all of its officers and men. If a division was in action for more than three months, the probability was that every one of its second lieutenants, all 132 of them, would be killed or wounded.[55] Farley Mowatt, the world-famous nature writer, entered combat during the July 1943 invasion of Sicily as an infantry platoon lieutenant with the First Canadian Infantry Division. In his book, *My Father's Son: Memories of War and Peace*, Mowatt states that six months later, "I was the sole officer survivor of those who landed in the assault wave at Pachino and took part in every major party thereafter." And the fact that he was able to survive this long may have been attributable to his transfer back to his old job as battalion intelligence officer (a relatively safer assignment) midway through the five-week Sicilian campaign, which ended in August 1943.[56]

Fortunately, American infantry divisions in Italy such as ours were getting replacements for the men lost. Mowatt says that by July 1944 the flow of volunteers from Canada had been greatly reduced and those that did come were mostly being sent to join Canadian units serving with the Allied armies in France rather than Italy. As a consequence, the few coming to the First Canadian Division "consisted mostly of soldiers wounded once, and even twice, who were now being returned to face the guns once more."[57]

Former Senator Robert Dole, running for President of the United States in 1996, had the unhappy experience of being sent from a replacement depot to the 3d Battalion of our 85th Mountain Regiment as a second lieutenant to head a rifle platoon in Company I. (The previous lieutenant had been promoted to command the company after its captain had been killed in the assault on Belvedere.) Dole had a feeling that a bullet would have his number on it, and he was right. Of the original 200 men in the company who landed in Italy, there were 183 casualties in the four months before the war ended.

Dole's company was in a relatively stable position during his first month with his platoon, occupying foxholes and dugouts where they stayed low to avoid the shellfire. In the attack which followed, however, as will be described later, he was badly wounded in the first few hours of the advance.

Our replacements were not only fresh recruits, but unlike the original volunteers for the ski troops, represented a cross section of American society. Since few skiers could still be found, or were willing to volunteer for the 10th, the new arrivals boasted such disparate backgrounds as a hillbilly from Appalachia (who had wild tales to tell of internecine warfare there), three former bartenders, an ex-missionary, and of course a number of college graduates, including one holding an M.A. in mechanical engineering and another a graduate degree in economics.

Since we had a few days before launching another attack on the German defenses, we were ordered to occupy the newcomers in close-order drill, weapons inspections, calisthenics, and other activities likely to take their minds (and ours) off the horrors to come. My performance, at least in drilling the newly reconstituted machine gun squad, didn't suit the standards of Colonel Barlow, the regimental commander. He apparently believed that precision in this task, as well as attention to other details, was a good antidote to the fear and depression caused by our introduction to the reality of modern war.

The rest camp let us catch up on mail from home—always a major morale booster—and find out what was happening in the outside world. One of the letters I received from Mother, postmarked February 6, 1945, some three weeks before it was delivered to me, had the words "Hospital, Missing, or Killed" penciled below my name and army address on the envelope. Fortunately, it was not returned to her with those notations. The words did nothing to diminish my growing realization that we were in a terrifying business and that the next time the mail clerk's notations might be right.

To further divert our minds from the battles that loomed ahead, the Red Cross sent some of their doughnut girls to the rest area, and we were even given the opportunity to see some show-business acts. In one, a well-known actress, Annabella, starred in the play *Blithe Spirit*; in another a magician using the name "Ber-Mar" foretold, as part of his act, that the Germans would surrender by April 15, 1945. The latter prediction was obviously one we wanted to believe, but with cruel irony, fate chose April 15 as the day after we began the major attack in which the future Senator Dole was wounded and we lost many others who had escaped unscathed so far.

In Campo Tizzoro I had the opportunity to make some additional entries about the Monte Belvedere-della Torraccia battle in my diary and write a letter about it to Mother and Dad and another one to Margaret. Mother included a typed copy of my letter, along with emotional comments giving thanks for my survival, as part of one she wrote to my brothers and sister. Her letter was dated March 19 so my letter must have taken about three weeks to reach her and Dad.

(Diary)

February 18—We've just been informed of our first major Division mission. We're going to attack on the right flank of the 5th Army in an attempt to take a high ridge that is the last barrier before the Po valley. It is a division objective in a night attack. This is the big test. Over the top. If I go, I hope I can sell my life dearly.

February 19—We moved up by truck and bivouacked at the base of Belvedere. Slept there and moved up this morning. First Battalion and Third took Belvedere and the ridge. Six dead GI's carried down on mules. Dug with my helmet. Moved thru the 3rd and 1st Bn's to the attack. Terrific "88" pounding. Lost contact. Passed Jud coming back. Said it was hell.

Stopped and dug in. Grede and Oman killed here. Slept on the fringe of a slope with the gun. All night terrific shelling. Olsen heart attack. H Company stopped the counter-attack.

Moved on through and hit "Bloody Ridge." Pierce killed. Nevada, Carney, Krusell, Steiner, Legassey, Canham and many others wounded and

Front and back of letter from Jessie Ellis, with mail clerk's penciled notes, that author received after Belvedere battle.

killed by 88's there. Steiner died in Orwig's arms. I followed Hanks and lived. Dug in on crest of ridge with Oldham. Scared to death. Cold. No bags or blankets. Colonel blew himself a hole. Three of us left in my squad; nine in platoon of 32 men. Horrible slaughter.

Moved over ridge in morning and 1st [squad] captured three Huns. MG's popping all around. Held at edge of ridge. Prout nearby. Jensen killed ten yards from me. Dug in fast. 88's pounded us terribly.

Slept that night and captured 14 Germans by yelling at them and firing machine gun. Killed my first Jerry on the ridge (Division objective).

Moved the gun up to a new position and 15 minutes later a mortar hit my old foxhole and wounded Staebell and Giddix.

Two [of our rifle] platoons attacked and were zeroed in by artillery. Boney and Step were riddled. Also others. George and I covered the ridge but couldn't stop the Burp guns.

Hanks [Lieutenant] hard as nails. Counterattack surrounded us. Prayed in my foxhole and read my Bible. Shrapnel dropped on my stomach. Can't take it any longer. All night we sweated out the relief (86th). Capt. King crying. Prout knocked senseless. Chaplain cried.

Pulled out at 5 A.M. Followed by 88's till we reached the town. Then the heartbreaking reunions and experiences were exchanged. Sixteen dead and 48 wounded [out of company]. Prout wept with his arms around me as did Wally and Larry.

Rode back to Campo Tizzoro (rest camp). Wonderful here but our hearts are heavy. God saved my life. We broke strongest defenses in Italy at a great cost. Called by Mark Clark the greatest unit to ever fight in Italy. Mt. della Torrachia was the final objective.

This rest camp is all right. Doughnuts and coffee. Took a good hot shower. Still can't believe I'm alive. Silver Star and Bronze Star in our company. Everyone is exhausted.

Praise is pouring in from generals and the press. I was made a sergeant. Replacements have come in. The squad is filled up again.

Plenty of letters from home. Kelly is still sick. Herrick and Westphall died. The toll mounts. Outfit looks strange now. Hanks is [now] CO of E Company.

Saw Annabella in "Blithe Spirit." Ber Mar, the magician, said war would be over by April 15.

Drilled the squad and got bawled out by the Colonel.

Wonder how Jud is?

(Mother's Letter)
Shreve, Ohio
March 19th, 1945

Dear Family,

This weekend was one of those which we will long remember. We had waited and waited for fresh word from Robert and knew the reason for the sudden and complete blackout of letters from him—that he was unable to write for when he is able he writes two to three letters to us a week. We were literally on our knees in our spirits and flesh while we waited, meanwhile keeping track of him daily through the radio, *New York Times* and *P.M.* And the news did not much reassure us of the terrific feats of endurance and daring to take those mountain peaks. Finally Margaret got a letter and telephoned its contents to us. Then next morning ours of the same date as hers reached us. I want to share it with you all. Here it is:

AMERICAN RED CROSS

(Campo Tizzoro)
February 26, 1945 (Italy)

Dear Mother and Dad,

I've just been into the valley of the shadow and out again. God is the only one who brought me back for death was all around. Read your

Some of author's ill-fated F/85 weapons platoon members at Camp Hale. Standing, left to right, Jorstad, Weidorn, Pierce, Staebell, Allen (sitting), Westphal, Carson (crouching), O'Brien, and Neilson. Pierce, Westphal, and Carson were killed in action on Belvedere; Staebell was badly wounded the following day near Monte della Torraccia, but was helped to an aid station by Neilson. Jorstad was wounded in the left shoulder by a dud 88mm, but later returned to combat after six weeks in a hospital.

newspapers for the Italian front news from the 19th on and you'll see what I've been through. I'll enclose some *Stars and Stripes* clippings. For five days and nights I was under constant fire in the attack. Some day I'll tell you the story fully. Once I passed Jud in the night and he said, "Boy am I glad to see you—in fact I'm glad to be able to say that."

Little did I dream what I was walking into. How I lived I'll never know—my lieutenant, hard as nails and cool saved my life for I just followed him through what we call Bloody Ridge. The Germans were really tough to get out, but the 88mm artillery was something indescribable. My last night there I had shrapnel [censored for nearly a line] snow, dirt, and everything else, but none penetrated. Prout is OK and the last I heard Jud is too. My platoon aided in capturing 14 Germans.

Once I thought the end had really come. I thought of you all and got ready to die. I had my Bible in my hand and read in Paul's letter to the Galatians. I prayed and hoped and God answered.

We are now in the rest camp, and everyone is treating us like kings and heroes, which is so true of many of the men. The bravest men I have ever seen.

The Red Cross girls are here and we get wonderful food—hot coffee, doughnuts, etc. I feel fine, so try not to worry too much. Pray for me and my comrades, and that the war may end. No one can possibly imagine the sacrifice these men are making. I dedicate the rest of my life to the effort of stopping war. Enough on that.

I received almost 30 letters when I returned to this rest camp. They certainly were wonderful. I love you all, and hope the end of this comes soon.

[Mother continues]

Wilder and I read this with eyes and hearts running over. The prayer that I keep on my lips all the time is this: "Cover his defenseless head with the shadow of Thy Wing." That helps keep me steady. I pray night and day and I am sure it is helping him and his comrades and us too. It is all that we can now do and our daily letters.

I have sent him some food lately as part of the time he is starved. Last week I canned fried chicken and pressure cooked it and also put in nuts and raisins Persian style for him. Another box I sent was cookies full of nuts, raisins and figs and also a can of pineapple. This week I am going to send him a jar of his beloved pears.

If his life may only be spared to do constructive work now, for which he is so eager to fit himself, we shall be so very thankful. If he lives, his life will always seem more precious to him, and peace and the "mere joy of living" will have taken on new value. His religious life will have been strengthened and deepened. But if he does not live, we will have the memory of a beautiful life and one which trusted in God in life or death and was ready, and that to us is a wonderful comfort. He did not find God first in a fox hole, but with his mother and father at home, and for that we are glad too.

I am sure you will write to him and give him courage. He won the Combat Infantryman's Badge and he has been made a Sergeant. His address is Sergeant Robert B. Ellis, ASNO 16169350, Company F, APO 345, C/O Postmaster, New York City, N. Y.

Gen. Hays' commendations to them *were wonderful.*

(Letter)
Campo Tizzoro
February 27th, 1945

Dear Margaret,

I suppose Mother sends on some of my letters so some of what I say you'll probably hear again. I've been in a very stiff fight and am now in a rest camp. How I came back I'll never know but here I am. I'll send along some clippings, etc. which don't tell the real story of suffering, courage, and sadness but will have to suffice until I get home.

I was interested in a propaganda leaflet the Germans dropped which welcomed our division to Italy and seemed to know everything about Camp Hale, our route here, etc. They're no dummies and I must admit it didn't do my morale any good.

I'm now a sergeant and also hold the Combat Infantryman's Badge. Neither, however, is worth going through that again. Yet I suppose that is the lot of every infantryman.

Nor can anyone possibly imagine what it's really like. There is only one word—hell; its every conceivable form is there.

This rest camp is nice while it lasts but I'll never get a rest until I board that ship for home. If and when.

A German officer's diary was captured in the Monte Belvedere-della Torraccia battle which expresses many of the same sentiments about the terrors of infantry combat I described in my diary and letters. The following are some excerpts from that German diary.

Feb. 13, 1945—One starts to think about the war: one thinks of the future. (Do we have any future at all?) One starts philosophizing, but what good is Schopenhauer's philosophy, Goethe's *Faust*, Nietzsche's *Superman*, and Fichte's well-meant speeches? We all, whether young or old, whether officer or enlisted man, are subject to the laws of this embittered war. Its iron fist forces us into the smallest hole when the splinters start flying. When the Yankee pulls the lanyard, we become animals. For seconds all instincts are being put *ad acta*. And then you think, once more it did not get you!

Feb. 20, 1945—To my right, I don't know exactly where, the Americans are again reported to have penetrated our positions…. Their machine guns are hammering without let-up. Just now Adam came in and reported that somewhere the rat-tat-tat of American MGs and MPs was heard. All indications are that sometime soon something will break loose in the sunny South. Those on the other side know as well as we just how much the wheat fields of the Po Valley mean to us….

Feb. 23, 1945—It is 2000 hours. The fore-runners are on the way. The whole neighborhood is alive with crashes. The bunker is shaking…. At last I have more details on the enemy penetration. Mt. Belvedere, Capello, Conchidos, Mt. della Torraccia, and Mt. Castello are in the hands of the 10th American Mountain Division. The 1044th Regiment is almost completely destroyed. Two companies (4th and 6th) have gone over to the enemy. Only 3rd company of 1044 is still intact….

Feb. 26, 1945—I can hardly believe in final victory. It must be much the same on all the other fronts. God in heaven may give that the end may be at least halfway bearable for my Germany!

A terrible explosion and fire all around me. A human being cried for help. This war is terrible. Whoever has not gone through it as a front line infantryman cannot possibly picture it. What human beings can do to one another. They are hurling death and destruction-bringing material at each other. Damned humanity, what insanity are you committing!!![58]

7

A Rat Walked Over My Face

*Mt. Della Spe and Defensive Life in
the Trenches, March–April 1945*

The new troops follow after, and tread the land we won,
To them 'tis so much hillside re-wrested from the Hun;
We only walk with reverence this sullen mile of mud;
The shell-holes hold our history, and half of them our blood.
—A. P. Herbert, *Beaucourt Revisited*

Having captured the dominating peaks and ridges in the enemy's Gothic Line, General Hays now planned a new advance on a northeasterly axis toward the road junction town of Vergato, on Highway 64, twelve miles northeast of Monte Belvedere. The objective was another line of peaks, roughly four miles from the positions gained in the first phase, from which the spring offensive could then be launched against the last defense lines before the Po Valley. These peaks included Monte della Castellana, Monte Grande d'Aiano, and the final objective—Monte della Spe.

In this action General Hays decided to employ two regiments abreast, the 86th Mountain Infantry on the left and the 87th on the right, while the Brazilian Expeditionary Force would advance along with the mountain infantry to protect our right flank. My 85th Regiment, which had borne the principal responsibility in the first attack and had suffered the majority of casualties, was placed in division reserve prepared to counterattack if required and to pass through the other units and carry on the advance when ordered. Facing us were two German divisions, the 232d Infantry and the 714th Jaeger Division. The German commander, Field Marshal Kesselring, had been planning to replace the two with a fresh division, the 29th Panzer Grenadier Division, then undergoing reorganization, but our attack opened before he was able to do so.[1]

Our involvement in this second battle began on March 2, when we were trucked at night from our happy sojourn in the Campo Tizzoro rest camp to the village of Gaggio Montano. Despite the addition of new men from the Repple Depple, our Company F was not up to the strength we had had when assaulting Monte Belvedere. We had been assigned only 181 men compared to 201, and of these, only 164 were actually available for duty. Thirteen were sick, two were missing, and two were on temporary duty elsewhere.

From Gaggio Montano we walked in the rain to a nearby ridge where we prepared to dig in for the night. Wally Krusell, my 6'7" first gunner who had experienced some shell shock in that terrible place where our weapons platoon had been decimated, now suggested that we share a foxhole. He thought my luck thus far in escaping injury boded well for anyone who stayed close to me. I agreed, but had my worries about whether we could dig a hole deep enough for his Bunyanesque frame. As it turned out, the ground was so filled with rocks, we had to settle for a shallow slit trench in which we spent a virtually sleepless night because of the steady downpour. Luckily, we were not in the forefront of the advance, so there was little shelling in our area.

The following afternoon we were given the now familiar and dreaded order, "Packs on," which one of my Latin scholar buddies joked was a garbled version of the true order, "*Pax vobiscum* (Peace be with you)." Regrettably, that was never the case, and we spent the next two days following the other two regiments, who soon captured all the intermediate division objectives as well as over a thousand prisoners. In the afternoon of March 4, our regimental commander, Colonel Barlow, received his orders for us to take over the attack the following morning, with the 1st Battalion to capture Monte della Spe and my battalion, the 2d, to seize Monte della Castellana, a short distance to the southeast.[2]

We moved out in the middle of the night and by 3:00 A.M. reached the so-called line of departure for the attack to follow. At 8:00 A.M. we crossed the LD, which was in a narrow ravine, and began our advance. Soon after, we came across an abandoned A-6 Browning machine gun which I "liberated" for the use of our squad, leaving behind the A-4 we had been carrying. While similar to our old gun, the A-6 boasted a number of modifications which made it more attractive. These included a removable metal shoulder stock, a removable handle which had been added to enable easier carrying of a hot gun, a barrel which could be changed when hot by grasping the muzzle and (with asbestos mittens or other protection) unscrewing the barrel and sliding it forward out of the jacket, and—most importantly—a removable bipod supporting the end of the barrel. This last feature obviated the need to carry a separate tripod (which weighed 14 lbs.) to support the gun. All together, the A-6 (with metal stock and bipod) weighed slightly over 32 pounds, versus some 31 pounds for the A-4 without its tripod.

In World War I, where the battle lines were largely static, machine guns dominated no-man's land, causing the legendary slaughter of infantry in head-on assaults from one trench to another. In World War II, armies made rapid and frequent movements, and the weight of machine guns carried by the

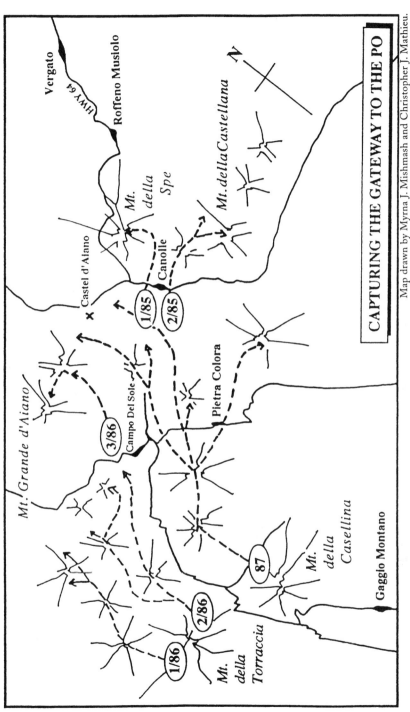

CAPTURING THE GATEWAY TO THE PO

Map drawn by Myrna J. Mishmash and Christopher J. Mathieu.

Troopers from the 10th dashing over a ridgetop after passing a dead German killed in our della Spe offensive (courtesy Denver Public Library, Western History Department).

infantry was a significant factor affecting their use. To make them as light as possible, the ones carried by a rifle company's weapons platoon were air cooled, but this meant that we also had to carry one or more spare barrels. Sustained fire would make the barrel too hot to operate, and it would have to be replaced by a cool one. The barrel burden was shared by various members of the machine gun squad, who were also responsible for carrying the boxes of belt-fed ammunition. Each belt contained 250 rounds of 30-caliber bullets. As the gun could fire some 400-500 rounds a minute, the squad had to carry numerous boxes to keep it supplied in a sustained fire-fight.[3]

Since I had been promoted to squad leader, Krusell was now responsible for carrying the gun. Because the gun was so heavy, he carried only a .45-caliber pistol for his personal defense. The second gunner carried a spare barrel, a rifle to help protect the gun position, and some ammunition. He also helped load the gun. I was charged with deciding where the gun should be emplaced, observing the fall of shot and, in general, directing the fire. While a machine gun squad was capable of operating on its own, it was safer to protect it with riflemen, and we were often attached to a rifle platoon—as we were in this advance—for mutual support in an attack.

Members of a machine gun squad cover surrendering Germans walking to rear (courtesy Denver Public Library, Western History Department).

Unlike our experience on Monte Belvedere and Monte della Torraccia, we were not subjected to continuous intense artillery and mortar fire in the sector to which we were assigned, although our initial route brought us under 88mm fire. After withdrawing and taking another approach, we experienced less shelling. The Germans were entrenched, however, in various farmhouses from which came heavy machine gun and rifle fire, and we had to dislodge them from such strong points in order to advance up the steep slope. My squad was successful in providing answering machine gun fire, and one of our mortar men, a tall, rather effeminate soldier with a mincing walk, demonstrated great bravery as well as skill when he fired his mortar from an exposed site. He managed to drop some rounds in a courtyard, and even in the doorway of one of the buildings.

What was also different about this assault on the German positions was that we had a greater feeling of operating as a team, of companionship, as we advanced across the battlefield. On occasion we could actually see the enemy in their defensive positions, and this increased our excitement and sense of purpose. As I soon learned, there is no soldier who is valiant under all conditions of combat, and one may act like a lion in one situation and like a scared rabbit under similar circumstances in another. Studies of soldiers under fire have indicated that "these lightning emotional changes are common wherever men fight," and this time at least we exhibited considerable audacity and resolution.[4]

One of the characteristics of the battlefield which comes as a particular shock to the soldier experiencing it for the first time is that it is a lonely place. Nothing he is subjected to in training prepares him for this. He is used to the nearly continuous close presence of his comrades, not simply on the drill field, but even in mock battle exercises. Suddenly, once he becomes the object of enemy artillery and small arms fire, most of his companions have disappeared. They've all gone to ground to escape the deadly missiles coming their way. The enemy too is for the most part invisible. Such isolation in the midst of mortal peril is all the more stunning because it is unexpected.

Situations like this advance, where the targets are numerous and visible and your friends are observable on every side and to the rear, usually occur because you have achieved a breakthrough and are moving rapidly to exploit the situation.

By late afternoon on March 5, the third day of our assault, the 1st Battalion of the 85th stood on top of Monte della Spe and my 2d Battalion had carried Monte della Castellana. In the advance, however, the division lost its most famous ski trooper, Tech Sergeant Torger D. Tokle. Tokle, who had emigrated from Norway to the U.S. after the outbreak of the war in September 1939, joined the 10th Mountain Division in April 1943, the same month he became an American citizen. Tokle had been a great skier in his homeland, but it was not until he came to America that he became internationally known as one of the greatest ski jumpers in the world. Before his entry into military service in October 1942, he had won 36 ski-jumping events in three years of competition—breaking course records at such places as Iron Mountain, Michigan; Lake Placid, New York; Steamboat Springs, Colorado; and Leavenworth, Washington—and had twice set the national ski jumping record with leaps of 288 and 289 feet.

Tokle was a platoon sergeant in Company A of the 86th. When his platoon was pinned down by heavy machine gun fire, he and a bazooka gunner crawled to a forward position and opened fire on the German gun. Shortly after they did so, a fragment from a heavy concentration of shells the enemy had been pouring on our advancing troops struck and killed them both.[5] Another trooper with the 86th killed by a sniper in this advance was Private First Class John Compton, the grandson of W. H. Danforth, chairman of the board of the Ralston Purina Company, and son of Randolph P. Compton, the former president of the brokerage house, Kidder, Peabody & Company. (Following the war, John's parents visited the village where their son was killed and restored the war-damaged roof of the village church as a memorial to him.)[6]

However limited the scope of our operation was from the viewpoint of the U.S. Fifth Army, the official history of the campaign, *Cassino to the Alps*, states that General Kesselring saw the fight as having developed into "a battle for possession of the gateway into the Po Valley at both the operationally and tactically most unfavorable point."[7] For this reason he believed he had no choice but to rush his principal reserve, the 29th Panzer Grenadier Division, into the battle. Four counterattacks were launched that night by this division, accompanied by heavy artillery and mortar fire, against Monte della Spe, which was defended in large part by the 1st Battalion of the 85th. The first enemy effort brought them to within 15 yards of our defensive positions and resulted in a severe struggle featuring bayonets and grenades. In this action, the executive officer of Company B, Lieutenant John Creaghe, distinguished himself by taking charge of defenders on the left flank of his company, and as a consequence, he suffered wounds in the right leg, chest, and right arm, and lost the use of his left eye. After receiving some first aid, he crawled into a foxhole and refused to be evacuated until the following morning in order not to deprive the defense of needed men.[8]

The counterattacks kept up the rest of the night, and as each was beaten off, mortar and artillery fire intensified on the summit of della Spe and the adjacent ridges. The harassing fire and counterattacks, though gradually diminishing, continued in the days to come, with the result that the 85th Regiment suffered casualties at a high rate. Over 90 percent of these came from the 1st Battalion, with Company B alone losing over 50 percent of its men.[9] Nevertheless, the objectives of the limited offensive were in hand. At a cost of another 549 casualties, including 106 killed, our mountain division had brought the right wing of the IV Corps abreast of the II Corps and in control of excellent jump-off positions for the spring offensive.[10] As a reporter for the *New York Times* described it: "From vantage points taken by the 10th Mountain Division in a grueling three-day attack that ended Monday, the Apennine ridges yet to be crossed appear foothills in comparison with the brutal terrain already won.... It is already possible to view the outlines of the Bologna and Po Valley objective."[11]

Field Marshal Kesselring, nicknamed "Smiling Albert" by the Allies, was obviously not smiling now. In his *Memoirs* he admitted: "To my surprise—in deep snow—the remarkably good American 10th Mountain Division launched an attack against the left flank of the 'static' 232nd Infantry Division, which speedily led to the loss of the dominating heights of Monte Belvedere." The follow-on advance towards della Spe was in his view, "an emergency where, to safeguard the possession of the gateway to the Po we just had to commit the 29th Panzer Division, which had been resting for some weeks—a hard but inevitable decision." The result was, he said, that the Panzers "suffered such serious losses that they lost their value as a strategic reserve."[12]

General Truscott, commanding the 5th Army, could have let the 10th continue ahead under the momentum they had already created, but he thought the objectives of the limited offensive had been achieved, and he did not want the Germans to think that the main thrust of the spring offensive would come in this area west of Highway 64. Highway 65 to the east offered the more direct approach to Bologna, and on this road we were only 12 miles from the city, whereas on Highway 64 our most advanced elements were still some 20 miles away. Highway 65 boasted the best road net in the 5th Army sector, but it was also the route where the Germans expected the principal Allied effort to be made. To protect the city, they had prepared a bristling array of defenses, which they called the Genghis Khan Line, on all the dominating ground along that highway and extending east as far as Lake Comacchio.[13]

My diary notes briefly summarized the three-day battle in which we had achieved all that our Allied commanders had hoped to accomplish in preparation for the spring offensive yet to come.

(Diary)
March 2—We're moving out again on another mission. What a feeling. Hope I can bring this squad back intact. Roy Manse [a new replacement] is from Canton [Ohio].

Trucks took us and we hiked a little past Gaggio Montana. Worst foxhole I've ever had. Rained. Moved out this afternoon and hiked near Highway 64 in reserve of 86th and 87th. They were advancing rapidly and captured many prisoners—1,058 in three days. Moved out at night and hiked to the L.D. in a narrow draw. Picked up an A-6 for the squad.

Easily occupied first ridge. Attached to 1st platoon. Ran into heavy 88 fire on second ridge. Held up by "Burp" gun [German machine gun] fire. Flanked to the right and after a terrific climb, we captured our company objective. Also seven Germans, four machine guns, etc. Cleaned out a strong point with the A-6. Directed fire. Everyone seemed scared except my squad. Got commended by Orwig and the platoon leader for my handling of the squad. Dug in, in a Jerry hole.

As was customary following a major battle, especially where you had emerged victorious, we received ponderous letters of commendation from all levels of command higher up for both the Belvedere and della Spe operations. Each general, no doubt exulting over the accomplishment in the hope that his superior up the line would accord him some credit for its success, not only thanked us for our efforts but, lest we forget that the war was not over, included exhortations to continue our aggressive action against the enemy. The following commendations were received:

• The supreme allied commander, Mediterranean theatre of operations, Field Marshal Alexander, used such words as "heartiest congratulations ... a very well planned and well executed operation."

• The commander, Mediterranean theater of operations, U.S. Army (MTOUSA), Lieutenant General McNarney, wrote that the 10th had shown by its "first battle test, offensive capability which will be a constant source of real concern to our enemies."

• The commander, 15th Army Group, Lieutenant General Mark Clark, offered his "congratulations to the officers and men of the 10th ... on ... the capture of Mt. Belvedere.... Your Division ... has acquitted itself with the courage and daring of a veteran combat unit. This speaks more eloquently than words of the ... spirit of officers and men."

• The commanding general, 5th Army, Lieutenant General Truscott, Jr., described the task as "a very difficult assignment [in which] you have seized every objective in record time.... The 10th Mountain Division in its first operation has been an inspiration to the entire Fifth Army."

• The commanding general, IVth Corps, Major General Crittenberger, waxing even more eloquent, told us: "The enemy estimate of 'elite mountain troops,' applied by him to your division after short but bitter experience, is a deserved compliment.... It is a great pleasure for me hereby to commend you ... not only for a precise and masterly execution of your mission, but as well for the dash and vigor that never for a moment left the issue in doubt." Crittenberger added: "Four attempts have been made to take this high ground but you are the only ones who have held it for long. I have had thirty divisions in the Corps and this is one of the best."

• And our own commanding general of the 10th Mountain Division, Major General Hays, said he took pride in these commendations from generals "who have personally engaged in some of the heaviest fighting and most difficult operations of this war.... May we all look forward with renewed confidence in our ability to undertake whatever tasks may lie ahead."[14]

What we faced for the next month or so was a static battle, since the forward movement of the division had ceased for a while. Now the problem of defense became the prime consideration.

The Germans always left beautifully protected bunkers and trenches on the hills we captured from them, but they were on what was to us the forward-facing slope rather than the rear, where we wanted to be. This effectively made them useless to us. If, in our offensive posture, we were to occupy foxholes or other dugouts on the forward slope of a ridge or mountain, the retreating enemy could fire directly into our position. Thus, we had to dig new foxholes on the backsides of these hills to reduce the danger from artillery and mortar shells being lobbed in our direction. (Of course, 88mm fire was not lobbed at all; it came in at you in a flat trajectory like a rifle bullet.) This meant that whenever we captured a hill, we had to dig fresh emplacements, while the tempting but unusable German ones stayed mockingly empty.

To add to the irritation, we had to use our own muscle power, while the Germans used forced Italian labor to dig their bunkers and trenches for them. These defenses, which were immediately available when they chose to retreat, also reduced the time their troops were exposed above ground to our artillery fire in their fall-back positions.* The opposite was true for us. Once we had

---

*Field Marshal Kesselring referred to such prepared positions in his Memoirs, commenting that their construction south and north of the Po had been going on "with remarkable success" all during the summer of 1944.[15]

Orwig shaving within diving reach of his bunker on Monte della Castellana.

seized the heights they had held, we had to dig in as quickly as possible, because their artillery rounds would start falling on us within a few minutes of our arrival. Unfortunately, we could rarely dig in fast enough, and this is how we lost many of our men.

During this period of maintaining the status quo, much effort was devoted to customizing foxholes. Wally and I concentrated on adding sandbags around our position and digging as far as we could to protect our bodies. Further back from these forward positions, some men were able to make fairly comfortable dugouts and to cover the tops with logs. On these they piled sandbags and anything else which might protect them from shells bursting in the air overhead or deflect direct hits. None of this could keep out the rain, however, and because it was springtime in the Apennines, we were often wet, cold, and covered with mud. Such conditions might seem a guarantee of pneumonia, but cases of serious illness were uncommon.

We lay in the cold, stony ground of our foxholes 24 hours a day, usually with one sleeping and the other keeping watch, sometimes using binoculars to see what the Germans were up to. There had long been a rumor in the army that color-blind people like me were not fooled by efforts to camouflage gun positions, but after many days of watching the German lines, I reluctantly concluded that the rumor was false. One welcome replacement who came to our squad from the 8th Replacement Depot, a Private First Class Joseph Mofford, had incredible eyesight without the aid of field glasses and frequently pointed out enemy soldiers in hiding where we had seen nothing. As a result, he soon earned the nickname "Eagle Eye" Mofford.

Our food was entirely from cans: C-rations consisting of beef stew, spaghetti and meatballs, or other cold concoctions. If you tried to raise your head above ground, you risked being shot by a sniper, getting a rain of machine gun bullets through your body, or having a shell explode in your vicinity. We learned to appreciate more than ever that, whereas to the average observer the infantry appears to be the main element in modern battle, in fact the artillery has been responsible for about 80 percent of the slaughter in both world wars. As one military analyst has put it, "the role of the infantry [is] as the staked goat with artillery as the hunter."[16]

To get rid of our trash, we threw the empty cans of C-rations and other debris out of our holes, and on occasion an incoming shell exploding nearby would blow them back in our chambers. We also had to face the very real danger that we might suffer a direct hit, even though we remained below ground. These and other fears became our constant companions and even they, as Macbeth observed, were "less than horrible imaginings."

Every day someone would get wounded or killed by the random explosions in our midst, and the sound of both our outgoing missiles and the enemy's incoming ones was the music to which we danced. My diary log covering a six-day period (March 7–12) at this time noted:

> *(Diary)*
> 88's killed Struller today and wounded Gallagher [March 7]. Kept improving the position. Worked like a horse. Mother writes often.
> Wagle killed [March 10] and Stavola wounded [March 11]. Also Lt. Cassidy [March 12]. Sandbagged Wally's and my position.

We were under orders not to light cigarettes at night, because the enemy might see the glow and send some rounds our way, but such orders were often disobeyed. On one occasion when Wally or I violated the instruction—although doing our best to hide the light—our action was followed almost immediately by a shell whistling over our heads which we later believed might have been one which struck the bunker of some of our cooks not far to our rear. The shell fragments and splinters from the log cover caused the cooks some serious wounds. While it may have been simply a random missile that the Germans chose to send over at that particular time, that possibility did not ease the guilt we both felt.

Staff Sergeant Don Chrisler, a friend who was an 81mm mortarman in Company H of our battalion, had a somewhat different but equally close shave resulting from lighting a cigarette at night when in close proximity to the enemy. He told me some 50 years later that during our March attack, he had been ordered during the night to run a telephone line from his mortar's position up to an observation post. "Pissing and moaning," he said, "we got a reel of wire and some phones and headed up the hill. We noticed a few pieces of German equipment scattered about, but thought little of it as we settled into a shell crater for a smoke. Lighting up, we cupped our hands around the cigarettes to hide the glow and ... stopped breathing when a German patrol skirted the upper edge of our crater. Thanks to the darkness and our training in shielding nighttime smokes, they missed us. If they had skirted the lower end of the crater, they would have tripped over our wire. Also, being good mortarmen, we had left our rifles leaning against the side of the hole, well out of reach. The question is, would we have used the rifles if they had been within reach? I can't speak for Tom, but I'm sure I would have just held my breath, as in the actual event."[17]

Even though artillery rounds were often falling on our positions, during the daylight hours the situation was stable enough that we managed to clean our weapons, shave every once in a while, and write occasional letters home. The following are some that I wrote from my foxhole to Mother, Margaret, and Paul some 10 days after we seized Monte della Spe and Monte della Castellana.

(Letter)
Monte della Castellana
March 15th, 1945   V-MAIL
   I'm beginning to find myself in need of a watch and a pen. In the confusion of battle I lost my pen which I regarded as an old friend. It was the one I had won on the SS *Scythia* in the shuffleboard tournament. I really could use a watch—a shockproof watch if you can get a hold of a good one. I know pens are pretty difficult to get.
   Your air and V-mail letters arrive in approximately the same time, to answer your oft-repeated question. Frankly I prefer your air letters.
   I seem to remain well and rather healthy. Everyone else, luckily perhaps, gets something wrong with his feet or teeth, etc., and gets a nice rest in a hospital, safe from shells and enfiltrating patrols. As my friend, Larry Boyajian, puts it, perhaps a strategic wound wouldn't be so bad. I frankly envy Kelly and his hospitalized dysentery.
   Margaret still seems to find time to rebuke me in her scarce letters for not writing a thank-you note for her Xmas present. Would that she could share this foxhole with me for a few moments.

(Letter)
Monte della Castellana
Thursday, March 15th, 1945

Dear Margaret,

   Glad to hear that you're back in your little home again. I'm writing this letter with some Heine ink I found in an abandoned fox hole nearby. But there's not much of it and I had to dilute it in order to get enough for my pen.
   This is the first time I've ever written from a fox hole. Usually I've never stayed long in any one hole. The lovely weather high in these Apennines is spoiled by the sounds of shells, ours mostly, thank God, whistling over head.
   War is certainly a shock when you first face it in its stark nakedness. For instance, the first time you step over an old friend lying there bloody and still as you press forward in the attack. You wonder if you'll be next

and if you've got the courage to go over the little protecting rise of ground in front of you, beyond which death hails from everywhere. You feel as though you're holding your life by a piece of string and someone is taking swipes at it with a knife. And even as you go forward steadily, yet warily, you think of how all your hopes and dreams, memories, the things you want to do—your awful love of life—hang there unprotected, all to be lost with the whine of an '88 and the rain of shrapnel death. This is when you wonder if anything, any ideal, is worth to you the price of life. You try to put it all aside—to make your mind a blank—and press forward to deal death yourself.

Sorry about the Xmas present—the holder was swell.

(Letter)
Monte della Castellana
March 15th, 1945   V-MAIL

Dear Paul,

It is the end of another day, and I'm writing you with some Heine ink I found in a nearby foxhole. As usual he makes everything uncomfortable, for he didn't leave enough and I've had to dilute it with water.

Speaking of fox holes, I think we should hurry now and make the world safe from all future threats of war and pestilence. To use the fox hole as a simile, we should build, construct, and dig deep into solid foundations of brotherhood, and be protected like the walls of Mother Earth by cooperation and amicable discussion.

Frankly I'm getting a little tired of eating from a can, and crackers don't exactly take the place of my great appetite for bread. I think I'd be perfectly content to wait for Mary Liz to fix dinner. Just to eat from a table and to see your smiling parental faces would be enough. Probably, however, I'll be eating Chinese rice after I finish with this Italian food.

I'm really isolated from my old friends. I haven't seen John Horrall since I left the States.

Send some pictures.

At night we sent out patrols to feel out the German positions and to determine what regiments and divisions were facing us, and the Germans tried to get behind our lines for the same purpose. It was about this time that Lieutenant Robert Dole, a candidate for President in 1996, was sent to Company I of our 85th Regiment as a replacement lieutenant.

In the regimental history covering the period from January 4 to May 28, 1945, compiled by Captain John Woodruff, Dole is mentioned a number of times as having been ordered to lead ambush and combat patrols of 12 to 20 or more men from our positions in the Monte della Spe and Monte della Castellano sector to try and capture prisoners of war (PWs) for interrogation. This was one of the more unpleasant duties of second lieutenants in the various rifle companies, not to mention the men chosen to accompany them.

The patrols were dangerous business. They were conducted at night, preferably when there was little moonlight, and because you had little idea where the enemy might be hiding or the location of mine fields, you could expect sudden death to greet you in the darkness at any moment. Moreover, since your mission was usually to take prisoners, you had to be aggressive and attack a known enemy position or hide in ambush and try to surprise any of the enemy who happened to pass by. Either way, you had to expect a fire fight, and the likelihood that more than one of you would be hurt or killed was great.

Many patrols returned without accomplishing their goals, and this was apparently true of the ones Woodruff's history describes as being led by Dole. One that he led the night of March 17 is a good example.

> Company I sent out an ambush patrol at 1900 hours [7 P.M.] 17 March of 16 men, led by Lt. Dole. An ambush was set ... with part of the patrol and the rest moved forward. Enemy machine gun and mortar fire suddenly opened up on the patrol, inflicting four light casualties. No prisoners were taken but one German was killed or badly wounded. The patrol was forced to withdraw because of mortar fire.[18]

Not infrequently all three companies in a battalion would send out patrols the same night, and on occasion these teams risked getting entangled with one another. This is what happened to another patrol led by Dole. It ran into a 25-man patrol from K Company which had got into a fire fight in which an estimated eight enemy were killed, while three of their own men were wounded by a German grenade. Dole's group was fired upon, and, thinking it might be the Company K patrol, he withdrew his men to avoid a battle with friendly forces.[19]

Despite their increasingly difficult situation, the German troops facing us had been tenacious in defending the ridges and mountains under their control. One possible explanation for this determination came when we captured a German soldier's diary which revealed that he and his comrades had been warned that the 10th Mountain Division was about to attack and that they would not take any prisoners. In an attempt to counter this propaganda, leaflets were dropped by our airplanes over the German lines urging them to surrender. One that I picked up read as follows in English and German on one side:

SAFE CONDUCT

> The German soldier who carries this safe-conduct is using it as a sign of his genuine wish to give himself up. He is to be disarmed, to be well looked after, to receive food and medical attention as required, and is to be removed from the danger-zone as soon as possible.
>
> [Signed]
> H. R. Alexander
> Commander-in-Chief, Allied Armies in Italy

On the other side, in German, it asked whether "Getting killed, shortly before the end" was what the German soldier wanted, or—in accordance with the Geneva Convention—to be guaranteed food, prepared by their own cooks, in "the same portions as … received by Allied soldiers," to receive "payment for labor," as well as "opportunity for sport and games," and "to get home soon after the end of the war."

Not to be outdone, the Germans saw to it that similar passes, in this case bearing inducements to find peace and happiness in the Fatherland, got into our hands. One that I sent home—a bit more imaginative than the American propaganda—bore a picture on one side of what were supposed to be Scottish PWs, playing bagpipes and marching through a crowd of happy onlookers, and on the other side this inviting message in English:

PRISONERS-OF-WAR GET A SQUARE DEAL
GERMANY STRICTLY OBSERVES
GENEVA CONVENTION

Prisoners-of-war tell us they expected to be shot by the Germans as their officers had warned them they would.

These "dead" men have a grand time celebrating one of their national holidays in a German camp. Piping is going on as merrily as ever in front of the well-constructed barracks.

Later on the boys will attend a variety show in the entertainment hall of the camp. There are many good amateur actors among them. The decorations and stage requisites are made by the POW themselves. The costumes are lent them by German theatres.

No. 5 of a series of twelve leaflets showing the life of prisoners-of-war in German camps.

By the middle of March, the front had quieted down some, and General Hays ordered that one battalion in a regiment at a time be rotated back to rest areas at Campo Tizzoro and the city of Montecatini and that individual soldiers be given short leaves to go to Rome, Florence, and other towns in the rear to have a few days freedom from shelling.[20] Unlike combat air crews in the Army Air Corps, where the completion of a set number of missions guaranteed your escape from a war zone, the infantry had not yet learned that if no reprieve is ultimately granted, men will inevitably go mad in battle and that no appeal to heroism, love of country, or obligation to one's comrades will matter in the end.*

General Hays could not grant a release after a set period of time in combat, but he did have the sense to permit us at least a brief respite from duty on the front line. War reporter Ernie Pyle, who visited many infantrymen in

---

Such a change finally came, first in the Korean conflict and then in Vietnam, when combat troops were deemed to have fulfilled their combat obligations when they had served 365 days in the theater of war, even though often less than that in actual combat.

Italy who had been too long in the line, commented that you could tell them by a look in their eyes that anyone could discern. "It's a look that is the display room for what lies behind it—exhaustion, lack of sleep, tension for too long, weariness that is too great, fear beyond fear, misery to the point of numbness, a look of surpassing indifference to anything anybody can do. It's a look I dread to see on men."[21]

My turn to get away came on March 18, when I spent two days at the Campo Tizzoro rest center. It was only a short distance from the front lines and offered only the barest of facilities, but these included a hot shower, fresh clothes, and hot food. Then—much to my surprise—on March 22, almost immediately following my return to our entrenched positions, I was given one week's leave to go to Rome. This was quite a different situation, and a great improvement over anything in the way of a reprieve from combat I had previously experienced.

In Rome I stayed at the Foro Italico (also called the Foro Mussolini), an ambitious sports complex on the Tiber River. Built in 1931 by a fascist organization, the former Accademia Fascista della Farnesina, it had been commandeered by the Allied forces as a retreat for soldiers on leave from the front. Among its Fascist-inspired statuary was a marble monolith some 60 feet high, inscribed "Mussolini Dux," rising at its entrance in front of an imposing avenue paved with marble inlaid with mosaics. The center featured a 20,000-seat stadium, the Stadio dei Marmi, whose tiers were decorated with 60 colossal statues of athletes. The complex also contained indoor and outdoor swimming pools, tennis and basketball courts, running tracks, gymnasia, fencing halls, reading rooms, and other facilities.[22]

Both of these brief respites from the front were reported in my diary and letters home.

(Diary)
March 18—Went to Battalion rest camp. Canham returned and LeGassey. Got the flashlight. Rat walked over my face. Climbed back up the mountain.

March 22—Told to pack and go to Rome on seven-day leave. Rode by truck to Tizzoro and took train from Montecatini. Beautiful ride down along the coast (17 hours). Taken to the Forum Mussolini (rest camp) on the Tiber. Took bus to town and wandered around. Bought a cameo and bracelet to send to Mother and Dad. Had my picture taken.
Took the tour to the Vatican, St. Peter's, Roman Forum, Garibaldi's monument. Went to an Italian movie theatre. Took the tour along the Appian Way and the tombs of St. Peter and St. Paul. Saw the Pope in a little room in the Vatican. Seemed like a very kind man, but tired and old. Heard an operatic troupe. Saw an Italian stage show—"Follies of 1945." Woman sang "Ave Maria" in it, much to my amazement. Visited the Catacombs. (Beautiful place to go AWOL.)
Rome seems unharmed, the people well-fed and clothed. Children seem to have *rien* to do.

Couldn't get in touch with McSweeney. Visited the Coliseum, Circus Maximus, etc. Saw the balcony where Mussolini used to rave. Prices enormous—sweater costs $69. Mussolini's Victor Emmanuel Monument is really quite a figure of art.

Italian girls love the Negroes. Went to a night club ("Melody Club") and drank champagne—one bottle in 15 minutes. Couldn't find my way back to the bus. A British officer steered me back.

Gorged myself at the snack bar. Tried to get tickets to "Carmen" at the Royal Opera house, but failed. News stands sell bright publications comparable to *Time*, *Life*, etc. Many young Italian men seem to be wandering around with nothing to do. You see the hammer and sickle chalked on walls and other political posters up favoring this or that party.

Started back by train to Montecatini. Had to sleep in the aisle. Arrived at the front and climbed in the dark to relieve the 3rd. Battalion. Rather dangerous positions. Heavy shelling and machine guns over our heads.

Got about 40 letters. One from Howie Wells and Jack Millar. Paul Barnes died.* Family seems pretty worried. Not that I blame them. I'm worried too.

(Letter)
Campo Tizzoro, Italy
March 18th, 1945

The war may seem very close to the end but to the men here who watch their comrades die each day the end is far away. I'm back at a rest camp again for a two day breather, which really isn't much of a rest but it does give you a chance to get clean clothes and to get a change in diet from rations in tins. The accommodations are none too great—in fact a rat ran over my face last night, so I almost prefer to be in my fox hole. However, I'll take rats over the German artillery any day.

I have heard nothing from the people you know in Italy. Kelly is still sick somewhere. We're having beautiful spring weather here and the mountains and valleys are covered with violets and daisies.

I hope that Ed doesn't have to get into this mess. It will do him no good. If he does have to go he should do his best to get into the artillery.† With German air power cut down it's the best place to be. The infantryman is the only one whose lot never changes, and I wouldn't want anyone to undergo this.

I'm enclosing a clipping about a diary of a German officer we captured. It's pretty interesting. I expect some mail from you in a few hours so I'll delay the end of this letter to see what you have to say.

Any more word on Bob McDowell?** That really is a shame. I hope he turns up all right. How is Margie Rath taking it?

Just received your flashlight and a letter from you. Thanks a million.

Wells was a Western Reserve Academy classmate who, as a conscientious objector, refused to take up arms and instead volunteered to serve in Italy with an ambulance crew. Barnes, also in my class at WRA, was killed fighting with an infantry division in France.

†War reporter Ernie Pyle noted, while visiting an artillery regiment in Italy, that they had not lost a single officer in more than a year of combat.[23]

**McDowell, like me, was the son of a physician who had been a medical missionary to Persia. A close friend, he was piloting a DC-3 which disappeared over the island of Biak near New Guinea. The wreckage was never found.

(Letter)
Rome
March [date censored], 1945   V-Mail
    Guess where I was the last seven days. Out of the blue came a seven-day [one word censored] leave in Rome. It really was wonderful seeing all the famous works of art again—the Sistine Chapel, St. Peters, Catacombs, Raphael's works, etc. This time I really enjoyed and appreciated them. Nothing seemed damaged and some of Mussolini's additions—such as a beautiful collection of buildings called the "Foro," dedicated to the youth of Italy—where we stayed during our rest, are a nice addition.
    Prices of course are fabulous. I saw a girl's sweater in a window priced at $69.
    I am sending you a bracelet and the Combat Infantry Badge that was awarded me. Also some pictures I had taken in Rome are on the way.
    If you never received the $90 that I sent you in January, write me about it. I still have the postal money order stub. Also, now that I'm having a sergeant's pay, I'm sending home around $75 in bonds a month instead of $37.50. So tell me about that when you receive it. The extra bonds will start with April.

As indicated in my diary note before I left for Rome, two former members of my platoon, Ray Canham (a machine gun ammunition carrier) and George LeGassey (a mortarman)—both of whom had been wounded in that terrible place on Monte Belvedere where machine gun sergeant Leonard Pierce had been killed—returned to duty. Both had been hit by shell fragments in the buttocks, a nasty place, we learned, since the healing process there seemed to stretch out interminably. The wound threatened to break open every time you tried to sit down or subject it to any other kind of pressure. We told Canham, whom we called "Comfortable" because he always seemed to be able to find an accommodating spot in which to curl up, that he had to wear his Purple Heart where he had been wounded.

    During our long train ride down the leg of the Italian peninsula to Rome, we were shunted off to a siding at one point to let another train pass by. It happened that we stopped right next to a grassy field where some rear-echelon troops were playing baseball. For the combat infantrymen on board, the opportunity to observe and comment, in a mostly humorous vein, on this wholly different world of military activity, where no bombs or other instruments of death fell, was too great to resist. As a consequence a number of exchanges took place, with each side kidding the other. One train passenger yelled: "Hey, be careful now, I wouldn't want to see any of you hurt running like that."

    One of the ball players called back, "Where you going? What outfit are you with?"

    "We're with the 10th, and we're going to Rome on leave!"

    Cheers and catcalls in response.

    A young GI came up beside my car and joked: "How come you ski boys are back down here? You're supposed to be up there fighting those *Germans*. Who's gonna stop 'em from heading this way and killing us?"

"Maybe that would do you some good," I said, "you'd find out what you're fighting for."

"Are you crazy?" the GI answered, "It's been so long since I've had 'basic,' I wouldn't know which end of the gun the bullet comes out. That's what *you're* trained to do—protect us from those Goddamn Nazis. You shouldn't be down here at all!"

Even though we got a lot of laughs out of the joking back and forth, I was reminded of Charles Montague's bitter statement, "War hath no fury like a non-combatant."[24] We front-line troops thought we were terribly discriminated against and that there was a disproportionate number of men in the rear versus the forward areas. We had good reason for this belief. With the growth of military technology in World War II, the size of the noncombatant tail dragged along by the forward echelons grew to almost a 10:1 ratio.[25] For those engaged in supply, transport, and other administrative operations, the war imposed unpleasant housing, onerous discipline, and often boring duties. But to the few who had to actually fight the enemy—only some 700,000 in the infantry (and many fewer than that in rifle companies) out of some 11,000,000 men in the army—it was a contest with mortal implications, and violent dismemberment of one's body was a likely outcome.[26]

The "Foro" rest center in Rome provided a variety of delights, one of which was an advertised opportunity to "Dance with Beautiful Roman Girls." I did exactly that one night and found unreal the sudden move from the foxhole on Monte della Spe to a dance floor with "a Roman girl" in my arms.

As I wrote Mother, although I had been taken as a child through countless European art galleries, cathedrals, and monuments on our travels to and from Persia, it was a pleasure to see them again as a young adult, even under war-time conditions. But watching a performer sing "Ave Maria" in what was essentially a burlesque show with half-nude dancing girls was a bit of a shock. And, of course, I did not tell Mother and Dad about drinking an entire liter of champagne in 15 minutes. This last, together with earlier shots of various liquors, had me so drunk I wandered for hours vainly seeking the pickup point for the bus that would take me back to the rest center. Without the help of a British officer whom I accosted in my stupor, I would have collapsed unconscious in some Roman alley.

Alas, my brief escape in Rome from the war had to end, and my return on March 27 coincided with my Company F (and the 2d Battalion) being ordered to move from the rest center in Montecatini to relieve the 3d Battalion on Monte della Spe. We had the unenviable pleasure of climbing the mountain in the dark and the rain and having to occupy strange foxholes and dugouts in what was clearly an exposed position, with large caliber shells and bullets—the latter emanating from machine guns and snipers—being directed at us with some regularity.[27] The intense artillery fire that had accompanied the many attempts to take back the mountain had scarred and denuded the summit, which had been a forest of chestnut trees. Now not a tree was still standing.

Two nights after occupying these positions, I and others in our two machine gun squads were chosen to accompany a 62-man night patrol, led by a thoroughly incompetent lieutenant, to raid enemy positions and capture PWs. My diary summarized the experience.

> *(Diary)*
> March 29—Sixty-two men went out on a raid. Mission was to wipe out two villages, clear a ridge and capture a prisoner. Led by Lt. D—, we set out at 9 P.M. with tremendous firepower (six BAR's, two MG's, three rifle squads, three litter teams, two medics, and two bazooka teams). Beautiful full moon. Very slow movement. No opposition. Our artillery smashed the villages when we reached Phase II. Then the Heines threw phosphorous at us. Came pretty close and panic started. W—set off some trip flares. Many took off and never returned. Finally we reorganized. I found the machine gun and one man in my squad and we withdrew, never accomplishing our mission.

The official regimental history, in its description of this patrol, states that supporting artillery fire was laid down at 1:30 A.M. on one of the targets but that "intense enemy artillery fell on the patrol position and they were forced to withdraw and reorganize." As a result, this account went on, "Time did not permit further action before daylight and the patrol was ordered to return."[28]

The failure of the patrol was mainly a result of the excruciatingly slow pace set by our excessively cautious lieutenant. This led all to believe that nothing useful was being accomplished. Our snail-like progress stretched almost beyond endurance nerves already heightened by the tension which invariably accompanied a nighttime attack. When some incoming phosphorous shells landed in our midst, this provided the trigger which caused many to scatter and seek protective cover. Phosphorous fragments were particularly frightening, not only because the steel splinters thrown off were white hot, but the phosphorus itself could burn you severely. When one of the men in the patrol accidentally tripped a wire that caused some flares to explode into the air, exposing our position in the naked light of the slowly descending flares, this escalated the panic and further contributed to the unit's disorder.

After some exploration of the shrubbery nearby, I was able to locate our squad's machine gun, and we reassembled. By this time the hour was so late and our numbers so reduced, the lieutenant decided we should abandon the raid and return to our defensive positions on Monte della Spe.

Rather than court-martial those who had fled the patrol, another patrol of some 50 men, which was led by the same lieutenant and included those who had disappeared after the shelling, was sent out two nights later with much the same mission. While they did not return with any prisoners, they experienced a firefight in which they were attacked by Panzerfausts—the German anti-tank guns—and light mortars, but they returned fire and the Germans evacuated the buildings they were holding. One of the men from my squad who was forced to accompany the patrol for the second time told me, when he returned in the wee hours of the morning, that it hadn't gone too badly until, as they were proceeding down a narrow draw, a rocket aimed right at them came whistling down the ravine. Fortunately, it just cleared their heads and they continued forward to carry out their assignment.

During this period of over a month, when the division manned a relatively stable six-mile front extending from the eastern end of the Monte Belvedere Ridge to the summit of Monte della Spe and Highway 64, more replacements arrived. F Company received them in two batches, some 32 enlisted men on March 13 and another large group a month later.[29] Regrettably, few were sent to join us at the right time. The best method would have been to have them report when your unit was behind the lines for an extended rest period. In this way they could get to know the veterans, could form natural friendships, and could feel some sense of identity with their new comrades when they went into battle for the first time.

Anyone faced with the likelihood of death prefers not to be alone. To risk losing one's life in the dark of night in a foreign land, frightened and confused, with no friends around and facing this most critical moment entirely alone, takes extraordinary strength. Too often the new recruits would arrive with others at night, have a brief session (if at all) with the company commander, who would inform them of the respective platoons and squads into whose ranks they would be placed, and then the appropriate sergeants or platoon leaders would take them to their assigned foxholes or other entrenchments. As a result they often met few, if any, of their immediate comrades and could be thrust into battle the next day almost as a total stranger.

General S. L. A. Marshall, the military student of why men fight, complained that too often a line company paid little heed to the way in which it greeted a new replacement and failed to recognize "the inherent unwillingness of the soldier to risk danger on behalf of men with whom he has no social identity." It is this, he said, which is the heart of the matter in developing an effective fighting force, and not the accepted infantry school dogma concerning how the soldier should maneuver his weapons in relationship to himself, to others, and to the ground in order to achieve maximum fire power. The latter proposition, he said, "is absolutely false." It is personal *honor*, he said, coupled with sympathetic understanding and knowledge of each other, that is the most important force driving the soldier, and it is the one thing that enables him to face the risks of battle. Only when primary stress is placed on the human, rather than the material, aspects of the engagement, will you find the necessary combination of psychological as well as mechanical elements needed for aggressive action and ultimate victory.[30]

Despite this injunction, neither the 10th Mountain Division nor other infantry units in the Italian theater paid much attention to what seemed the commonsense approach. No special effort was made to introduce me to the new men who joined our platoon, including a new platoon leader assigned us from the Eighth Replacement Depot, a second lieutenant named Wayne Jinkins, who had held his commission only four months. I admit that the circumstances, namely a substantial number of shells and bullets coming our way, were hardly conducive to socializing. Still, about all I learned of our newly appointed leader was that he had been a window dresser for a department store in Chicago. After observing him from our respective foxholes for some days, my associates and I concluded that he was "very nervous in the service," not surprising, given where and how he joined us. He soon acquired the nickname (not divulged to him) of "the turtle" for his habit of rarely sticking his head— much less the rest of his body—out of his hole.

The addition of new men to our company and the dispatch of some of us to be trained in such esoteric subjects as flame throwing—this at a school site near Pisa—made it evident, even to the most optimistic, that we were being prepared for another offensive. In the closing days of March and the beginning of April, however, I managed to occupy myself by helping dig new outposts and trenches connecting our positions, getting in some reading from pocketbooks (one found near my foxhole), writing a few letters describing my experiences and commenting on the war situation and the news from home, and making some diary entries about recent events.

> *(Letter)*
> *Monte della Spe*
> *March 26, 1945*
>
> I'm enclosing a picture I had taken while in Rome. It portrays, perhaps not to its best advantage, but at least portrays anyway, the latest addition to my upper lip. If only I could have shown you the full red beard I had two weeks ago. That really would have frightened the daguerreotype. However, it frightened the Colonel too, and he asked me to part with it during my Army career.
>
> The news this morning about our crossing the Rhine is certainly great. The papers are so optimistic that I'm beginning to feel that this may well be the end. I just hope that we don't launch some bloody useless drive down here.
>
> *Time* magazine, I notice, dated March 19th, finally gave us a write-up. The papers here claim it was the greatest thing since Wolfe took Quebec and *Time*, I see, parallels them also. As far as I could see it just took a lot of guts, which my buddies certainly have, and other outfits here seem to lack.
>
> Give everyone my love. How's Ed's draft status coming along? There is a small chance that I may be discharged come the end of the European war. I've had 2½ years' service almost, from the time of my enlistment December 12th, and by the end of hostilities here I'll have had about six months overseas.

Time magazine reported: "Using tactics old when General James Wolfe scaled Quebec's heights in 1759, Major General George P. Hayes's [*sic*] 10th Mountain Division was jolting the German [Field Marshal Kesselring] loose from the Apennine positions upon which he had based the center of his line.

South of Bologna, expert climbers set ropes on sheer cliff faces. Up those ropes swarmed the troops to catch the Nazis by surprise, smash them back five miles through jagged country."[31]

In a letter apparently sent to Paul about the same time, the first part of which is missing, I wrote about some of the macabre humor we experienced and the mixed feelings that stemmed from contemplating the possibility of being wounded.

(Letter)
Monte della Spe

If I'm hit, so what. But your body and will to live put up a terrific struggle with your conscience and knowledge of what you know you must do.

There is still humor though, and it furnishes the only relief. It so happens the first person I fired at in this war was an old woman carrying a large sack of something in the middle of an '88 bombardment.... [On another occasion] while attacking I walked by a group of houses on the side of a hill and an Italian family stood there and watched me and my squad go by. They seemed very pleased and said "*buon giorno*" very pleasantly, thinking the war was finally over for them. About 10 minutes later, as we climbed higher up the hill, a shell came whistling over our heads and landed kerplunk in the middle of these houses we'd passed. I could see them scampering in all directions. Funny huh? Laugh fool.

I asked an Italian partisan soldier what he thought the best thing was to do when I met the Heines. Laughing like mad, he said, "Put your head under ground." Not bad advice as a matter of fact.

Hope it won't be long before we can gag it up together.

P.S. The picture was taken at the Catacombs while I was in Rome on a seven-day rest leave. Can you find me? Too bad you can't see my Gable moustache from there.

(Letter)
Monte della Spe
April 2, 1945   V-Mail

I'm sorry to hear that Edwin has to join up. That will be a big hardship for you all, and Army life is something I wouldn't wish on my worst enemy. Let's hope the war won't take too long now.

By the way, you're spelling "sergeant" wrong. And to think you taught me spelling at one time.

When I wrote you that I had been in Rome, I was actually still there but couldn't say so because of censorship regulations. I really had a wonderful time there. We were treated like kings and had a good rest. I tried to get in touch with McSweeney but the Red Cross couldn't find him and his name wasn't listed in the directory....

I'm back on the line in a foxhole at present. The war news is certainly terrific. I expect we'll drive soon, but these mountains are awful tough going.

Early in 1945 my brother Edwin received a notice from his draft board in California, where he had been located before being hired by the Western Reserve Academy, to come there for a physical exam. He managed to get the location of the physical changed to Cleveland which, happily, caused some additional delay. Finally, however, he could no longer escape the exam. As it developed, the fears he had experienced for years about having to leave his wife and two young children for military service turned out to be unwarranted. I learned later that the examining physician, after viewing the unusually dry skin on Edwin's legs, declared that he was too susceptible to the skin diseases prevalent in the tropical combat areas of the Pacific and classified him 4-F (physically unqualified for military service).

(Letter)
Monte della Spe
April 7th, 1945   V-Mail
 I happened to find a book lying on the ground near my foxhole. It's *The Crock of Gold*, by James Stephens, and amazingly enough turned out to be the most philosophically thought-provoking book I've ever read. I wish you'd send for it and add it to my library. I surely hope you are collecting these books that I write you about from time to time, and not thinking that it's an idle whim or fancy. Please do collect them—a little constructive reading now and then is about all I get out of this war, and I expect to see a choice selection of my favorite reading when I get home.
 I'm certainly glad Ed made such a fine showing with his wrestling team. He really is a fine coach in that field, I believe. Paul's church seems to be a rapidly growing institution. He's making such a success of it that I expect him to be working on 5th Avenue before long. I imagine that Mary Elizabeth plays no small role in it either.
 Haven't heard the news for four days, but I imagine big things are taking place.

(Diary)
 March 31—War news is terrific. I think a big push will start all along this line soon.

 April 1—Spent Easter in our foxholes. Very heavy artillery. Haines killed. Linscott hurt. Very sick. Threw up all night.
 W[—] and others almost courtmartialed, but went out on a raid again. No one hurt but Heines threw bazookas and much else at them.
 Kelly still sick. Ed to be inducted. Got three new replacement officers in.

 April 2—Had quite a detail. In charge of burying a Heine at 1 A.M.

 April 6—Bobo [Boyajian] returned from Rome. Umberto [Militari] got the Bronze Star. Decker knocked out by an '88. Limber [Krusell] went to the funeral of our dead. Eighth Army made an amphibious landing.* Russians heading for Trieste. Rumors circulate wildly about what we'll do next. We're still a light division and can't do much in flatland terrain.
 Prout talked to Clare Boothe.† Dotty Duft married Dana. Wonder if

---

 This was the first of two operations, preliminary to the main attack, scheduled for each of the coastal flanks, which began the night of April 1 when a flotilla of LVTs (landing vehicle, tracked) crossed the Comacchio Lagoon on the Eighth Army's Adriatic flank.
 †*Clare Booth Luce, a member of Congress from Connecticut and wife of Henry Luce, publisher of Time magazine, visited the 10th briefly as part of a so-called fact-finding tour of the battle front.*

I'll ever see altar and with whom. Reminds me of that church near Catigliano where we ate chow in the pews and Bobo put a grenade on the altar. What a war!

Some Moanin Minnies went over last nite. Kelly still at large.

Got a new platoon louie (Jinkins). Very "nervous in the service."

April 10—Nevada returned. Eighth Army jumped off. Also Nisei and 92nd Division.

Talk about the 92nd is that when ordered to attack, they "lean forward in their foxholes." High illiteracy a reason. We're getting set for a rugged attack. Tanks and planes to back us up.

Mortars almost got Wally and me today. Blew C-ration cans in our hole.

Met Decker at Battalion rest camp. He's Staff [Sergeant] now. Exchanged experiences. Division has lost 876 dead to date. We've lost 23 to rank as highest company.

Kelly wrote a letter to Don saying he'd been on Belvedere, and was wounded by a Heine concussion grenade. Makes me mad when I think of Wiksell and others who died, and he lies about it. He's no good.

April 13—Attack postponed. Signed up for the Allied Forces tennis meet. Patton crossed the Elbe, and is 60 miles from Berlin. Reminds me of *All Quiet [on the Western Front]* when the soldier reached for the butterfly on the last day of the war, and was killed by a sniper.*

Iwo Jima taken. Okinawa attack going well. Russia breaks her pact with Japan. President Roosevelt died.

My comment to Mother and Dad about hoping, given the predicament Germany was in, that we would not launch some useless attack which would waste many lives expressed a view that, in retrospect, has received some support in postwar assessments of the Italian campaign. It had long been true that the principal mission of the Allied armies in Italy had been to occupy as many of the German divisions as possible to keep them from being used on what were considered more critical fronts, namely in the east, where the Russian armies were approaching, or in France and the Low Countries against the forces under General Eisenhower. As far as Italy itself was concerned, the American view had always been to drive straight toward the Alps and thence into Germany. The British had disagreed vigorously with this strategy, Churchill in particular feeling that the peninsula should serve as a springboard for an advance into Yugoslavia and the Danube basin, to prevent the Soviets from dominating those areas in the postwar period, but they eventually yielded to the Americans.

Even after the American view prevailed, however, it could be argued that the Allied armies could have stopped at any number of places in Italy and kept as many German divisions occupied as they did in their costly, foot-slogging pace up the mountainous peninsula with much greater loss of life. Senior

*I was referring here to the 1930 movie with that title, starring Lew Ayres, and not to the novel which contains no mention of such an incident. In a very moving final scene in the movie, Ayres, playing a German soldier, extends his hand from his foxhole to a butterfly and is shot dead by a French sniper.

German generals were already negotiating with the American OSS representative, Allen Dulles, for the possible surrender of the German army in Italy. Both the Americans and Russians were nearing Berlin (the latter having also seized Vienna on April 13), and the U.S. Third Army was sweeping down the Danube to meet the Russians in Austria. Obviously, the European war was nearing an end. Once again the Allies had an opportunity, this time in the northern Apennines, to stand fast while containing large numbers of German forces with relatively few Allied divisions. There was also the risk that if we did manage to break out of the mountains and reach the Po River or the Alps, either of these natural bastions could provide the Germans with positions which they could defend with far less manpower than they were forced to expend in the Apennines and might release some of their divisions to other fronts.* In short, unless there was a real prospect that the Nazi regime intended to retreat into an Alpine redoubt where they might make a final stand of indefinite duration—a prospect which intelligence specialists never took seriously—it made little strategic sense to sacrifice thousands of lives to break this last mountain barrier.

As it happened, such reasoning—and it is questionable whether it was ever given serious consideration—failed to influence the responsible Allied commanders in Italy, and the planning continued for breaking the German defenses which prevented our advance into the Po Valley.

While awaiting the orders for this new offensive, we welcomed back some of our wounded who had been returned to the front lines to face the music again, exchanged stories and rumors, and carried out various assignments both pleasant and unpleasant. Sergeant John Nevada, one of our platoon's two machine gun squad leaders, who had been hit in the leg with a mortar fragment in the Monte Belvedere battle, returned to duty on April 10 in the midst of heightened preparations for our next attack. My foxhole companion, Krusell, was selected to attend a division memorial service held on April 6 at a U.S. military cemetery established just south of Florence. Attendance at the service included our regimental commander Colonel Barlow, an officer representing each battalion as well as one representing each company, and an enlisted man (such as Krusell) from each squad that had a member killed in action up to that date. After the service, a parade and formation were held with awards and decorations being presented to men in the division.[33] My old friend Umberto Milletari, the ASTP returnee who dropped out with me from that terrible Easter Sunday climb in a raging blizzard during the never-to-be-forgotten "D-Series" maneuvers at Camp Hale, was one of those decorated with the Bronze Star.

---

*Field Marshal Kesselring, reflecting in his Memoirs on his defense strategy of defending the whole of Italy, disputed this reasoning. To have retreated to the Alps, he said, would have given the Allies freedom of movement in the direction of France and the Balkans, sacrificed an indispensably deep battle zone, and unleashed the air war early on all of southern Germany and Austria.[32]

Perhaps the most disagreeable work assignment—or "detail" as they were called in the army—I was ever given while subject to military orders occurred during this period when we were saddled with the task of trying to hang on to our newly won positions on Monte della Spe. One night about 2 A.M. I was awoken by my lieutenant coming to my foxhole and telling me to go see the company commander, Captain King. This I did and was informed that somewhere nearby was a corpse of a German soldier whose odor was no longer tolerable and that I was to take some men, find the body, and bury it.

As sergeant in command, I went back to our trenches, picked three or four of our new replacements, and gathered some entrenching tools and other implements to help us dig a grave. Then we set off to try and locate the body. It was almost pitch dark, and we had considerable difficulty locating the corpse, despite that sickeningly sweet odor typically thrown off by human remains which have lain too long in the open. When we finally located the body, we discovered, as expected, that it had swollen in death to a great size, and we now faced the risk of it exploding if it were accidentally struck by a careless shovel, or clod of dirt, in the dark.

I ordered the men to dig a trench right next to the body to minimize the distance it would have to be moved. Standing as far off as possible, I had them set about the task. Unfortunately, the ground—as so often in the Apennines—was almost solid rock or shale. On and on the men struggled with their inadequate tools in the black of night, trying to carve at least some semblance of a cavity into which the body could be nudged. Finally I became convinced that it was impossible to break through the rock and hardpan further. To bring the smell and the rest of the nasty business to an end as quickly as possible, we dragged the body with great care, and without accident, into the limited depression they had managed to make in the ground. I then had them heap the dirt they had managed to excavate over the remains to at least give the illusion of a burial and to mask the odor sufficiently that we would escape criticism. What we left was more of a burial mound than a grave, but since I heard no complaint, I can only assume the company commander either was satisfied or had other concerns of higher priority.

On or about April 10, we received word for the first time from Jack Kelly, who had left us in the grips of dysentery on February 15, a few days before our attack on Monte Belvedere. Much to our astonishment, Kelly had written one of our friends in another company, as my diary entry noted, that he had actually participated in the Belvedere battle, but had been evacuated after being knocked unconscious by a German concussion grenade. There was also a story circulating that he had gone AWOL and been arrested.

Why Jack assumed anyone would believe his tale of having been in combat, since it could easily be proved false by checking with persons in the unit in which he supposedly served, none of us could fathom. And to say that its impact on his many friends and acquaintances was profound would be understating the case. Naturally, I took it particularly hard.

If combat does nothing else, it draws all its participants together in a bond of intimacy unlike that realized in any other shared experience, and it results in a fraternity to which no outsider can gain entry. While few of us begrudged Jack's successful escape from the horrors of battle—an objective virtually all sought mightily to achieve—to claim he had shared in that awful experience where so many of his and our closest friends had died was inexcusable. Was he aware of how badly our squad and company had been battered, we wondered? Did he know his own squad leader and many others were lost? As might be expected, overnight his popularity as a great actor and comedian and his talent for demonstrating how to escape many of the unpleasantries of military service by fooling the Army brass were forgotten. He became a pariah, and one story we heard that he had landed a job as a jeep driver for some rear-echelon general only magnified the feelings of resentment. Henceforth his name was rarely mentioned, and he was an outcast as far as the company was concerned.

The disillusionment stemming from Kelly's action, the death of President Roosevelt (who had been our commander in chief as long as most of us could remember), and the obvious signs that we were about to launch another attack with likely bloody consequences, all combined to lower morale to a level not previously experienced. In a last letter before we launched our assault on the German lines the following morning, I made an effort to see some good in the future but could not refrain from expressing bitterness about the Kelly episode.

(Letter)
Monte della Spe
April 13th, 1945   V-Mail
    You probably won't hear from me for a while after this letter, but try not to get too worried or wrought up. It's rather cold and damp in this fox hole at the moment. I'm afraid the rainy season is about to break on us. I'll be glad to get out of these cold mountains and get on flat land. I think these years in the Army have given me my fill of mountains. From now on I'll simply be content to ride through them very rapidly in a car.
    Jack Kelly seems to have given us all a knife in the back. It's strange how men change over here and show their true nature. They do anything to get out of being on the front line or being in an attack. Jack went AWOL and was caught by the MP's. Where he is now I don't know, but I'm sorry he let us down and has lost so many friends. It's a great temptation to try to get out of the danger, especially when your life is at stake, but someone has to do the job and the majority of infantrymen never waver.

8

Packs On

The Breakout, April 1945

When I am dead and over me bright April
Shakes out her rain-drenched hair,
Though you should lean above me broken-hearted,
I shall not care.
— Sara Teasdale, *I Shall Not Care*

The plan for the spring offensive to break through the last German defenses in the Apennines and into the Po Valley provided for the British 8th Army, in a secondary role, to begin the attack on the right flank on April 1 with an amphibious assault in an attempt to establish bridgeheads across the Santerno River. During this phase the British were to be provided all available air support, including heavy bombers. Once the Santerno was crossed, the emphasis on air support as well as the principal attention in the entire attack would shift to the American 5th Army, which would attempt to advance into the Po Valley and either capture or isolate the heavily defended city of Bologna, with its main objective being to encircle major elements of the German armies south of the Po.

To help draw some of the enemy strength from the central part of the front where the Allied offensive by the 5th Army would be concentrated, General Truscott had the 92d Division, made up entirely of black enlisted men, with white and black officers, and the Japanese-American 442d Regimental Combat Team, begin the 5th Army's attack on the extreme west flank on April 5.

The 92d Division had been activated at Fort McClellan, Alabama, in October 1942 from a cadre of officers and men drawn from the 93d Infantry Division, the first black combat division to be organized in World War II. The 92d had an unusually high percentage of poorly educated men. An investigation by Truman Gibson, a black civilian aide to Secretary of War Stimson, revealed that 17 percent were illiterate and 75 percent semiliterate, while among army white soldiers, 4 percent were illiterate and 16 percent semiliterate.

Since the 92d's ill-starred offensive effort in early February 1945, it had been reorganized with the best men of the three original regiments gathered together into the 370th Infantry Regiment. Demonstrating not even a minimal understanding of human psychology, a failing characteristic of many military decisions during World War II, the army made the problem even worse by replacing all black company commanders in the 370th with white officers in a misdirected effort to improve its fighting spirit. Instead, this almost insured poor performance, because it suggested a total lack of confidence in black leadership and willingness to fight.[1] As the Republican presidential candidate, Wendell Willkie, said, "From the battlefields of Italy to the gold-star homes here in America, [Negroes] have learned that there is nothing more democratic than a bullet or a splinter of steel."[2]

Because the 92d had not done well in previous offensive actions, encouraging racist jokes such as the one I quoted in my April 10 diary entry, the 442d had been attached to it to help strengthen it in the attack. Their offensive on the extreme left flank of the Gothic Line, as well as that of the British on the extreme right, was soon stopped by the Germans. But the deceptions accomplished their purpose by drawing off half of the German reserve forces to reinforce their defenses against the British and the other half to shore up their positions on the west coast against the Americans.

In an attempt to confuse the enemy further, this time as to when the main attack would commence, General Truscott ordered that instead of a heavy artillery bombardment immediately preceding the offensive, there would be "a 20-day program of gradually increasing intensity, building to a crescendo during the final week preceding D-day."[3] D-day itself was scheduled for April 12, the day Roosevelt died, but fog forced cancellation of all air activity for two days, so the attack actually began April 14.

Truscott, in a final message to all of us in the 5th Army before we did battle, told us, "Today we are on the eve of our last great battle." By destroying "this last great enemy force in Italy," he explained, "we shall ... prevent withdrawal to oppose our forces on other fronts ... and prevent further ruin and destruction in this unhappy country." Whatever our feelings were about getting killed this close to the war's end, it did not affect his message, which he closed with the injunction: "Be aggressive... aim to kill and destroy, and to take your objective at all costs."[4]

As it happened, we did in fact accomplish the objective, but only at great cost, for the attack turned out to be the deadliest combat experience of the war for the 85th Regiment. It began at 8:30 A.M. with wave after wave of bombing runs, as well as sorties by tactical aircraft, and then a 35-minute artillery, mortar, and machine gun barrage directed at the enemy positions. The machine guns were the heavy 50-caliber variety and only a short distance apart, all of which added to the din being created by the more than 2,000 pieces of artillery, ranging from our division's 75mm pack howitzers to the 5th Army's 8-inch guns, firing over our heads.[5] We had never witnessed a bombardment to compare with it.

The night preceding the attack, I and other noncoms and officers had attended a company briefing at which we were told the attack plan. I took notes on the briefing and made a rough sketch of the plan, entering both in my pocket diary:

(Diary)
April 13—Artillery terrifically close and heavy. Grid 61-63 (2,000). 3rd Battalion on left. 86th and 87th [Regiments] on right. 1st Battalion in reserve.

Probably not committed before Monte Teroni (63-30), about 2,000 yds. from objective. From Mt. della Spe to objective is 5,000 yds.

Seem to be few mine fields.... L.D. is road to our front. Main mission to move generally along line of road, cleaning out pockets and houses of resistance. Plenty of fire thrown immediately on targets of opportunity. One tank out there—61.5—22.8.

Wear mountain jacket. 2 pair socks. Check on wound tablets. Flank security if alone as a platoon. Keep lieutenant informed all the time.

Check for rain coat. Get pistol, machete, pack boards, extra gun barrel, mountain jacket.

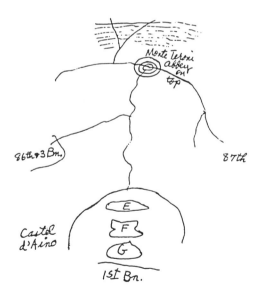

April 14—In a few minutes we will attack. It is now 7 A.M. Dawn is breaking and the men are nervous, wondering what lies ahead and who won't come back. Hope my luck stays with me. We're splitting the section again. Here goes.

The 10th Mountain Division attack plan called for the 85th Regiment on the left and 87th on the right to attack abreast, with the 86th following to mop up the area between the 87th and the 1st Armored Division to the east. At 9:45 A.M., when the aerial and artillery bombardments lifted, we climbed out of our foxholes in response to the familiar order "Packs on" and began our advance down the forward slopes of Monte della Spe with two battalions of the 85th abreast, my 2d Battalion on the right and the 3d Battalion on the left. Despite the heavy fire we had inflicted on the Germans in advance of our attack, their construction of an intricate system of bunkers and covered gun emplacements had enabled them to withstand all but direct hits by heavy artillery and bombs and to inflict many casualties on us from machine guns and mortars as we walked toward them.[6] Before we even reached the road that technically constituted the LD for our attack, one of our company officers, Lieutenant William Callahan, was killed by a mortar round only a short distance to my rear.[7]

Our route took us down into the Pra del Bianco basin, a small bowl-shaped valley just northeast of Castel d'Aiano. As the dust and smoke cleared from the preliminary bombardment, we were subjected to increasing enemy fire and then ran into extensive mine fields and booby traps which were planted in virtually all areas through which we had to pass in order to reach the various hilltops we were ordered to capture.[8] The briefing we had been given that there were few mine fields was completely wrong—not only did the extensive mine fields enable the Germans to gain time to man their weapons within the main line of resistance, they prevented our tank battalions from accompanying us in the advance and bringing their fire to bear on strong points. As a result, our advance was checked temporarily just short of the crest of hills overlooking the basin.[9]

By 12:30 P.M., Company I, of our 3d Battalion, which had advanced to within 200 yards of its first objective, Hill 883, had suffered so many casualties that the battalion commander ordered Company K to pass through it and attack the hill from the southwest.[10] Company I was Lieutenant Robert Dole's company, and he was experiencing his first hours of an advance by infantry into battle. Richard Cramer, who described the run Dole and others made for the presidency in 1988, states in his book, *What It Takes: The Way to the White House*, that Dole was leading a squad in his rifle platoon in an attack on a machine gun nest when enemy troops spotted them. The Germans opened fire, wounding some of Dole's men. Dole dragged his wounded runner into a shell hole, but then, while on all fours, scrambling from the hole, he was hit in the back behind the right shoulder. "Whatever hit him exploded inside, broke his collarbone and the shoulder behind it, not to mention his arm. Worst thing was, it smashed into his vertebrae, crushed a piece of his spine, it was broken, the spinal cord was knocked out. He couldn't move. He couldn't feel anything below his neck."[11]

When Dole finally reached a field hospital, the surgeon did not believe he would make it, but he managed to survive and subsequently underwent many operations (including the removal of one kidney) and experienced much suffering. He was a tall man, standing six feet, two inches, and he weighed 194 pounds before being injured, but his weight during his convalescence was reduced at one point to 122 pounds.[12] In the end he recovered some of his physical abilities, but his right shoulder and arm remain essentially useless.

Regrettably, some of Dole's fellow officers were even less fortunate. Lieutenant Kvan, Company I's weapons platoon leader, was killed instantly by a mine or booby trap when he bumped its release string, and Lieutenant Mitchell, a rifle platoon leader, was killed by a sniper's bullet. Thus three of the company's four platoon lieutenants had either been killed or wounded in that Saturday action.[13] As for the 3d Battalion as a whole, some indication of the cost being paid for the ground gained on that one day is reflected in its figures for officer casualties: of the 28 company officers in the battalion, 12 were lost, 5 of them killed, including the captain commanding one of their four companies.[14]

My battalion, the 2d, which was advancing slightly to the east, was not finding the going much better. My Company F had hardly left Monte della Spe before the leader of our 3d platoon, Lieutenant Pierce, was wounded by mortar fire. Fortunately, however, we began the advance as the battalion reserve, with our fellow companies, E and G, leading the way through what turned out to be deadly mine fields. E Company went through the first one with heavy casualties but reached the summit of its objective, Hill 860, by 11:30 A.M. By the end of the day, their casualties totaled 34 wounded and 7 killed. In addition, 3 of their men were captured by the Germans. I learned later that among those E Company men who died was Bill Luth, my old friend from Camp Hale days, when he and I were initially attached to Company M of the 86th Regiment.[15] Luth, who had been attending Ripon College in Wisconsin before the war, had shared Mother's birthday cake on my 19th birthday (his 19th was only two days later) with John Horrall and me and had been one of my companions on what few weekend passes we managed to get to Colorado Springs and Denver.

Company G was commanded by Captain Otis Halverson, who had been a lieutenant commanding that same Company M of the 86th back in July 1943. Their initial objective was Hill 909, and by noon they had managed to advance halfway up the hill but they were then pinned down by sniper and machine gun fire. Captain Halverson, after refusing evacuation despite being wounded by a mortar shell, subsequently lost his life when he was hit by a sniper's bullet while checking out a safer approach route. Of the remaining five officers in his company, only two escaped being wounded during this attempt to capture Hill 909. In this same action, a Company G enlisted man, Private First Class John Magrath, who enlisted from East Norwalk, Connecticut, performed some extraordinary deeds which earned him the Congressional Medal of Honor. He was the only 10th Mountain Division soldier to be so honored.

Magrath, volunteering as a scout, accompanied a lieutenant who had replaced Captain Halverson on a reconnaissance mission. When the party was stopped by heavy artillery, mortar, and small-arms fire, Magrath, instead of taking cover, leaped up and attacked a machine gun nest armed only with his rifle, killing two men and wounding three. He then took the enemy gun across an open field through heavy fire and used it to knock out two more machine gun positions. Circling behind four other Germans, he killed them with a burst as they were firing on his company. Spotting another enemy position to his right, he kneeled with the machine gun in his arms and exchanged fire with the Germans until he had killed two and wounded three. Later in the day he volunteered to collect data on casualties, but while carrying out this task, he was killed by mortar shells landing at his feet.[16]

Some of F Company's effort on the first day of the attack to capture its assigned objectives, and my involvement therein, was described in the opening of this memoir. The experience of that day and the one which followed was also summarized in the following diary entry prepared after the action.

(Diary)
April 16—We attacked and before we reached the L.D. one lieutenant was killed 50 yards behind me. Dug in in a draw. Shells very close. Crossed the road and dug in again. Orwig, Eyer, [Olsen] (shell-shocked), Oldham hit. G Company taking a terrific beating. Dead GI's all around.

Held down by MG fire. Dug in on reverse slope just around corner from Burp fire. [Paulsen] shot himself. I walked over thinking a hidden Heine had shot him and found one in a dugout. As he turned toward me I shot him with my .45 through the head.

This morning Capt. King got MG slugs thru his stomach about two feet from my foxhole. Under cover of four 30's [30 calibre machine guns] we assaulted the next hill and took 60 prisoners. Dug in quickly on reverse slope. Lost contact with the company. Wondering what to do. Found out where the company was and rejoined them in a very dangerous position. Many dead—Taylor, Moses, Koski and others. Our casualties so heavy we were relieved and went to a rearward assembly area.

Luth, one of my oldest friends, and Goodal killed. 74 men left.

Shortly after my run-in with the supposed sniper in the bunker, our regimental commander, Colonel Barlow, ordered Lieutenant Colonel Roche to push our 2d Battalion's attack until 7 P.M. and then "button up for the night." Accordingly, as I later wrote my brother Edwin, "We started advancing again, and occupied some positions that were under direct fire from some German machine guns and artillery. I set up my machine gun in what turned out to be a very unhealthy spot. The situation looked something like this:

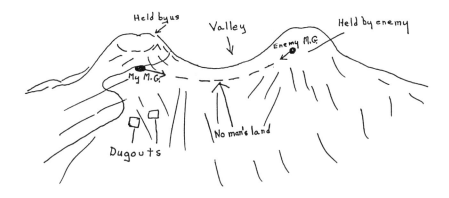

From where my gun was located I could see very clearly the enemy positions by use of field glasses. However the Heine MGs fired directly on my position intermittently."

And so ended the first day of the offensive. Continued resistance and the coming of darkness prevented further advance. Those of us in the 85th Regiment at least were quite discouraged because of the slight amount of ground gained and our heavy losses. The cost to the 10th as a whole had been 553 mountain infantrymen killed, wounded, or missing. Unknown to us, however, the division had opened a serious breach between the 334th and 94th Divisions of the German army.[17] My regiment alone had taken a total of 114 prisoners by midnight. Ironically, none had been informed of the transfer of their beloved general, Field Marshal Kesselring, to command the western front, where the Ardennes counteroffensive had failed and the Allied armies under Eisenhower were forcing the Germans back into the Reich itself. But they had been told immediately of Roosevelt's death.[18]

When morning came, I was able to get a better view of our situation. As the drawing I made for Edwin shows, my squad's position was below the crest of Hill 909 in a highly exposed situation from which we could easily see what turned out to be our next objective, Hill 915, on our right flank and the saddle we would have to cross to attack it. My foxhole, in particular, had an excellent view of where the enemy was located. The only problem was that they could see my position equally well, and as I wrote to Edwin, "It was disconcerting to have the dirt knocked off the rim of your hole by MG bullets." For this reason, I did not poke my head up except when necessary.

Because I occupied such an excellent observation post, and in the absence (because of wounds) of any forward artillery observer with our unit, I was asked to perform the usual function of such observers: locating where our mortar and artillery rounds were landing and passing the word to someone with a radio so the fire could be redirected as required. Artillery units are usually located a few miles back of the front-line infantry. In Italy at least, because of the hilly country, in about 99 percent of the cases they never saw, or even knew, what they were firing at. Artillery observers up on the front lines with the infantry or in spotter aircraft gave firing orders which were sent back by radio and telephone through division and regimental command posts to the artillery battery's executive post. Those orders simply consisted of a set of figures, which the chief of each gun crew in a pit received through his headphone.

This was the task I tried to carry out, as best I could, starting as soon as daylight illuminated the scene. Sometime around 8 A.M., after the entire battalion had been ordered to renew the attack, my company commander, Captain King, walked up to a spot next to my foxhole. He stood there for a moment to get a better view of Hill 915 and to point out the location of an enemy machine gun position to Lieutenant Balch, a machine gun platoon leader in Company H, our battalion's heavy weapons company.[19] Captain King had been there only a few minutes before one of the German machine guns that had been raking the area periodically fired a burst which hit him in the abdomen. Seriously wounded, he was taken to the rear, and Lieutenant Wayne Mackin, the Company F executive officer, then took command of our company.

We now faced the heart-stopping task of getting out of our protective foxholes in the face of machine gun fire and bursting artillery shells and advancing across the saddle and up the slopes of Hill 915 which lay before us. The best solution was to advance as fast as possible to minimize the time we would be exposed to the incoming fire, and we knew that it was solely a matter of chance whether we'd be hit. Combat experience, or what the press liked to call "battle-seasoning," offered no advantage in an action of this kind. It was luck, pure and simple, which would determine our fate.

As we awaited the order to attack, I wondered again, as I had before under similar circumstances, why the army never encouraged a spirit of excitement and group identity in an action of this kind to help lessen the stress. The reality of battle, as General S. L. A. Marshall noted, is that the other combatants are not often seen, and one misses the presence and warmth of human companionship. Elementary psychology seemed to suggest that some feeling of spiritual unity—similar to that derived from mob action—was needed if the courage of the soldiers making up the unit was to be contagious and they were to do an effective job of moving and fighting.

Whatever happened, I asked myself, to the rebel yells of the Civil War, the bugle call and drum roll, and the flag bearer leading the assault? If we had to cross this ground of great danger and there was no way to use one's battle experience, brainpower, physical ability, or other talents to lessen the risk, why not do it with dash and vigor, shouting a battle cry or other yell which would at least stir the blood? To be sure, many would be cut down, but would we lose any more than would be slaughtered in an otherwise silent and lonely march forward? Surely there were times, and this seemed to be one of them, when the job could be done best, not by the "thinking soldier," but by angry and excited mass action.

Unfortunately, this was not the army's way, at least in our experience, and

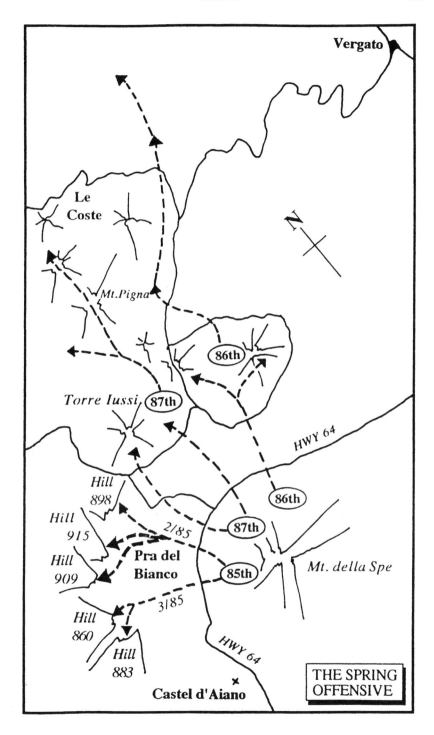

Vergato

Le Coste

N

Mt.Pigna

86th

Torre Iussi 87th

HWY 64

Hill 898

86th

Hill 915

2/85

Hill 909

Pra del Bianco

87th

Hill 860

3/85

85th

Mt. della Spe

Hill 883

Castel d'Aiano

HWY 64

THE SPRING OFFENSIVE

we marched forth to destiny. The 85th Regimental history describes the assault—one which took Hill 915—as consisting of the 2d platoon of Company F, supported by fire from the rest of Company F and Company E, and machine guns of Company H. My machine gun squad was attached to this rifle platoon, and we managed to reach the side of Hill 915 without any casualties. There we were met by a group of German soldiers shouting *"Kamerad"* with their hands raised wanting to surrender. A few members of our company were assigned the task of escorting the prisoners to the rear, and they had no sooner left than the German artillery stepped up its firing, this time on our new positions from which they had just retreated.

Then followed one or more of my less heroic hours in combat. Having no time to dig any foxholes as the shells began falling, I and other members of my squad dove into some large bomb craters apparently caused by our aircraft in their softening-up exercise preceding our attack from Monte della Spe. (I was sharing my crater with one other man.) The craters were fairly shallow, so we hugged the ground face down as best we could, fearing dismemberment at any moment. The noise was deafening from the explosions all around and much dust and debris were being flung about. Suddenly I felt a hard blow in my lower back and concluded the end was near, but glancing up saw a terribly frightened rabbit that had leapt off my body and was dashing across the slope in search of some safer hiding place. This was the only time I observed wildlife, other than occasional birds, on the battlefield.

Much relieved, we remained below ground a little longer and then set off to find out where the others were located. They were in positions up the hill a ways, and we learned that the shelling had killed and wounded many of the riflemen. Among the dead were an unusually high percentage of noncoms, including one of our longtime platoon sergeants, Technical Sergeant Arthur Taylor, and a section sergeant who was a particular friend of mine, Staff Sergeant Lawrence Moses. Two other staff sergeants and three "buck" sergeants were wounded, all casualties in this one day of action. I was criticized by a lieutenant for not having kept my squad in closer proximity to his riflemen, but my own weapons platoon commander, Lieutenant Jinkins, took a different stance, complimenting me on my actions during the past two days. Jinkins praised my aggressiveness in seeking out and killing what he believed to be a sniper and my serving as an artillery observer for the company and said he was recommending me for the Bronze Star. While I felt there was some justification for his fellow platoon leader's criticism and didn't think I had done anything remarkable enough to justify a medal, I wasn't about to argue the matter since such decorations for valor increased the number of points needed for discharge from our beloved Army of the United States.

F Company then pushed on and captured another enemy strong point, Hill 898, wiping out a full company of Germans. This was followed by a strong enemy counterattack being launched against us which we managed to repulse, but with additional heavy casualties to our company.

Early in the afternoon of April 15, our 2d Battalion commander, Lieutenant Colonel Roche, who had apparently been viewed with some disfavor by General Hays since the first days of our assault on Monte Belvedere, was relieved and replaced by Lieutenant Colonel Seiss Wagner, who had been our regimental commander's executive officer. Since the battalion had suffered extremely heavy losses, one rumor we heard later was that Roche had been relieved because he had lost too many men in hopeless assaults, but this seemed unlikely. Our commanders never appeared that disturbed by high casualty figures. Rather, the historical record suggests that it was general incompetence, as perceived by his superiors, that was his undoing.*

In any event, Colonel Wagner was determined to push the battalion further to bring it abreast of the 3d Battalion on the left and the 87th Mountain Infantry on the right. He ordered all three companies to advance, and this led Lieutenant Beck, who had taken over command of Company G since the death of Captain Halverson the day before, to a heroic exploit. With his company strength now down to only 58 men, he led them in a rush through point-blank fire down the slopes of Hill 909 in a desperate effort to close the gap between the 2d and 3d Battalions. Beck and others were hit during this charge, but the remainder reached the foot of their objective, Hill 762. There the few who had survived managed to hold their ground until dark.[20] Meanwhile, Company E had taken Hill 801, and my Company F had taken Hill 810.

At 7 P.M. word was received that changed the regimental mission. Both the 86th and 87th Regiments appeared to have broken through the principal enemy defenses in their sectors, while the high cost in casualties in the 85th's salient had convinced the IV Corps that further effort on the 85th's part to move directly north would incur too many casualties to be justifiable. Accordingly, units of the 85th were ordered initially to remain in their relative positions and then to begin a side-slipping maneuver which consisted of moving to the northeast, relieving elements of the 87th as they did so, and then helping to exploit the breakthrough.

The first movement began on April 16 while the main body of the 85th Regiment was resting and reorganizing. During this time my Company F was occupied, among other things, in absorbing replacements for our losses, receiving 25 new men around April 16 and then 21 additional from the 8th Replacement Depot a few days later.[21] These made up for most of our losses, which had been high. During the two-day attack on April 14–15, the 85th Mountain Infantry had sustained a total of 462 casualties, 98 of them killed. Of these my battalion suffered 42 killed and 169 wounded.

The 2d Battalion was now ordered to move to an assembly area from which we would be transported to a new location to help the 87th Regiment

---

*One member of G Company, Thomas Brooks, believes that Roche was relieved because he would not renew the attack of Brooks' company which Roche visited on the first day of the attack and which, Brooks says, had only 3 officers and 64 other men left.[22]

continue its drive towards the Po Valley. The Brazilian Expeditionary Force (BEF) took over the positions we had captured, and we began a long march toward the place we were to assemble. Once there I made another entry in my diary.

(Diary)
April 18—Heard that the Ninth Army is in Berlin. This whole front is blazing. The 87th and 86th seem to have broken through and are going like mad. Lt. Jinkins recommended me for the Bronze Star. What a laugh.

We're moving to the 87th area on trucks. 1st Armored Div. is massed around here. Am sitting on a beautiful sunny slope at the moment hoping for my first hot chow in six weeks but don't think I'll get it.

Kelly was reclassified Class 2B to a rear echelon job. Don't know why.

At 2:15 A.M. we departed by trucks for another assembly location near the 87th Mountain Infantry on our right. We arrived at 9:30 A.M. and then left that location at 4:50 P.M., arriving at our final stop in the evening at 7:15 P.M.[23] It took a great deal of time to make the trip because the roads were filled with mules, marching men, and every kind of vehicle, including tanks, half-tracks, and self-propelled artillery. German prisoners, who by this time totaled almost 3,000 captured by the division,[24] were streaming back to the division's rear, and troops and supplies were being rushed forward. With the rapid movement of our division's 86th and 87th Regiments, the BEF on our left and the 1st Armored Division on our right were being hard pressed to come abreast.[25]

The 5th Army battle plan now called for enveloping the city of Bologna from the southwest, instead of assaulting the defenses frontally where the Germans had concentrated their strongest positions. While I had assumed that once we broke into the Po Valley, we would let the 1st Armored and other divisions, who had plenty of tanks and other motorized vehicles, lead the attack, General Hays, who was the first division commander to break the German mountain defenses and was on the verge of being the first to enter the Po Valley, had other ideas. "The breakthrough has been accomplished," he told Colonel Fowler, commander of the 87th. "All regiments must keep pushing and exploit it."[26]

With our arrival on April 19 at our assigned assembly area, the 85th was now ordered to push through the leading units of the 86th and 87th and continue the attack through the last ridges remaining before the Po Valley. To carry out this command, we began a succession of round-the-clock marches with no chance to rest and the least sleep I have ever experienced.

(Diary)
March 19—Moved out. No sleep. Took one ridge, just got lying down and had to move out again. Took the last ridge in front of the Po Valley and 14 prisoners. Tried to sleep but sun too hot. One man hurt by a Heine MG. It is our first view of the flat stretches of the Po and Bologna to the

Mountain troopers on the offensive passing by dead Germans, March 1945 (courtesy National Archives).

> northeast. Saw a plane shot down but pilot bailed out. Absolutely exhausted. No sleep for 40 hours and now we're marching to Bologna.

Our final day and a half in the foothills of the Apennines was characterized with a few exchanges of gunfire with the rapidly retreating enemy and almost continuous movement. By noon on the nineteenth, when our front-running 85th Regiment had taken Monte San Michele, "a dominating height [which was the] ... key to a position the Germans had hoped to hold at length—the *Michelstellung**—the German defense collapsed."[27] At midnight on April 19, our battalion began marching in a column of companies to Ost, which we reached at about 1 A.M. Shortly thereafter, the battalion fanned out to secure by daylight a 3,000-yard frontage of ridges to be used by the 86th Regiment as their follow-up line of departure. My Company F took M. Avesiano after one serious firefight, and the other companies secured their objectives without suffering any significant casualties.[28]

When morning came, I was near the point of collapse from lack of sleep and physical effort, but the foxhole I occupied on the ridge, where for the first

---

*This was the last of the German army's prepared positions in the hills south of the Po Valley and was less a continuous line than a series of lightly held strongpoints.[29]

time I could see the valley spread out before us, was in the midst of some baked earth, and the threat of fire from the enemy rear guard and the heat from the blazing sun prevented me from getting any sleep. Five days of attack had cost the 10th Mountain Division 1,283 in killed or wounded, and we survivors were close to exhaustion, but the enemy withdrawal had become a rout. As described in *Salerno to the Alps*, a condensation of the nine-volume *Fifth Army History* prepared by the army's Historical Section, "In seven days the 10th Mountain Division had broken through the main enemy defense line in the Apennines and had advanced 16 miles from Castel d'Aiano to Highway 9. In the lead all the way, the mountain troops were still ahead of the armor on their left and the 85th Division on their right."[30]

The regiment was now under orders from General Hays to have one company seize a crossroads immediately to our front in the Po Valley. According to various sources, it was Company A of our 1st Battalion that was the first to leave the last of the Apennine ridges at 6 A.M. on April 20 to enter the Lombardy plain where the Po River was located and make history. By 6 A.M. they had taken the road junction, and the months of seemingly endless and costly warfare up and down the mountainous spine of Italy were at an end.[31]

9

I've Never Seen
Such a Madhouse

The Race to the Alps, April–May 1945

I am tired and sick of war. Its glory is all moonshine. It is
only those who have neither fired a shot nor heard the shrieks
and groans of the wounded who cry aloud for blood, more
vengeance, more desolation. War is hell.
—General William Tecumseh Sherman

To begin the next phase of the operation, other divisions were shifted
around on the battle front. The 1st Armored Division, which had taken the
key enemy strong point of Vergato commanding a network of roads and valleys leading north, was shifted ten miles to the west, where the terrain was more
favorable for armored operations and where it could cover the extended left
flank of the 10th Mountain Division. The 85th Infantry ("Custer") Division
moved up in place of the 1st Armored to the right of the 10th Mountain,
which was to become the spearhead of the 5th Army's offensive.[1]

April 20 turned out to be "the turning point in the Allied spring offensive
across the entire front."[2] As the army magazine, *Yank*, put it: "Before the fifth
day of the offensive was over the 10th Mountain Division—a newcomer to Italy
but a division rated as 'amazing' and the 'cat's whiskers' by the highest ranking generals in the theater—jumped off southwest of Bologna to start the main
drive."[3] The tiresome struggle up and down rock-strewn hillsides to dig out a
determined enemy turned into a pursuit of a disorganized army. Tanks could
now be used as tanks and not simply as artillery pieces. The object would be
to trap sizable elements of the German forces, as well as their heavy equipment, artillery, and transport, south of the Po River, and then to get across the
river and race to the Alps before that seemingly impenetrable barrier of mountains could be made into a lasting redoubt.

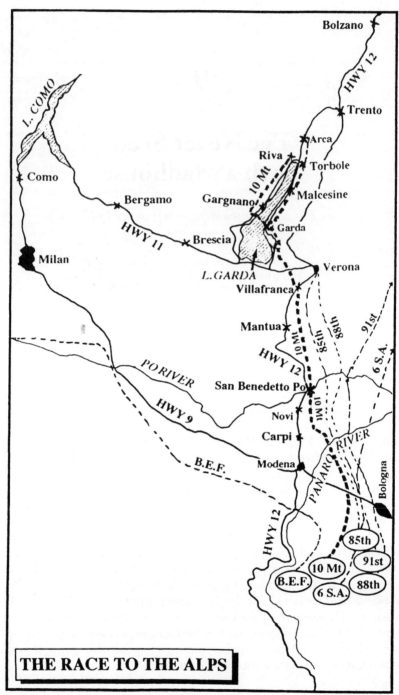

THE RACE TO THE ALPS

Map drawn by Myrna J. Mishmash and Christopher J. Mathieu.

General Clark had told General Hays that our division had performed heroically in breaking the German mountain defenses and that now it was appropriate that others lead the attack. General Hays, however, had no intention of having his troops bring up the rear. Instead he organized a fast-moving combat unit composed of a battalion of infantry from the 86th Regiment, a company of light tanks, a platoon of tank destroyers, a company from the division's 126th Mountain Engineer Battalion, and motorized reconnaissance troops to serve as the advance element of the division.[4]

Since as a "light division," we lacked much in the way of motor transport, General Hays gave the unit—which was named *Task Force Duff* for General Duff, the assistant division commander he named to head it—trucks which he had commandeered from the division's artillery to facilitate the rapid movement of its infantry forward. The mission he gave the task force was to try and reach the Po River before its bridges could be destroyed. The rest of the division was to follow, corralling prisoners and mopping up strong points which the task force had bypassed in its haste to reach the Po.

What followed was a wild and exhausting march through the countryside on dusty roads and through vineyards and farmers' fields, occasionally interrupted by brief skirmishes. It was an exhilarating experience to be moving fast without continually being subjected to artillery and mortar fire. During the advance, we had our first opportunities for occasional rides on tanks, since an armored platoon had been attached to our 2d Battalion to help protect our forward drive. I was much impressed by their power, particularly after observing one back into a high wall while trying to turn around in a narrow village street. It gave the wall what seemed only a slight nudge, but the entire wall collapsed.

Aiming at a spot some miles to the west of Bologna, the first objective of the 10th and its Task Force Duff was to save a bridge over the Panaro River at the town of Bomporto. This was over 25 miles away, so our work was cut out for us as we began our forced march at about 6:30 A.M. on March 21. We were already terribly worn from fighting since leaving our defensive positions on Monte della Spe seven days earlier, and we had traveled many sleepless miles afoot in the mountains. But there was no time for rest because we were now being asked to pursue the retreating Germans without respite.

In addition to my pack and other gear, I was carrying in each hand a box of belted machine gun ammunition which I gripped by folding steel handles. This additional burden amounted to a total dead weight of some 30 pounds which, as the hours passed, became ever more oppressive. On the rare occasions when we halted for a moment, I had difficulty uncurling my fingers, and before long I feared they would be permanently misshapen.

Italian peasants and other local residents, jubilant over our long-awaited arrival and their delivery from the Germans, assembled along the paths we were taking through their grape arbors and other fields and inundated us with flowers, wine, food, water, and kisses of gratitude. Their greetings and delight

10th Mountain infantrymen stopping to rest and eat (courtesy Denver Public Library, Western History Department).

were unquestionably genuine, and so infectious and overwhelming that it made us believe that at least some of what we had been through had been worthwhile. Our orders, however, would not permit us to stop, so we were forced to keep marching at a rapid pace, with many in these friendly throngs that greeted us hanging on our arms or running beside us for a time to express their gratitude.

The experience was repeated countless times as we passed through each field belonging to a different family or through the villages en route. Many of those who welcomed us held out cheese, eggs, loaves of hard bread, or other food to grab as we hurried by, and seemingly everyone offered glasses of water or the local vino. Any liquids were particularly welcome because we soon had emptied our canteens and there was a hot sun beating down on our sweating bodies. Since we were also traveling on largely empty stomachs, it wasn't long before we began to feel the effects of all the wine we had been drinking and, in our inebriated state, began to forget our weariness.

This attitude of bravura reached its climax in my case after one family offered some clear liquid in a glass. Naively assuming it to be another glass of water, I gulped it down in one great swallow and was shocked to feel my throat afire as it traveled down my gullet. The lady who had offered the drink— which I mistakenly called *cognac* but am sure now was *grappa* since it was colorless—laughed delightedly at my surprised reaction, and as a warm feeling spread through my tired body, I quickly forgave her. For the next few hours, I was another Sergeant York, ready to take on the Hun and win the war single-handedly. This display of militant aggressiveness, so unlike my normally cautious attitude when in any kind of danger, amused all my brothers-in-arms no end.

Another delight as we hurried forward was to discover that the Germans had abandoned all kinds of vehicles, including trucks, motorcycles, carts, bicycles, riding horses, horse-drawn wagons, and cars. Many had apparently been forsaken as our Allied fighter-bombers bombed and strafed the fleeing German columns, forcing them to try and find some sort of shelter and continue their retreat on foot. The effect of these air attacks, which totaled almost 12,000 sorties since April 14 and greatly impeded the chances of the German forces reaching the Po River with their armor, artillery, and other heavy weapons intact, was evident everywhere.[5] Horses, cows, and other livestock lay dead on the roads and in the fields. Burned tanks, guns, and vehicles of every description littered the route forward. The air attacks also scared us periodically when the planes, confused by all the columns of troops and equipment streaming across the Lombardy plain, came diving in our direction, causing us to jump into nearby ditches to escape their fire in case they did not recognize us as "friendlies."

I climbed up on one German tank which had been hit and burned and looked down into its interior through the open hatch. For once I thought someone had a worse occupation than we infantrymen when I saw the effects of being entombed and burned alive in that enclosed space. Later, when we came across a truck with enemy dead in the back and many small arms lying about, I first removed a campaign ribbon from a dead officer and a belt buckle bearing the emblem of a swastika and then tried to take the rest of the scene in quickly to see if I wanted to appropriate any of the pistols or other gear as souvenirs. There were many other GIs surrounding the truck with the same objective in mind, and as I stood there attempting to make up my mind, a hand reached out beside me and seized one of the prized objects of collection, a German officer's Luger pistol lying right before my eyes. It was the only one there, and I came away with little of consequence in comparison.

The various forms of transportation left behind that seemed relatively untouched were now available for the taking, and for once, our commanders had no objection to our dispensing with the foot-slogging ways of the infantry and riding in or on any of these conveyances that we could manage to get moving. Some, we discovered, had run out of fuel, but many were still operable when subjected to the skills of American backyard mechanics. Larry and I could not believe our luck when we came upon a German landau, a general's staff car with an open top, that was ready to go. In we piled, and with Larry at the wheel and me in the back, feeling like Erich Von Stroheim, we roared down the road, exchanging wiseacre remarks with our brother infantrymen such as: "Don't you salute a German officer when you see one?" Of course we received obscene replies. The adventure struck us as something approaching heaven on earth until we ran out of gas and had to start trudging again on our own two feet. But not long afterwards, we found a German motorcycle with side car which started up immediately and provided almost an equal delight. Off we sped, with Larry again driving, through farmyards and villages with their smiling inhabitants showering us with happy greetings and flowers. Not having time to write any letters during this madcap race across country, I tried to record the highlights of our experience during those two days in a few brief diary notes.

> *(Diary)*
> April 21—The 10th is really moving. Chris just stopped a bullet from hitting me. Tanks look good. On and on. Terribly tired. Little opposition. What confusion. Everyone going pell mell across this flat country. The paisans give us water and vino. Just got a campaign ribbon off a dead Heine officer. Marched from dawn to dusk. Never in my life so tired. Everyone getting high on vino. A glass of cognac really hit me. Our own planes scare us. Roads littered with wreckage of animals and vehicles. Lush country.
>
> April 22—I've never seen such a madhouse racing after the Heines. They're leaving everything. We're riding captured vehicles now. Larry and I got a command car. Then a motorcycle. The Ities are mad with joy to see us. Give us eggs, milk. Some girls just threw flowers on me and the church bells are ringing in freedom. People hug you. I'm now on the front tank of the front spearhead racing to the Po.

By nightfall on the twenty-first, Task Force Duff had reached Bomporto and seized intact the bridge over the Panaro River. Prisoners captured during this advance were sent to the rear without guards, to be picked up by us and the other regiments which followed.[6] Our 85th Regiment marched until about ten o'clock that night after a day's advance of some 15 miles. We were then told to close down our operation, but that the following morning our 3d Battalion would move forward on trucks to Bomporto to relieve the 86th's infantry attached to General Duff's Task Force. Our 2d Battalion was informed that we would continue the march on foot.

The next day our battalion started off again at dawn, crossing the Panaro bridge that had been seized by the task force. The tank platoon accompanying us went ahead and then waited for the majority of us foot troops to catch up. Some of us, of course, not on tanks or walking, were riding in various forms of captured transportation and the situation became sufficiently confusing that in the early afternoon we were ordered to display either red or yellow identification panels on our vehicles.

While we were moving at a quick-step pace, Task Force Duff, which was serving as the spearhead of the entire Allied drive across the valley, was racing to reach the Po River and seize a place to cross. En route, however, the leading armored vehicles were ambushed and the column halted. The commander of the 85th's 3d Battalion, Lieutenant Colonel Shelor, was ordered to send some of his infantry to wipe out the enemy strongpoint. The operation was successful, but Col. Shelor, who had just come under fire and had taken to a ditch from his jeep, was wounded as the result of a direct hit on his jeep by a German Panzerfaust, and his executive officer took command of the battalion.

After meeting more spots of resistance which were overcome by the infantry, supported by fire from tanks, the task force reached the great river near the town of San Benedetto Po shortly after midnight.[7] But an hour or so earlier, General Duff had been badly wounded while standing near a lead tank which ran over a mine. General Ruffner, our artillery commander, was named by Hays to succeed him temporarily. Near the town, the task force set up a defensive ring around the area for the crossing, having arrived too late to prevent the bridges from being destroyed.[8]

Our 2d Battalion reached the city of Carpi, which had been bypassed by the task force, in mid-afternoon, and Company E was dropped off to capture the town. That took them till nightfall while the rest of us pressed on. After an exhausting day's march of 23 miles, we billeted north of the town of Novi. The next morning, April 23, we continued our rapid advance, finally reaching an assembly area at the river around noon.[9] Thus, in two-and-a-half days we had covered some 50 miles, traversing the entire southern half of the valley to finally stand on the banks of the river which had so long existed only in our imagination. Now we set about establishing some defensive positions and awaited our turn to cross.

At this point we had reached a stage of exhaustion that is almost incomprehensible to the noncombatant, much less the civilian. Many years later General Hays acknowledged that he thought to himself at the time: "What'll I do with these men? They're absolutely worn out with 10 days of fighting and two long days of marching.... So I gave orders ... the men were to ... go to sleep. I woke up about 7:30 A.M. and I've never seen so many men so sound asleep in my life."

Our exhaustion actually penetrated the mind and soul as well as affecting us physically. We kept going only because we recognized this kind of warfare was preferable to what we had experienced in the mountains, because of loyalty to each other, and because we had no choice. But the never-ending dust, the perpetual movement with no chance to ever settle down, and the food snatched on the run, remaining ill-digested in the stomach, all combined to form a depressing tapestry which seemed to have no end. Now we faced a river crossing in open boats, with the enemy waiting on the other side and undoubtedly prepared to make the trip very unpleasant.

The Po River wanders through northern Italy in a series of great bends and twists. Happily for us, in this spring of 1945 its water level was at the lowest ebb it had been for fifty years. The Po featured a shallow, slow-moving

Riflemen from the 2d Battalion survey the Po barrier (courtesy National Archives).

current, with low banks on either side where we prepared to cross, a spot located within a 20-mile stretch previously selected by 5th Army engineers from aerial and map reconnaissances. The river's width was about 100 yards, presenting a major tactical problem with the limited amphibious equipment available and our minimal training in such assaults.[10] As we waited with considerable trepidation on its bank, I could not help but think of the only instruction we had ever been given on river crossings, when we had practiced on the Colorado River in Texas and I had subsequently come down with a terrible case of poison oak. There, too, the river had been about 100 yards wide, although the current had been much faster.

Since no one had expected the 10th Mountain to get to the Po so quickly, all the heavy bridge equipment was located with the II Corps far to the east, where it had been anticipated the crossing would be made by other units. As a result, General Hays had to make do with what his own battalion of engineers, the 126th, had available or could obtain quickly. These turned out to be 50 canvas assault boats, each of which could theoretically carry eight infantrymen plus a crew of three combat engineers. (The combat engineers had the highly unpleasant task of paddling the boats back, thus being exposed to fire until the entire operation had been completed.) The boats had no motors; propulsion had to come from the men using paddles. Apart from the gamble of the crossing itself, all vehicles and heavy equipment, including artillery, had to be left behind until some type of bridging had been accomplished, so our arrival on the other side also posed some serious risks. Virtually no information was available as to the power of the German forces awaiting us and whether they would try and make this a last stand.[11]

General Hays decided the risk was worth taking, and at about noon on April 23, he ordered the colonel commanding the 126th Engineers to tell his men to load the first boats and "we'll see what happens."[12] Before the crossing could begin, some enemy 20mm cannon and 88mm guns began firing at us from the north side of the river, hitting quite a few of us waiting in foxholes and slit trenches on the south side. Nevertheless, the first assault wave, consisting of two companies of men from the 1st Battalion of the 87th Regiment, began paddling for the opposite shore, and despite heavy flak from shells exploding only a few feet above the water, as well as small arms and machine gun fire, they experienced no casualties. This was partly because of good luck, but also because few of the many firing positions on the north bank that the Germans had prepared were occupied.

By two o'clock in the afternoon, a beachhead had been pretty well secured by the 1st Battalion of the 87th, and other battalions in the regiment began crossing. After the entire 87th had reached the northern shore, our 85th Regiment was told to start loading the boats. F Company's turn didn't come until night had fallen, and we climbed aboard much concerned about being exposed to machine gun fire while on the water, as well as air bursts we had seen from the artillery shells timed to explode over the heads of people in the boats.[13]

Most of the men in our craft were heavily burdened with packs, ammunition belts, and other gear (even including rifles) weighting them down. Before boarding, I had noticed that many of the craft seemed to be overloaded and at risk of being swamped if anyone made a wrong move, because the water was only a few inches below the sides of the boats. Not being a terribly strong swimmer and not wanting to meet my end festooned with a lot of military equipment of which I was never enamored, I decided to improve my chances of reaching the other shore by loosening my boots and removing my ammunition belt (including attached pistol), backpack, and anything else I thought might impede my progress through the water if I ended up in it.

As we began paddling and got well out into the river, the enemy barrages continued to be fairly heavy, but no one in my boat was hit. At this point I began to worry more about someone upsetting the boat, and this began to happen to some boats even though the river had a fairly slow current and the water was calm. Since it was very dark, we could not see who was in the water or, under the circumstances, do anything to assist them, but we began to hear some terrible cries and screams for help. This chilled our spirits, but on we pressed until we reached the opposite shore. There we quickly waded in, gathered up our gear again while reassembling our squads and platoons, and then began moving out to occupy the defensive positions assigned us. As we did so, we learned that some of our men were missing and presumed drowned, two of

Paul Williams' sketch of the "10th Mountain Navy" crossing the Po (courtesy Denver Public Library, Western History Department).

whom—Sergeant Robert Rapp and Private First Class Harold Brezina—I knew quite well. I later learned that four other enlisted men from our company, perhaps all in the same boat, were lost also. The company, and later the division, record listed all as "missing in action."

A *New York Times* editorial, commenting a few days later on the river crossing, stated: "Three days ago the Tenth American Mountain Division, in the face of concentrated German fire, fought its way across the Po." That advance, the editorial continued, "ended any hope the enemy may have had of holding a river line in Italy." One of the *Times'* own reporters, who actually accompanied our division in the crossing, summarized the action as follows:

PO CROSSING MADE UNDER HEAVY FIRE
Anti-Aircraft Guns Employed as Artillery
Inflicted Loss on Assault Boats
by Milton Bracker

WITH THE FIFTH ARMY, Across the Po River, April 24 (Delayed)—The greatest river in Italy was crossed by American troops for the first time shortly after noon yesterday when two companies of a Tenth Mountain Division regiment braved a murderous hail of anti-aircraft fire (used as short-range artillery) to reach the north bank in assault boats....

The crossing took place on barely a half hour's notice. It was accomplished without air support or artillery preparation and it should go down as the Remagen of this campaign even if no bridge was involved....

Before the first wave of men could clamber over the dyke to the soft, sandy beach a vicious barrage of enemy shells ripped down on them. Some mortars were interspersed, but for the most part the shells were all heavy anti-aircraft used as anti-personnel artillery. Each shell burst some thirty feet above the ground at a speed estimated at 2,000 feet per second and sent blazing fragments tearing like rain into the crowded Americans. The casualties were relatively serious before the first boat was loaded.

Nevertheless the men got over the dyke and into the boats.... Both the wind and current were against them, and the deadly air bursts continued.... At least one boatload was lost and the men were feared drowned.[14]

A strong counterattack by the Germans was anticipated, and the following morning we thought it had begun. A tremendous barrage of artillery shells, the heaviest we had ever encountered, began whistling over our heads and landing nearby. I and others in my squad dashed for a culvert under a nearby road and waited out the horrific bombardment there. When it finally let up, we discovered it had all been launched by the American 85th Infantry Division attempting to soften up its landing site preparatory to crossing the Po.[15] One can only wonder if West Point trained its future generals to communicate with one another and why the 5th Army commander, General Truscott, did not let his right hand know what his left hand was doing. Or perhaps the explanation was that even Truscott had trouble keeping up with General Hays, having reportedly charged into his headquarters the previous afternoon during the 10th's crossing of the Po and asked, "What the hell are you trying to do, George, win this war all by yourself?"[16]

Before most of the division and its fast-moving task force could move out, we had to await the building of a pontoon bridge and a treadway which would enable our artillery, tanks, and other heavy armor to cross. Early on the morning of April 24, engineer units began the construction, which was not completed until late in the afternoon of the following day. Meanwhile, since the task force was being delayed waiting for its armor and artillery to arrive, General Hays, confident that the Germans had left the area, ordered the 1st Battalion of our regiment, the 85th, to begin the pursuit without waiting any longer and to try and seize the Villafranca airfield some 25 miles away. The men began moving out at about 1 A.M. on the twenty-fifth, initially having to clear innumerable mines on the road, but by 7 A.M. they had passed through the mine field area and were able to travel much more quickly. After engaging in a number of firefights en route, they reached the airfield late in the afternoon and by 5 P.M., after quickly dispersing a German rear guard detachment, the airfield was in their hands. Thus ended a forced march, against opposition, of some 25 miles in less than 20 hours.[17]

While my company waited to begin the chase again, I finally had an opportunity to write a brief letter home.

(Letter)
San Benedetto Po
April 25th, 1945   V-Mail

   This is the first chance I've had to write. You've probably read about our rapid advance and the 10th Mountain has really been going to town. The other day I killed a sniper at about 15 feet with my .45 revolver. So I've really been having quite a time.

   Pat writes that some midshipman proposed to her but she refused him, thank heavens.

   We've really been having a madhouse here—you can read more about it in the papers, I guess, than I can tell you. But I've certainly been having experiences and I'll tell you about them some day soon, I hope. It looks as though we'll still have some stiff fighting though if these Heines hole up in the Alps.

   Larry and I captured a German command car in our wild dash, and drove it along the road with women throwing flowers on us and kissing us. Everywhere people are hysterical with joy to see us. It's quite moving.

   Send this letter to Pat and the family. Don't have time to write more.

To spearhead our drive to the Alps, General Hays once again decided to use his mobile task force, which, having been reunited with its needed armor, was ready to lead the advance with a new commander. He was Colonel William Darby, who held a staff job in Washington but happened to come by at this time as an escort for some visiting War Department dignitaries. General Hays asked generals Truscott and Clark if he could have Darby as his assistant division commander in place of the wounded Duff, and to his pleasure they and the War Department agreed. Darby had previously headed an elite force based on the British Commando model, the so-called Darby's Rangers, which had been effective in hit-and-run roles in North Africa and Sicily. When the Rangers had been mistakenly employed earlier in the Italian campaign as conventional infantry to spearhead the breakout from the Anzio beachhead, however, they had been caught by the Germans. Half were killed or wounded and virtually all the remainder taken prisoner.[18]

   The 10th had now been told to continue the pursuit by bypassing the city of Mantua and heading for Verona to cut the roads leading out of the latter to the Alps and the Brenner Pass. General Hays ordered the 86th Regiment to accompany the task force with a tank battalion leading the way. Our other two regiments were to follow, mopping up German forces bypassed, but moving up ahead by truck relays to help if any strong resistance were encountered. By nightfall on April 25, Darby's Task Force had reached the Villafranca Airfield to join the 1st Battalion of the 85th in its defensive positions, and at midnight, the task force continued on to Verona. Once there the division received new orders requiring us to take the road west to Lake Garda and then to move north along the highway, on the lake's eastern shore, towards the city of Trento and the Brenner Pass. East of Lake Garda this line of march and Highway 12 paralleling it some seven miles farther east were among the few escape routes left to the German army.

General Hays' plan for this stretch of our advance towards the Alps contemplated a leapfrogging movement in which each regiment would march as rapidly as possible for 8 hours and then rest for 16. In this way, he said, "I hope to advance 60 miles per day, 20 miles per night"—each regiment advancing 20 miles—and have fresh infantry leading each new advance every eight hours. Trucks would shuttle the infantry and artillery forward, the travel time needed to catch up with the advancing infantry being taken out of the rest period. The armor units supporting the infantry would be on 12 hours and off 12.

Before the new march began, the 87th Mountain Infantry and our 85th Regiment had been shuttled on April 26 to a bivouac area near Villafranca about ten miles south of Verona. There I again jotted a few notes in my diary describing what had occurred in the past few days.

> *(Diary)*
> April 26, 1945—Crossed the Po, Rapp and Brezina drowning. Their screaming was awful to hear. Plane strafed us. Rested a day. Modin returned, and Orwig. We're now near Verona heading for the Brenner Pass and Lake Garda. 10th was the first unit to cross the Po.

The 87th was now designated to begin its leapfrogging exercise at 8 A.M. on the twenty-seventh with our 85th Regiment to pass through the 87th late the same day. Again the pace was exhausting. As we marched and periodically rode through the countryside, more and more local villagers and farm families, greeting us happily, would call out, as some had done for some time, *Tedeschi kaputt*—"the Germans have surrendered." Having long since learned to be terribly cynical about any prospect of seeing an end to our daily way of life in which death was ever present, we dismissed it as cruel rumor-mongering which only a fool would be so naive as to believe. But as we kept hearing the same story, despite our rapid movement forward, I at least began to give it more credence, reasoning that since all telephone and power lines seemed to be down, I did not see how the word could be so widespread unless it had been announced in some radio broadcast. Moreover, we had not run into any German resistance for some hours.

At about 6 P.M., however, our trucks unloaded us at Lake Garda, where the 87th had been moving up the road on its eastern edge, and we learned that they had run into a strongly defended road block in part manned by Hitler's SS troops. Although they had managed to eliminate it after a short, bitter firefight, it was now our regiment's turn to serve as Task Force Darby's lead element, with our 2d Battalion serving as the spearhead, and it was clear the war was not over. Indeed, the realization that we could be in for some more nasty fighting, despite the fact that the war in Europe was obviously nearing its end, made us even more resentful of those who had tried to convince us otherwise. Having managed thus far to escape being killed or wounded, I did not want to end up shot during what appeared to be the last days of the war. Nevertheless, we all had no choice but to go forward and do our duty.

As the remnants of the German forces retreated toward the Alps, Allied headquarters issued a call for a general uprising throughout northern Italy, and partisan units in the villages and towns began seizing control in many areas. With most of the exits to the Alps closed, enemy units west of Lake Garda and in northeastern Italy as well had little alternative but to surrender either to the Italian partisans or to Allied forces. To our dismay, however, the one place where they decided to make a stand was in our narrow sector east of Lake Garda. Only there did the commander of the German forces in Italy, General von Vietinghoff, believe there was a chance of maintaining some semblance of resistance, using his XIV Panzer Corps which was all that was left of his 14th Army. This corps was commanded by Lieutenant General Fridolin von Senger, Oxford educated, who had master-minded the German defenses of Monte Cassino a little more than a year earlier.[19]

The terrain from which we had to oust the Germans—namely, the beginning of the Alps, one of the highest mountain ranges in the world—cast fear into all our hearts. I, for one, was fully aware that during World War I, in two years of bloody fighting in these mountains which used to be part of the Austrian Tyrol, the Italian army had been able to move only about 10 miles into Austrian territory. The Austrians had seized these heights from Italy in 1815, and one of the reasons the Italians entered the war in 1915 on the side of the Allies was that they had been secretly promised the return of this forbidding frontier. Despite their understandable determination, however, to recover what they had lost, they failed to appreciate what the effort might cost. The Austrians had dug out vast caverns in the mountains to house their men and equipment, and their strategically placed guns covered all routes of approach.

In the period from May to June 1916, when the Austrians launched an all-out attack in the Lake Garda sector, they only managed to penetrate an average of 12 miles and on June 25 began a general withdrawal, abandoning more than one-half the ground they had won. Casualties in these two months of action alone cost the Italians about 147,000 men killed, wounded, and missing while Austria's losses totaled 81,000.[20] In the end, along this entire Alpine redoubt, Italy sacrificed over 600,000 lives, and the Austrians about as many, without accomplishing any great changes along the battlefront.

Our line of march was now along a narrow road cut into these enormous Alpine cliffs which descended precipitously some 7,000 feet to the edge of the lake. We had never seen anything like these cliffs in the Apennines, which in comparison to the Alps, seemed like minor foothills.

Garda is the largest lake in northern Italy, being over 31 miles long and from 2 to 11 miles wide. Its southern end is wide and surrounded by relatively flat country, but the northern part is long and narrow, with steep sides, like a Norwegian fjord. Since we were essentially restricted in our advance to the road itself, the cliffs being too difficult to scale, we had to proceed in a narrow column of companies with the men in front likely to suffer the majority of casualties.

One of the tunnels along Lake Garda's eastern shore after 10th engineers cleaned it out (courtesy Denver Public Library, Western History Department).

It was raining heavily as we began to march, accompanied by tanks from the 751st Tank Battalion and gunners from the 1125th Field Artillery Battalion. It was quite cold, and my clothes were getting thoroughly drenched, but I discovered that if I stayed close to the rear of a tank its powerful exhaust would send a gale of hot air at me like a traveling blast furnace, so I was managing to get soaked and dried simultaneously. We ran into no trouble, and by midnight we had reached the resort town of Malcesine, about two-thirds of the way up the eastern shore of Lake Garda, ending a forced march of some 20 miles in six hours.

The 86th Regiment was now shuttled forward and late that night, after detrucking, passed through us to continue the attack the morning of April 28. Meanwhile, the 87th had been ordered to turn off to the northeast, which required climbing a steep rocky bluff, to pursue the enemy between the lake and Highway 12 a short distance away.

Shortly before noon, advance elements of the 86th reached the first of a series of tunnels where the road passed through the cliffs, and it was here that the Germans took advantage of terrain to make things extremely difficult and bloody. As our men approached the first tunnel, they ran into heavy automatic weapons fire, and the Germans set off demolitions collapsing both ends of the tunnel and effectively blocking the road. General Hays, having anticipated this possibility, had arranged for DUKWs (2-1/2 ton, amphibious six-wheel trucks) to accompany the division, and they were now used to ferry men of the 86th around the tunnel, completely surprising the Germans and forcing them to fall back. This process continued through and around five more tunnels, with the Germans demolishing bridges and blocking other tunnels where they could. In the last of the tunnels, disaster struck: a German 88mm shell exploded inside the tunnel while more than two companies of the 86th were advancing through its rubble. When Captain Albert Meinke, a battalion surgeon in the 86th, arrived on the scene, he found it comparable to "a nightmare or horror movie." More than a hundred of the men were lying scattered about, one on top of another, on the tunnel floor. Many were unconscious or suffering from concussion, but at least four were dead and some fifty or more were wounded. While efforts began to treat the wounded and evacuation of those most seriously injured commenced, advance units of the 86th Infantry entered the town of Torbole near the northern end of the Lake.[21]

In Torbole some hand-to-hand fighting ensued, but by the afternoon of April 30 the Germans had withdrawn and both Torbole and Riva, the latter being the town at the head of the lake, were occupied. That same afternoon, Colonel Darby, after conferring with the new commander of the 86th and other officers about continuing the pursuit the next day, was killed by a fragment from a single 88mm artillery shell that hit him in the chest as he entered a jeep parked in a hotel courtyard in Torbole. This parting shot from the Germans who had abandoned the town mortally wounded this famous World War II soldier just before the war ended. Two other officers were wounded by the same shell (including the new commander of the 86th), and the 86th's regimental sergeant major was also killed.

During the action by the 86th Mountain Infantry, my 85th Regiment received orders to send a reinforced company across Lake Garda to attack the village of Gargnano and try to catch Mussolini, whose villa and office were nearby, as well as other Italian officials who were rumored to be hiding in the town. Company K undertook the task, crossing the lake in 12 DUKWs, occupying the town, and seizing Mussolini's quarters. His villa contained many interesting items, including a Stradivarius violin, decorative swords given him as gifts by Hitler and Emperor Hirohito, and a giant four-poster bed in which some of the K Company GIs took turns sleeping. But *Il Duce* (The Leader) had already fled to Lake Como, some 60 miles to the west. There he made a desperate attempt in a German motorized column to escape our advance by getting to Switzerland over one of the passes to the north of that lake. He was within a few miles of safety when the column was stopped by Italian partisans. After a summary trial, Mussolini and his mistress, Clara Petacci, were shot and taken to Milan, where they were hung upside down in a service station for the public to see.

Later two more amphibious crossings of the lake were made on DUKWs by Companies L and I of the 85th under instructions from General Hays. They patrolled the entire area, searching for enemy forces, and on May 1 they advanced up the highway on the west side of the lake to Riva, where they met elements of the 86th Regiment which had taken the town the previous day.[22]

All this time, while the 86th men were being wounded and killed fighting their way through tunnels and towns on the east side of the lake, elements of the 87th were up on the ridges clawing their way north. My Company F, however, along with the rest of my 2d Battalion, was having a rather pleasant respite from the war awaiting our turn to proceed to the front. Our quarters were clearly the best we had experienced since arriving in Italy, General Hays having authorized our use of the many resorts along the lake during our inactive periods. I was housed on the ground floor of one of the hotels in Malcesine.

In a courtyard right outside my room, some enormous guns manned by British soldiers attached to the 178th Medium Battalion of Royal Artillery, which had been given to the division to provide close support, kept up a deafening roar aiding elements of our 86th Regiment fighting farther up the lake. During my first night in the hotel, I got little rest, finding it difficult to ignore the terrible noise and flame from each nearby gun when it went off. The concussion from their blasts would make the floor where we were sleeping tremble and almost levitate our bodies ever so slightly. But continuous firing, even that close, didn't keep us awake after we got used to it. It was the occasional blast, coming after some period of silence, that propelled you upright and caused your heart rate to increase dramatically.

Apart from the blasts emanating from the British guns, whose close proximity I had never before experienced, and worrying about when we would be called to resume leading the attack again, I was having quite a good time. After talking to the British gunners, I was ashamed to even mention the length of time I had been in military service and in combat. Virtually all of them had been overseas since 1940, fighting in North Africa, Sicily, and Italy, and had not seen their families for four or more years.

One of the things we enjoyed was trading canned food and other rations with our British friends, each side feeling that whatever the other army was eating had to be better—obviously less boring—than what they had been consuming ad nauseum. We also enjoyed wandering about town, talking to the Italian inhabitants, and visiting the waterfront. Malcesine is a lovely old fishing village (now a flourishing tourist resort) at the foot of Monte Baldo. Amid olive groves and gardens, it boasts a dominating thirteenth century castle (*Castello Scaligero*) on the water's edge containing dungeons, a high tower, and other exhibits of interest.[23] As for Lake Garda, it boasts some of the most beautiful scenery in the world, with well-kept villas, lakeside hotels, and tiered terraces covered with white pillars of glazed or latticed pergolas. The famous German poet, novelist, and playwright, Johann Goethe, visiting the lake (and Malcesine) for the first time in 1787, wrote of it: "Beside me lay Lake Garda, displaying nature to truly marvellous effect and with dramatic enchantment.... On both banks there are hills and mountains, littered with countless, sparkling little villages.... No words can describe the beauty of this ... district."[24]

Lake Garda's waters, when the sun shines, are called by many the bluest

Top: Original and replacement members of the author's machine gun squad with gun. Left to right: Manse, "Eagle Eye" Mofford, author, "Limber" Krusell, and Sven ("Holy sheeet") Modin, Malcesine, Italy, May 1945. *Bottom:* Author and fox-hole companion, 6'7" Wally Krusell, on castle grounds, Malcesine, Italy, May 1945.

of all the lakes of northern Italy. Indeed, we could not have found a lovelier spot to spend our final days of the war with Germany, as I noted in my diary and my next letter home.

(Diary)
April 30—Lake Garda is the most beautiful place I've ever seen. Received the camera. Marched 20 miles along Garda to town of Malcesine. Raining. Have cut off many Heine units. Made amphibious landings across Garda to Mussolini's private residence. He escaped but partisans caught him and shot him.

Still rough fighting up here. Heines stopped us by blowing up 5 tunnels.

(Letter)
Malcesine
April 30th, 1945
The news is sensationally good but men are still dying in this theatre and the load will be lifted from none of our soldiers until the last shot is fired. I keep thinking of the man in *All Quiet on the Western Front* who reached out of his trench on the day of the Armistice to catch a butterfly and was shot by a sniper.

I can't say where I am or what exactly I'm doing but you've probably read of our smash across the Po valley. As the papers say, the 10th Division was the first to cross the Po, which was quite an honor. I've had quite a time riding a tank, being hugged and kissed, flowers thrown on me and my buddies, etc. by the grateful populace in the towns we've freed. At first the newly freed are a little frightened but the moment they realize we're Americans their joy reaches no bounds. The Italian Partisans help a lot and according to the news last night caught Mussolini and hung him.

I managed to contact John Horrall last night and we had a fine time together. It was the first time I'd seen him since we left the States. Jack Kelly, whose reputation is very bad in this company because he hasn't been with us in any of our battles, has been reclassified into a clerical job because of a psychoneurotic condition brought on by the tension before battle. Tim Prout and Jud are both fine, but one of my oldest friends [Bill Luth] from Camp Hale was killed the other day. I can't mention his name.

I'm sorry that I can't follow the news and developments more closely. I usually get word only of the major happenings and then usually it's two or three days old.

I wish Edwin didn't have to go in, but on the other hand I don't see why any of us over here must go to the Pacific. We've fought a terrible long war here and those of us who have been lucky enough to survive should get a break.

Since the beginning of the spring offensive, by cutting off many of the German units at the Po and later blocking their escape routes to the Alps, we— together with the British 8th Army—had captured some 145,000 prisoners.[25] (The 10th Mountain Division alone captured 11,000.)[26] The situation was clearly becoming desperate for the Germans, but scattered survivors in the one narrow sector where we were advancing were still fighting on. For this reason, on May 1 Colonel Barlow, commander of our 85th Regiment, warned us that we would resume the attack that evening at 8 P.M. with the 87th on the ridge to the east, the 86th on a similar ridge to the west, and our 85th Mountain Infantry, accompanied by armor, advancing up the valley. What neither we nor Colonel Barlow probably knew, although we had heard a lot of rumors about the Germans finally giving up in Italy, was that documents agreeing to a capitulation had actually been signed on April 29 by representatives of General von Vietinghoff, commander of all German forces in Italy, and SS General (*Obergruppenfuehrer*) Karl Wolff, the senior SS official in Italy.

The story of how this unconditional surrender came about would make an excellent plot for a comic opera, were it not for the men dying while the principal characters played out their roles. It is a tale of deceptions and conflict within the German high command, including house arrests and countermanding orders, as well as unyielding and perhaps too dogmatic attitudes on the part of Allied commanders. Of perhaps the greatest interest to us, when we learned about it later, was the fact that as early as April 16 a representative of General Wolff, the German leader of the effort to end the hostilities in Italy, was urging the Allies through Allen Dulles, who headed the U.S. Office of Strategic Services (OSS) intelligence operations in Europe, not "to make useless sacrifices with their intensified offensives" because the Germans were ready to surrender. His offer fell for the most part on deaf ears, and Field Marshal Alexander saw it as simply an attempt by the Germans to upset his offensive.

Of course generals know their reputations can be made in combat, and here was a golden opportunity to win without much risk. Yet it is possible Alexander could have been right, for it took a while before General Vietinghoff was ready to agree to the Allies' uncompromising surrender conditions, and subsequently both Wolff and Vietinghoff were accused of treasonable actions by their superiors and arrest orders were issued. It can be argued that had Alexander not been so uncompromising and had he not pressed forward with such determination to cut off the German forces and render their situation so patently hopeless, Field Marshall Kesselring, who commanded the western front, and other die-hard commanders in the Italian theater who were zealous to fight on might have had their way. The German commanders who were ready to call it quits also had their enthusiasm tempered by Kesselring's actions on April 26 when he had some officers summarily executed who had attempted to seize control of Munich and order a cease-fire before the Allied forces arrived.

As late as April 30, General Schulz, who had officially been placed over Vietinghoff, ordered all units to keep on fighting. This resulted in his being placed under house arrest by General Wolff. Hitler committed suicide on the same day, and the local army commanders in Italy reached an agreement that they no longer considered their forces capable of meaningful resistance. After a raging two-hour telephone argument shortly after midnight on May 2 between Wolff and Kesselring, in which Schulz at long last supported Wolff, Kesselring finally authorized the cease-fire order. The Germans then broadcast the order to their troops at 2 P.M. on May 2. After their broadcast was heard by the Allies, Field Marshal Alexander repeated the announcement at 6:30 P.M. the same day.

We heard the welcome news that our terrible war in Italy was finally over from a BBC radio broadcast at that time, and naturally it was greeted with great yells and much firing of rifles and other weapons. Allen Dulles later said that of the congratulatory messages he received from Eisenhower, Alexander, and others, one that he would never forget was a telegram from the number two man in the OSS, Brigadier General John Magruder, who had a son in the 10th Mountain which, Dulles said, "was poised for attack when the cease-fire order came on May 2nd." The telegram said:

> COUNTLESS THOUSANDS OF PARENTS WOULD BLESS YOU WERE THEY PRIVILEGED TO KNOW WHAT YOU HAVE DONE. AS ONE OF THEM PRIVILEGED TO KNOW, AND WITH A BOY IN THE MOUNTAIN DIVISION, I DO BLESS YOU.[27]

The local citizens in Malcesine were equally joyous. Many Italian men had been taken as forced labor into Germany, so the cruelty of the Nazi regime to them, as well as to the civilian population in Italy itself, was deeply felt. Soon thereafter we saw liberated slave workers and dispossessed families come streaming through our lines heading south to return to their homes. At the same time, some more of our wounded returned from military hospitals, and even some of our men who had been captured by the Germans were released and returned to us.

10

We Who Are Left

Post–Surrender Fears of Invading Japan,
May–August 1945

> We who are left, how shall we look again
> Happily on the sun, or feel the rain,
> Without remembering how they who went
> Ungrudgingly, and spent
> Their all for us, loved, too, the sun and rain?
> —Wilfrid Wilson Gibson, *A Lament*

The following afternoon General Hays gave a short speech to the entire division, which, with the exception of those still on the west side of Lake Garda, was assembled in Malcesine. My diary indicates he told us that of all his battles, including the Meuse Argonne and Normandy invasion, this had been the fiercest. He boasted—and, naturally, we were not about to dispute his claim—that our record of breaking through the Apennines and Po Valley to the Alps would "ring in military history." General Hays pointed out that we had spearheaded the attack of the 5th Army and sped with both flanks and our rear unprotected to win.

I recorded that our battalion commander, Colonel Roche, had been relieved of his command because of suicidal tactics and incompetence. The division chaplain prayed at the end of General Hays' speech and urged us never to forget our comrades who had died on the threshold of this great victory. The diary entry ended with the words, "It is over at last, thanks be to God."

On the same day I wrote a letter home describing my feelings.

(Letter)
Malcesine
May 3, 1945   V-Mail
Last night we heard that all German troops in Italy have surrendered.

It was the news we've fought long and terrible battles for, and the dawn has broken through at last. The Italian people are of course wild with joy and we're not far behind. The Nazi beast has finally given himself up and this terrible holocaust of suffering and sacrifice is almost at an end.

If only all those fine young men who gave their lives in the past few months could be here to rejoice with us. I feel that very much, for many of my oldest and best friends of Camp Hale days have given their lives. At the moment I'm very well, am living amidst great natural beauty in one of the loveliest parts of Italy, and am very happy because we have brought our enemy to her knees.

The German representative at the formal surrender ceremony in Florence, where General Mark Clark had his headquarters, was General von Senger, commander of the XIV Panzer Corps, which was the only effective force left opposing the 10th Mountain Division. He represented General Vietinghoff and asked to be accompanied to the ceremony by our General Hays. One of von Senger's principal concerns was for his troops to retain some of their small arms to defend themselves from bands of Italian partisans until Allied forces arrived in the German-held areas. This posed some risks if our troops rushed into such areas before all our enemies had gotten the word about their surrender. General Clark, however, agreed to this request since he also had an interest in not letting too many such arms fall into the hands of the partisan forces controlled by the Communist party.[1]

On May 4, my Company F was given the unique assignment of traveling some 60 miles into German-held territory in the Alps to the city of Bolzano, near the Brenner Pass, to protect the headquarters of General Vietinghoff which were located there and to demonstrate through a show of force to the Italian partisans and local citizenry that the war in Italy was over. We left Lake Garda late in the day and were soon deep in the mountains, passing quickly from a soft southern scene of cypresses, vineyards, and churches with Italian campaniles to sharp Alpine air, wooden chalets, and the German tongue. It was a strange feeling to see fully armed German soldiers—not to mention their tanks and numerous other weapons—as we passed by, and we hoped desperately they had been told the war was over. Evidently they had, for they made no effort to impede our passage, and we reached Bolzano at about 11 P.M.

Early the next morning I was ordered to take a group of men from the company and march them about the city to show all concerned that the American army was here. As we marched we were greeted joyfully by the local inhabitants, including former prisoners of war who told us about the starvation rations on which they had been forced to subsist and other awful tales of what they had experienced. Numerous German soldiers also came up to us, exhibiting a fawning attitude in an attempt to make amends. One German officer even tried to get me to accept his pistol as a measure of his goodwill, but I told him to go to our command post and turn it in there. Some of the men in our company later joined some of the Germans in a tavern, where they

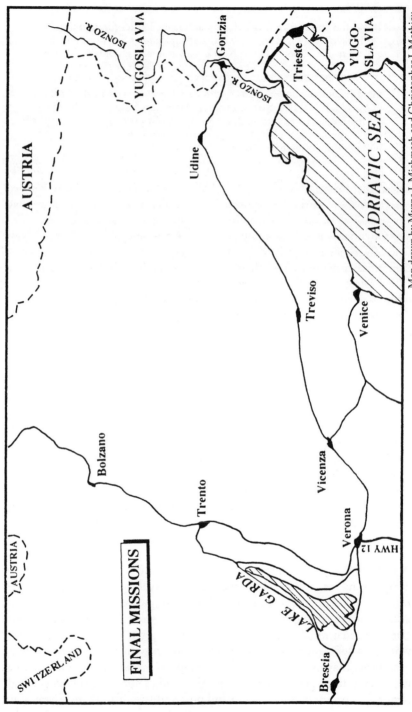

Map drawn by Myrna J. Mishmash and Christopher J. Mathieu.

drank beer together with seemingly no thought of the days just passed in which each side was determined to kill the other.

B-17 and B-24 bombers, flying over the Alps to attack targets in southern Germany, had often passed through the gap in the mountains where Bolzano was located and had been the objects of a kind of "skeet shoot" from 88mm guns located on the hillsides on both sides of the town. The bomber crews named these kinds of unavoidable mountain passes "flak alleys." Naturally, some effort had been made by the bombers to attack the antiaircraft positions that were giving them trouble, as well as other military targets, with the unavoidable result that some of Bolzano's churches and other buildings had been badly damaged. General Vietinghoff's command post, however, had been built into the mountainside with a system of underground tunnels and shelters, so it had escaped damage.

The town's citizenry were very fair-skinned, many of the women having light blond hair quite unlike that of the Italians further south. Since the city had not seen the evacuation of its German troops, we had the unusual experience of seeing some customary military activities as well as SS troops and other representatives of the Nazi regime that we had never had the opportunity to observe before. Early one morning, hearing a marching noise outside my window, I got up and leaned out over the window sill to see what was going on. To my amazement, it was a troop of heavy-set German women, in Stormtrooper or other special uniforms, heading off on some duty. To me they looked like the personification of some of the brutal females associated with the concentration camps, one of whom (Frau Ilse Koch, who had the skins of prisoners made into lamp shades) was known as the *Bitch of Buchenwald*. Later, during a walk around town with the camera sent me by Mother and Dad, I was able to photograph German soldiers in the streets still giving each other the "Heil Hitler" salute.

The Germans, for security reasons, had forced the local populace to surrender all their shotguns, rifles, pistols, and other weapons. These we found stored in a local warehouse, and many of the shotguns, in particular, were rare collectors' pieces, featuring beautiful silver inlay work. Some of the F Company men who were avid hunters and collectors of guns tried to ship them home as souvenirs, but most were "appropriated" en route by rear-echelon types and never reached their destinations. Bolzano also boasted a Beretta factory where we were able to commandeer all the pistols we would ever want. I took a number but later traded them for two revolvers that appeared to my untutored eye to be more valuable. In this I was sadly mistaken, and I was never able (or cared enough to make the required effort) to find ammunition for these weapons, which I still possess.

Near Bolzano, in a small stucco building in the Tyrolean village of Saint Leonhard, was an even more incredible collection of objects seized by the Germans, which some 10th Mountain troops were sent to guard, not to "liberate" as souvenirs. These consisted of hundreds of the world's greatest paintings and sculptures, by such artists as Michelangelo, Rubens, Raphael, Donatello, and others, which had been stolen from the galleries of Florence. Fifth Army headquarters was notified of the finding, and the collection, after being sorted, cleaned, and crated, was loaded into 13 boxcars and carried by rail back to Florence some two months later.[2]

After staying in Bolzano a few days to perform our mission, we returned to Malcesine. On May 7, I wrote home that none of us felt very much like celebrating. "Maybe if we were in the States we could get in the mood, but here, far from home, it seems a little flat and meaningless. Not that we're not all terribly relieved. It's just that we've given so much, and seen so many suffer and die, that even the end doesn't seem worthy of cheering." The only day that would really make me happy, I said, would be when I started homeward. "I feel like a runner, who ran as hard and as fast as he could and won the race, but was so exhausted that he couldn't celebrate."

Now everyone was worried about going to the Pacific theater. As I wrote Margaret, "I lived through this fight through the skin of my teeth. I know my luck will never hold out over there if I'm in a line company, and it'll take plenty to get me over there.... Maybe I'll desert to Persia."

The formal surrender of the German armed forces as a whole took effect at midnight, May 8, but we got the word a day earlier. May 9 was declared an official holiday, Victory in Europe (VE) day, and we spent the day relaxing and doing anything we chose. While we were obviously delighted to see the official end of this six-year struggle in Europe which brought death and destruction to so many, Japan remained as a powerful antagonist, and our unknown role in the Far East conflict with her now replaced the German nightmare that had occupied our thoughts. It didn't help our morale any to be shown the War Department film, *Two Down and One to Go*, reflecting the surrenders by Italy and Germany but not Japan. Knowing the army, we had little doubt that we might be sent directly to the Pacific theater. Alternatively, there was the highly unlikely possibility that we might be kept in Europe to serve as occupation troops or (as some dreamers suggested) we might even be demobilized.

One thing was certain, given the unyielding character of the Japanese, which would be magnified by their need to defend their homeland itself, we could expect a terribly bloody final struggle. Having learned only too well the odds against infantrymen surviving long in combat, we had to assume that if we were forced to participate in the invasion of that island nation, in all likelihood it would be a struggle from which we would not emerge alive.

While still in Malcesine, I took the opportunity to write the family a summary description of my experiences since arriving in Italy and to report that I had been given the official paper from General Hays (General Order No. 74) announcing that I had been awarded the Bronze Star. Edwin had just had his pre-induction physical up in Cleveland but had failed it because of excessively dry skin on his legs, so his worries about the army finally getting him were over. I congratulated him on his escaping induction. But I made it equally clear that if we now had to fight Japan, those of us who had managed thus far to survive combat would resent not being replaced by men who had obtained deferments for various reasons or by support troops who had never been on the front lines.

Since up to this time censored letters had precluded any reference to casualties, I was now able to tell Mother and Dad that my old and good friend Bill Luth from Camp Hale days, whom I had often mentioned in letters home, had been killed in the Mt. della Spe attack, but that Jud Decker, John Horrall, Wally Krusell, and Tim Prout had all survived. I warned them that my discharge points did not reach a very large total, mainly because I had no children, "so I'm afraid I'll be in the Pacific war eventually." At the same time, I thought there was a strong possibility of my getting a 30-day furlough in the States first. I also informed them on May 13 that I had received the paper work awarding me the Bronze Star, although the actual award ceremony would come later. "The War Department will notify you about it shortly," I said, "telling you why I received it, but don't get the idea that I'm out for medals.... My main worry is to get back alive."

The text of the citation read as follows:

HEADQUARTERS
10TH MOUNTAIN DIVISION
APO 345, U.S. Army

11 May 1945

CITATION

ROBERT B. ELLIS, 16169350, Sergeant, Infantry, United States Army. For heroic achievement in action on April 14th 1945, near Mt. Della Speé, Italy. On two different occasions during assaults by mountain infantry troops, Sergeant Ellis displayed outstanding heroism. While guiding a group of men from the rear of the company position to forward elements, enemy sniper fire seriously wounded one of his men. Altho armed only with a pistol he aggressively began a search for the sniper and locating him in a clump of bushes killed him by firing at close range. Returning to his squad he continued the attack. Later when the attack slowed because of hostile enemy machine gun fire, he, with no concern for his own safety, boldly occupied an exposed position from whence he directed accurate mortar fire on the enemy, liquidating their position, spiriting the attack to completion and allowing his company to take its objective. Entered the military service from Shreve, Ohio.

BY COMMAND OF MAJOR GENERAL HAYS:

CHARLES J. KNAPP
WOJG USA
ASS'T ADJ GEN

At about the time I received this citation, I was asked by our company commander to take on the duty of writing recommendations for military medals. Medals for valor, and even the Purple Heart for wounds received, not only honored the recipient, but had the added benefit of increasing the points needed for discharge. A Bronze Star, for example, was worth five points. Other ways of earning points included length in months of active service, months overseas, number of campaigns in which you had participated, and being a parent. I calculated that my total point score was only 44, computed by adding up my 25 months service, 4 months overseas, 10 points for two battle stars, and 5 points for the Bronze Star. This was not enough to get me a discharge by any means because you needed at least 85 points to qualify.

The point system inevitably led to much bad feeling. Support troops who never saw the front lines could earn battle stars, and the army brass saw to it that some high-ranking officers who had little exposure to shot and shell were given Bronze Stars. I was even asked to prepare one recommendation as late as October 1945, two months after Victory-Japan (VJ) Day. This prompted me to joke to some friends that I was seriously considering asking for a Purple Heart for the bad cut I received from my entrenching shovel while hastily digging that foxhole overlooking Monte della Torrachia.

Doing the needed paperwork, however, turned out to be an interesting exercise. After studying many examples of the kind of phraseology used to "sell the product," I soon learned that certain boilerplate expressions were desired by the army brass if the nominations were to receive command approval. These included (to my dismay) some of the language used in the write-up done on me, such as "displayed outstanding heroism," "with no concern for his own safety," and (a common finish) "allowing his company [or other unit] to take its objective." Other favorites were "gallantry in action" (a phrasing preferred for awards of the Silver Star), "at great risk to his own life," "his actions were an inspiration to all," and (another favored ending) "in the finest traditions of the United States Army."

Even though the vast majority of these awards, at least in the 10th Mountain Division, were properly due the recipient, after drafting many I could not help but get a little cynical, especially when I knew (as was often the case) that others not recommended for a citation were equally deserving. The particular actions which led to my receiving a decoration were in no sense unique, many others having performed feats meriting equal recognition, but that didn't prevent me from bringing my medal to the attention of most members of the family. And Mother, of course, saw to it that the story of the decoration and the achievements of the 10th Mountain Division in general, with some embellishments she had stolen from the *New York Times* and other news media, appeared in the local papers where she lived.

While waiting with dread to hear what the War Department was going to do with us next, we had a number of duties thrust upon us which occupied our time and attention. Some units of the division were sent to block international borders in our area and to meet troops of our 7th Army heading south through Austria. Each regiment was also assigned sectors where we were to patrol the roads and locate, disarm, and assemble the German troops for evacuation to prisoner-of-war camps. In our 85th regimental zone of responsibility, some 3,000 German officers and men were finally rounded up and assembled for delivery to these camps.

The next task for my battalion required us on May 15 to leave the delights of Lake Garda and our pleasant quarters in hotels and villas to guard German prisoners-of-war as they arrived by the thousands at the Ghedi Airport near the city of Brescia in the Po Valley. The airport was the initial concentration point for all the German POWs captured by the 5th Army. There we had to pitch two-man tents in our assigned divisional area in a field where we suffered the 100-degree heat of the Italian summer, which apparently had arrived. The posting did give us the opportunity to visit Brescia, a good-sized town offering a mosaic of diverse elements—ancient ruins, medieval and Renaissance architecture, rich museums, and a modern city center built during Mussolini's rule.

We were only in the prisoner guard business for about five days when we received new orders which were more exciting and required us to travel some 200 miles to the far northeast corner of Italy. Marshal Tito, leader of the powerful Communist faction of the Yugoslav resistance forces, was threatening to seize the strategic port of Trieste and perhaps other Italian territory in that area that Italy had obtained following the collapse of the Austro-Hungarian empire at the end of World War I. New Zealand elements of the British 8th Army had accepted the surrender of the German garrison in Trieste on May 2, after the German commander had refused to capitulate to the Yugoslav partisans. General Clark thought that there was a need for a larger force in that sector than just the 8th Army, in case further friction developed.[3] Accordingly, the 10th Mountain was ordered to travel to the vicinity of Udine, a city some 40 miles northwest of Trieste, and there to prevent—by peaceful means if possible—any further westward movement of Tito's forces or civilians into Italian territory.

Upon our arrival by truck at 2:30 in the morning on May 21, we were required to establish a tent bivouac on the east bank of the Torre River in a very wet and muddy area. The weather didn't help because we were inundated by rain much of the time. Wally Krusell and I tried to build earthen dykes around our tent to keep the water out but without much luck. In no time everything was soaked, and we felt miserable.

Each regiment was now formed into a regimental combat team, including medical personnel, engineers, artillery, and tanks, which could take action if the situation evolved into open warfare. Our job was to send out patrols in our regimental zone of operations to determine not only the strength and disposition of any Yugoslavian forces present, but also the whereabouts of Italian partisan units and elements of the British 8th Army. We were armed, and we were told to be alert to any possible hostile acts, but great stress was placed on our exercising tact and diplomacy to avoid any possible conflict.

The role I was asked to play in this patrol activity turned out to be quite a bit of fun. My job was to accompany one or another officer in a jeep and, using French, or what limited Italian I had managed to pick up, to interpret for him in contacts with partisan groups in attempting to find out the location of any Yugoslav units. After a while we were also told to look out for disaffected Fascists and robber bands in the area who were taking advantage of the disturbed situation to hold up, and occasionally kill, travelers.

Almost every village and town had its own partisan force with accompanying uniforms of unique design and self-bestowed symbols of rank. I was always careful to identify the name of the unit, the name and rank of the commander, and whether they were operating independently or were associated with either the Christian Democrats (who typically wore green scarves) or with the Garibaldis (the forces associated with the Italian Communist party). Often I exaggerated the power and authority of the officer accompanying me and frequently told other lies, some of which were designed to impress them with my importance. I did not convey most of this, of course, to the officer I was serving.

The partisan commanders seemed to enjoy playing the game, appearing to view it as one not to be taken too seriously and no doubt lying about a variety of matters to us as well. Some claimed the rank of *Generale*, although their usual titles were either *Colonello* or *Maggiore*, and they greeted us with formal saluting and other demonstrations of military respect. All tried to impress us with their heroic achievements in battling the German occupiers and the important roles they were playing now.

Many of these partisans had unquestionably helped their own and the Allied cause with acts of bravery. While Field Marshal Kesselring viewed the war they had conducted as "a complete violation of international law" and one which "contradicted every principle of clean soldierly fighting," he admitted a member of his staff had told him that from June to August 1944 alone the partisans had killed some 5,000 of his soldiers and wounded or kidnapped 25,000-30,000 others.[4] So we had to accept the claims of those we met at face value. They had clearly helped enormously in the final weeks of the war to harass the retreating elements of the German army and pressure thousands of soldiers into surrendering.

The local people appeared somewhat cool but definitely favored Americans over the other foreign nationals with whom they had had to deal. They clearly did not want Tito there and, in general, wanted to be left alone, having grown sick and tired of armies and confusion. While performing my interpreter duties, I met a young woman from Grenoble, France, who indicated she would like to go to America. I joked that I was terribly wealthy, but she said all she wanted was plenty to eat, a home, and happiness. Not surprisingly, that appeared to be the universal sentiment of all the refugees in the area.

The Allies concern about Tito even led to another hardly believable assignment I was given. I was sent out in a jeep on my own to try and find, with the help of the local inhabitants, defensive positions used by the Italians in World War I against the Austrians and Germans—positions that might be serviceable with some reconditioning. This "detail" offered an unparalleled opportunity to sightsee and to wander as I saw fit. It was one of those rare moments granted by the army which only Jack Kelly could have fully appreciated, and I took advantage of it. On one occasion, after having driven far outside the territory in which I was supposed to operate and having just let off a young woman to whom I had graciously given a lift, I was appalled to be confronted, as I rounded the next curve, by none other than the commander of the 87th Mountain Infantry Regiment, Colonel David Fowler, in a jeep accompanied by a driver. Naturally he asked what brought me to this remote spot high up in the hills, and I explained the task I had been given but added that I had somehow gotten disoriented and wasn't sure where I was. To my great delight he said he too was lost, and after discussing the likely routes to where we wanted to go, we parted on very amicable terms. (Perhaps he was shirking his duties also, but if so, he had undoubtedly earned the right to do just that.)

As for the emplacements I was supposed to locate, the few I found were so eroded as to be barely distinguishable and didn't deserve serious consideration. Fortunately, the Yugoslav forces withdrew from our area shortly after our arrival, so we never really ran into any trouble from that quarter, although there were a few minor skirmishes between Tito's men and Italian partisan units. At the same time, an uneasy confrontation persisted for some months between the Western Allies and the Yugoslavs along the Isonzo River at the head of the Adriatic Sea and the port of Trieste.[5]

The appallingly wet and muddy conditions of our bivouac area finally penetrated the minds of our superiors (I had even taken to sleeping in a river bed), and we were moved to a better location in the Tricesimo area, still close to Udine, on May 28. Some were even lucky enough to get quarters in buildings, but I still had to bed down in a tent. On June 3 I went to a ski meet located on Mount Mangart in the Julian Alps, near the Austria-Yugoslavian border. It was the first held by the 10th since Camp Hale days. Hundreds of us nonparticipants were trucked to the contest, which was won by First Sergeant Walter Prager, former ski coach at Dartmouth College and a two-time winner of Europe's Alberg-Kandahar race. The *Blizzard* later reported that only 25 of the 76 entrants were able to stay upright across the finish line, all the contestants having lost their form during the months of infantry combat.[6]

When I and a few friends returned from the meet to our company area, we were greeted by a scene never equaled in my experience. Almost everyone present, having consumed incredible quantities of alcohol, was either stumbling around completely smashed or had already lapsed into unconsciousness. Some had passed out inside the villa used for the party, others outside on the grounds. A few local women of less than outstanding repute had also been invited, and it was evident that they were, or had been, having sex with some

Paul Williams' drawing of some of the wild doings at the F/85 party (courtesy Denver Public Library, Western History Department).

of our men. For someone coming in perfectly sober, it was very late to "join the party," and some of the performances taking place could well convince one never to imbibe again. (At one point even the outside latrine blew up, which added to the din and injured one seated soldier.) We had to choose one of two alternatives: either leave the scene entirely and wait for all to sleep it off or start drinking and try to catch up. I chose the latter, but limited the amount I consumed in order to better observe and later report on the antics of those around me.

As we waited for the other shoe to drop with regard to what was going to happen to us next, we were all trying to find some way to get a transfer out of what the army referred to as our "Military Occupational Specialities" (MOS), namely those of riflemen, machine gunners, or mortarmen in a rifle company. It was an effort similar to what I had undertaken at the University of Nebraska when the ASTP was being broken up, but now virtually everyone in the division (having had a taste of combat) was using whatever contacts he could exploit to find something less dangerous. Among the jobs with some permanency that I explored were becoming one of the division's historians, getting into a military unit which would stay as part of the European Army of Occupation, being reassigned to a military police (MP) outfit outside of the 10th, and getting hooked up with Colonel McSweeney, Mother's friend, who evidently occupied some noncombatant position of importance. Both my diary entries and letters home now included many references to my attempts to accomplish any of these objectives, as well as visits to nearby towns and other amusements. Among other things, the 5th Army invited us to compete in various athletic contests, including track and field events and tennis, and I took them up on it.

(Diary)
June 2—Entered in the tennis tournament. No practice yet. Made application for the Army of Occupation. Everyone seems to be going home these days. What a blow to morale.

June 8—Gallagher went to the MP's. Larry's [Boyajian] bucking for it. Limber [Krusell] is pulling his height gag again.*

Still going on motor patrols. Trieste question has been settled and UN Conference is about over. Future looks rather promising. Truman seems to be doing a good job. B-29's are really blasting Japan, and Chinese are doing all right in their drive.

June 12—Am acting platoon leader with Orwig in Milan for the track meet. Am feeling a little more at ease in my orientation lectures.† Led a heated discussion on post-war military training. Most men think six months is enough and don't think a large standing army will prevent another war.

June 13—Larry Boyajian left today for the MP's of 5th Army. "Mother" [Eyer], George, Armstrong, and I toasted him in "P.M." and gave him a send off though it was very hard to see him go. Terrible on morale to see these men go home and elsewhere. Jock [Platoon Sergeant Jacques] Billings has gone.

June 14—Tomorrow I'm platoon leader in a Battalion field exercise with the General looking on.

Pat maintains again she doesn't love me, but hopes to when I return. Beginning to regard the bachelor's life as best. I'm getting used to it.

Jim Orwig, my platoon sergeant, was competing in the track and field competition and George Norton, my machine gun section sergeant, was on leave in Rome for seven days, so I was temporarily in charge of the platoon. Many others were given short leaves to rest centers in Rome, Florence, Lake Como, Venice, Trieste, and elsewhere, one of our lieutenants even getting a seven-day TDY in Cannes, France. Regular training, however, had also resumed, involving squad and battalion attack problems, road marches, and runs. In addition, we were required to attend courses in such esoteric subjects as mine warfare and demolition, flame thrower operations, and even glacier training and rock climbing, this last at schools in Austria. As none too subtle hints about where we might be going next, we were given a variety of shots for unnamed diseases (ones we assumed would not threaten us in the United States), heard an orientation on "Jap Tactics," and were shown a movie entitled *On the Road to Tokyo.*

---

*Meaning he was trying to use his height, which exceeded army regulations, to obtain a discharge.
†The division had resumed its effort to teach the GIs about current events, and I was again tapped for this role.

(Letter)
Tricesimo
Sunday, June 17, 1945

The tenseness of the situation over here has been definitely alleviated. Tito has withdrawn, as you've probably read in the papers, and some of us are a little disappointed. As long as he stirred up trouble our chances of hanging around were good. Now there's nothing to keep us here.

My application for the Army of Occupation fell through. It never even got out of my regiment, for the regimental commander refused to pass it on, saying I was too essential for the outfit. What a farce that is. If I was wounded or killed a replacement would take my place in no time and then *he'd* be considered essential. And so the Army has knifed me in the back again.

Larry Boyajian, the best friend I have left in the company, left a couple of days ago for MP duty with the 5th Army. Probably up in Austria somewhere. That was a big disappointment for me because so many of my few close friends have either been killed or wounded and never came back, and Larry was the only fellow I could really talk to. He's a wonderful fellow and got a good break by leaving the division, for he'll never go to the Pacific now. He doesn't know how he got it, for it's one of those chances in a thousand that you sometimes win. Some clerk puts some names down and Larry happened to be one of them.

He and I had some amazing experiences together. Once on the first day of our last jumpoff from the Apennines we were lying on a rock ledge together. They were shelling us with huge 120 mm mortars. [Here followed the description of our run through a mine field, detailed in the Preamble above.] So it's things like that, memories and close companionship, that make it hard to see a friend leave.

I wrote to Col. McSweeney to see if he could get me into his work, but that's hopeless too I guess. My only prayer now is that we'll return to the States before heading to the Pacific, and that the war ends soon over there.

What was especially damaging to morale was to see some of your old friends getting discharges because they had accumulated enough points or leaving because they had managed to obtain some miracle job which would remove them from the front lines. Boyajian's transfer fell in the latter category. If you had to go into battle again some place halfway around the world, it would help enormously to have the men with whom you had shared much pain and suffering in the past still by your side. I was now a candidate for the relatively safe jobs of battalion or division historian, but was told by my old ASTP friend, Milletari, that Colonel Barlow was turning me down because of my sergeant stripes.

My partner, John George, and I managed to win three straight matches in the tennis tournament and ended up champions of the 85th Regiment. At this time I also received the Bronze Star at a Second Battalion parade. Colonel Barlow would periodically convene, for ceremonial purposes, formations of his entire 85th Regiment, or of one of his battalions, at which he would present decorations for actions performed in the battles just ended. This is how I received the actual medal and accompanying ribbon as a follow-up to the written order. I would have gladly traded the medal, however, for the relatively safe assignment of battalion or division historian, but *that* generous Barlow was not about to be. Evidently he preferred that I stay a machine gun squad leader.

(Letter)
Tricesimo
Monday, June 26, 1945

Quite a number of interesting things have happened to me this past week. As I wrote you, I've been playing competition tennis. Well, my doubles partner and I have won the regimental championship, and tomorrow start playing for the divisional title. If we win there we have a chance to go to Cairo, Casablanca, and Paris for further competition. Of course the chances are we'll never get that far, but who knows?

I had, or rather almost had, a job as divisional historian working at Division Headquarters, but they didn't give it to me because of my sergeant stripes. The job didn't call for that high a rating. Of course if I'd known about it I would have gladly turned in my stripes, but I never knew I was up for it until today.

Larry Boyajian, my good friend who was transferred in some inexplicable way to II Corps MP duty, writes that he's trying to get me into a very good deal there—the "Information and Education" section. He spoke to the personnel officer there and told him of my qualifications, and the officer said he'd try to contact me and was very interested.

I'm also intending to get into the university training program over here at a school near Florence. That last deal of course is only temporary for I'll be simply on detached service for six weeks. What I'm trying to do is get out of the division and the infantry. And that is a major accomplishment the way the Army loves experienced combat infantry men, especially non-commissioned officers, and also especially the 10th Mountain Division from which it is notoriously difficult to transfer.

The latest rumor, and it seems to be almost fact, is that the 10th Division will be here until around November, when we'll return to the good old U.S.A. to remain as "strategic reserve" until called for. So maybe I'll be home for Christmas.

The university training in Florence to which I referred was a so-called GI university offering some higher education, and quite a number of men from the 5th Army had managed to be selected to attend the school. Unfortunately, it developed that the quota in the 10th Mountain was only one per company, so the chances of my going were minimal. It also had the drawback that you did not leave your unit permanently, meaning you could be returned in the event of a major move or sudden crisis.

The following day, however, I was offered a definite way out of my dangerous assignment that forced me to make one of life's major decisions, one that in truth could have meant life or death if I made the wrong choice.

(Letter)
Tricesimo
Tuesday, June 27th, 1945

About 10 minutes ago I was offered an appointment to West Point.

Well, I turned it down, though I may rue the day many times hence. Those decisions are awfully hard to make. It may change the whole course of my life, but I never intended to head even temporarily towards a military career.

The big point in its favor is that it might save my life. Points against it are: being in the regular army for seven years, including the four at West Point (and no way to get out unless I intentionally flunked out); studying a course of life I despise every part of; and living that monastic, pseudo-disciplinary hell for four long years. Having been through numerous vicious battles, I don't think I could take that last point.

So for better or for worse I made my decision, and I hope I did the right thing. I'm rather proud of it being offered for I was the only one in my outfit able to fill all the qualifications, but ...

Guess that's all tonight.

The offer came about when someone rapped on my tent and said my company commander wanted to see me. So I presented myself to him and he brought the matter up immediately, noting among other things that I had the required Army General Classification Test (AGCT) scores that would qualify me for West Point. By this time, of course, others who might have had acceptable scores had either been killed or were unable to continue service because of wounds, so I probably had few competitors.

When I asked how much time I had before I had to give him my answer, he said 15 minutes. I returned to my tent and, needless to say, gave it some careful thought. While it was still not certain what the army was going to do with us, the odds appeared to favor our being sent to help invade Japan and that posed a terrible risk if I couldn't transfer out of my machine-gun squad-leader assignment. If I were given the choice again today, I think I would probably say yes and then, despite the negative effect it might have on my prospects for getting into the best schools and on my future résumé, find some way to drop out or be ejected either because of unsatisfactory academic performance or some violation of military regulations.

At that time, I was more inclined to take chances and was heavily influenced not only by my dislike of the army way of life, but by a somewhat irrational (though natural) desire to continue sharing the war's vicissitudes with the men with whom I had already shared so much. And so the answer I finally gave my company commander, as I wrote Mother and Dad, was no.

(Letter)
Tricesimo
Sunday, July 1, 1945

Some good news came in last night via the *Stars & Stripes* newspaper. It stated that we may be occupation troops in the Trieste area. Of course that's wonderful for it means we won't go to the Pacific for a while anyway, even though we won't be going back to the States either. But I'd rather forego that pleasure with the assurance that I will be coming home eventually, and I'm sure you all feel that way too.

I've got all the medals I want, and I've seen enough ghastly battles and death to last me a long time. In a way I'm glad I did see combat for I've got the true picture of what war is like aside from all the hullabaloo and glamor. What the real infantryman, the basic element of battle, has to do, and it's far from a pretty sight. I never felt personal hatred toward the Germans even in the height of battle. War is such a grandiose thing in this modern age that the individual is lost. It's so impersonal, machine vs. machine, that you never can associate the enemy soldier with your hatred. You hate the shells screaming overhead, you hate the bullets singing by your ears coming from an unseen force, but you see the enemy only as a distant spot, like a target on the rifle range. When you rush the positions in the final assault, you charge across the battered earth with shells bursting death all around, and if you reach the enemy positions alive he throws down his arms and pleads "Kamerad." And your only revenge or satisfaction is that you've taken that little bit of ground behind you, and here is a badly frightened human being in front of you whom you can't correlate with the awful dying comrades of yours a few hours before.

War has lost, at least in this theater, that man against man, spear against spear philosophy. It is just a vast holocaust of destruction, pitting complex machines against each other while through it all move the bewildered soldiers. Acts of heroism are still there, of course, but it's usually a case of braving bullets and shells rather than killing a number of the enemy with your bayonet in a personal way. I must have killed many men, but the one I shot with my pistol was the only one whose face I could see at the time of killing.

Enough of that. George and I lost in the doubles yesterday. We were beaten by the former Eastern Junior Champion of the U.S. and another rather good player. We may still go to Milan with the team, however.

After having been offered West Point, I was now invited to serve as the master of ceremonies at the rest camp in Trieste but decided not to accept, hoping I could get into the GI university training. Unfortunately, the quota was only one per company, and I was not selected.

In a local movie theatre, I saw atrocity pictures taken at the Buchenwald concentration camp. The Italians attending were greatly upset, one shouting "A morte Fascismo" ["Death to Fascism"].

(Letter)
Tricesimo
Wednesday, July 10th, 1945

Dear Paul,

We have a rather good chaplain in our regiment. I've heard quite a number of his sermons and they're all fine. He reminds me of the preacher at the 1st Presbyterian Church in Chapel Hill, N.C. This one feels the tragedy of war very deeply. On Mt. Belvedere he was crying a great deal as the broken bodies were brought back to the battalion aid station. And yet he had great courage and never seemed to understand why he couldn't give sermons right on the front lines.

July 11th—I went to a flame thrower school today. We studied the weapon and then saw it demonstrated. It certainly is a lethal weapon, but very heavy. It weighs about 72 lbs. and that's a very heavy load in combat. Impossible actually for any great length of time....

I see in the paper tonight that the Jap war is predicted to be over by the summer of '46. That's good timing if true. I've lost all hope though in predictions from any source. If the collapse of Japan proper means the end of resistance also in Manchuria and elsewhere, then I think next summer could mean the end—but otherwise not. Either way a lot of men will die taking Japan. They say the mountains there are as rough as Italy. Personally I'd prefer to sweat out the war from Trieste.

With the end of the war in Italy, the Brazilian government decided to invite 2 officers and 42 enlisted men of the 10th Mountain Division (along with 4 enlisted men from a signal detachment) who had fought alongside the BEF to represent the American army at ceremonies in Rio de Janeiro celebrating the occasion. One person from our Company F, Private First Class Charles O'Brien, a handsome fellow who had always amazed me with his ability to latch on to an attractive Italian female within minutes after entering a town, was selected and left on June 27 to make the trip, along with Generals Clark and Crittenberger.[7] At the ceremonies, held on July 27th and presided over by the Brazilian war minister, O'Brien and the others had their medals, which had been especially struck for the Brazilian veterans of the Italian campaign— pinned on by Brazilian officers, and they were declared "blood brothers of the BEF on the field of battle." According to the *New York Times* reporter describing the event, in the accompanying parade (which was delayed by frantic crowds fighting for the best viewing positions), "When the first unit appeared ... it was a moment for American hearts to skip a beat. Attired in combat dress and preceded by the Stars and Stripes, 42 picked men of the 10th Mountain Division came into view."[8] As for O'Brien, I can only assume he was as successful in finding affectionate and admiring women in Brazil as he was in Italy.

To insure that I would not forget a number of the men with whom I shared combat and life in Italy, I made some notes in my war diary at this time about the members of our weapons platoon. These give some idea of the diverse backgrounds represented in front-line infantry units (at least in the 10th Mountain Division) in World War II.

> There are three bartenders and a missionary in my squad. Our platoon is a cohesive group of strange personalities. It's traditionally the character platoon and has more old men left than any other. Practically all of them were wounded, but we only lost three dead. We have men from 18 to 36 with one B.A. in Psychology, one in Economics, one M.A. in Mechanical Engineering, and former students from Illinois, Chicago, Minnesota, and Stanford. Some of the others include a lieutenant who is a window dresser from Chicago, one Maine trapper, a bellboy, a Swedish merchant mariner, one newspaperman, etc. What a cross section.
>
> Two old men died on Belvedere. Giddix lost his arm, Staebell an elbow, and as you see the men in the showers, almost everyone bears a scar—some fearful looking. All have unlimited humor and live for each day.

On July 13 the terrible news came that we had all been dreading: we would be sent to the Pacific for the invasion of Japan and we would be converted to a regular infantry division. The only consolation was that we would get a furlough first and then some field training in how to handle the heavier weapons and increased motor transport before being shipped off to the Far East. Our route homeward would take us first to Florence, where the redeployment and staging area was located, and then to Naples, where we would board a troopship for the trip back to the United States.

We arrived in Florence late at night on July 14 and found our camp site, where we erected tents, was in a city park right across the street from where the GI university that I had hoped to attend was located. Here we were put to work cleaning our weapons, turning in our equipment, and making other preparations for the movement back to the U.S. And here I wrote the family a brief note announcing both the good and the bad news.

> *(Letter)*
> *Florence*
> *July 16th, 1945*
>   Probably you've read the papers about us. We're coming home, leaving here—the *Stars and Stripes* says—about August 15. I'll get a 21-day furlough upon arriving, and then we're supposed to have three months training as a regular infantry division in the States, following which we go overseas to the Pacific again.
>   It's very bad news but the prospect of coming home is wonderful. I hope Pat will be there, for I want to be with her too.
>   Keep your eye on the papers for our arrival.

The coincidence of our being located next to the GI university was further magnified when I made contact with Jack Kelly, who, it turned out, was enrolled there. (Larry Boyajian had also managed to get detached duty from his MP unit to attend the university.) Jack attempted to justify his failure to return to the division and account for some of the stories he had told, but his explanations were inadequate and I told him so. Nevertheless, despite the reputation he had earned in the company where he had previously been so popular, he could not resist the opportunity to come over and see some of his old friends and asked me to take him around for that purpose. I reluctantly agreed, warning him that his erstwhile buddies might not be very accommodating and suggested some of the things he might emphasize in any accounting he might offer for what had happened.

The reality turned out to be even worse than I had anticipated. One of the cooks, an old crony with whom he had always enjoyed exchanging humorous insults, when approached by Jack simply turned away, and virtually everyone else was equally hostile. Finally, when it became clear to him that the atmosphere was too cold to bear any longer, he left the company area and I said good-bye.

I also saw many other friends, such as John Horrall, whom I had not seen since arriving in Italy, and we exchanged tales of our adventures as well as gossip about our commanders. Some stories concerned General Hays. In essence they reported that while a heavy drinker, he was very aggressive (something we obviously knew) and a brilliant tactician. Not surprisingly, he was also said to play favorites, this being the supposed reason a Major Skinner had shot himself. The hottest rumor was that Hays was being sent straight to the Pacific and that the well-publicized Terry Allen, who had commanded the famous ("old Red One") 1st Infantry Division in Tunisia and Sicily, and later the 104th Infantry Division in France, was taking over the 10th. Major General Allen was another highly aggressive general who, in General Omar Bradley's view, gave his men too much free rein, but Bradley also admitted, "none excelled the unpredictable Terry Allen in the leadership of troops."[9]

I had no way of knowing whether there was any truth to these stories about General Hays. While it was obvious he was an impatient and daring leader in combat, and no doubt had favorite subordinates who shared his adventurous spirit, if he had alcohol problems they apparently didn't affect his success in planning and implementing actions which would bring the enemy to his knees. Moreover, if he had had any serious weaknesses, it is doubtful that he would have been selected by the top brass in the theater to lead the way in the attack across the Po Valley to the Alps, which he accomplished so successfully and for which he received such high praise. The respect he earned from General von Senger, his principal opponent in the final days of the war, which led to the German commander's request that his escort to the final surrender ceremony be General Hays, is also convincing evidence that he was one of the outstanding infantry generals of World War II.

Three days before we left Florence for Naples where we would sail for home, I wrote my last letter home, passing on some details of the trip back and trying to suggest some plans for the homecoming.

(Letter)
Florence
Thursday, July 19th, 1945
This is an important letter for it will be the last one from me before I see you again. Exciting thought isn't it? My big problem is how I can be with you all the time and Pat also. I don't have time to fix it up, so I hope you get in touch with her and figure out a method....

We'll dock at some port unknown to me, from where we'll be rushed to the nearest camp. From there I'll entrain immediately for a camp near home. Either Fort Sheridan near Chicago, or Benjamin Harrison in Pennsylvania. Within 24 hours I'll pull out of there on the last lap home. So it shouldn't take much over two days from the time I dock to the time I get home. I'll telegraph you when I arrive.

As to what I want to do, I really don't exactly know. Of course I want to see all the family, but I'm not running all over the country to do that. There is too little time and I intend on staying put for awhile anyway. I expect to be home from 21 to 30 days and then to report back to a camp for our supposed three months retraining.

Italian boxcars used to transport men of the 10th to Naples en route home (courtesy Denver Public Library, Western History Department).

At the moment I'm in the "Florence redeployment and staging area." Guess that's all from Italy. See you very soon.

Our trip to Naples down the center of Italy, by rail in an ancient Italian freight train, was an uncomfortable but surprisingly happy experience, despite the conditions of travel and the terrible scenes of wartime destruction through which we passed. It took approximately 34 hours, interrupted by numerous stops, to travel the distance of some 260 miles (as the crow flies) to our destination, and the heat traveling in the middle of July was terrific. But we were going home, and there was also a marvelous feeling of comradeship which stemmed from our common experiences; we laughed and shared memories throughout the trip. In a way it was reminiscent of journeys I had experienced with missionaries in Persia, with whom we shared similar warm feelings and often sang favorite songs and hymns along the way. That was done on this occasion too, and I recorded some of the details.

(Diary)
The ride to Naples just about climaxed my fantastic experiences. We rode in Italian box cars in 100 degree heat. 26 men in a car. Morale is fantastically high. Everyone looking forward to home.

We're riding through the old battlefields. Obviously rough fighting. The plain below Rome is still littered with tanks and shells and casings. Foxholes half-filled from erosion. Towns terribly battered, especially

Cisterna. People hungry and poverty stricken. Living in caves. To our right we can see Anzio and to our left, just out of sight, is Cassino.

Sang spirituals and hymns in the evening with our loved C.O., Lieutenant Mackin. Woman at one stop said she came from Brooklyn and swore that the last seven years here were hell. Every day, she said, she died a little more. Modin said he'd put her in his barracks bag.

Naples and the bay in the moonlight. We're now staying in an old university.

While waiting a week in Naples for our troopship to arrive and be prepared for our transport, I wandered many areas of the city, much of which was still in ruins, and I was greatly depressed by the hunger and poverty which caused extensive prostitution and countless young children to pimp for their sisters, mothers, or aunts. I was repeatedly approached by the inquiry, "*figi, figi, meester?* followed by assurances that the solicitor had a sister only 14 years old or some other inducement to follow him or her. One cute little girl explained that she had to sell trinkets because her father died in Germany and her mother was sick. Even Pompeii, we learned, was overrun with prostitutes.

We had been warned that anyone infected with a venereal disease would not be allowed to board ship, and whether true or not, the warning gave some of my companions real concern. Wally Krusell asked me one day to give his penis a close inspection to determine whether he might have the beginnings of something that might prevent his departure. Needless to say I had never had such an unusual request before, but not feeling I could refuse my old foxhole companion, I did a quick examination and found nothing, at least to my untrained eyes, to get disturbed about. After that inspection, I could understand why the fair ladies of Bagni di Lucca and other Italian towns used to giggle when he walked by.

One curious incident occurred while I was ambling about the city. I entered an alley with many badly damaged buildings and came upon a long line of GIs waiting their turn at a house whose women were offering sexual favors. As I walked along wondering how one could be enticed to wait in line for such an activity and then enjoy some woman who had just had sex with numerous others, I heard piano music. Somewhere in the surrounding devastation, someone was playing a piece of haunting beauty by Rachmaninoff. The whole experience seemed like a dream, but I finally found the source in a partially ruined building nearby, where a young Italian man was playing an undamaged grand piano. I watched and listened spellbound for a while, but did not intrude on his playing.

On July 30 the long-awaited word was given to board the ship for home. My diary took note of our departure and of some of the events which transpired during the voyage across the Atlantic.

(Diary)

July 31—Yesterday we rode down on trucks to the pier. The *Marine Fox* (like a Liberty ship) is taking the whole regiment. It's double loaded and I have to sleep on deck. What a madhouse it is. Terrifically crowded. Dining hall is like a boiler room. Slept in a raft last night.

August 3—Am reading everything I can get my hands on. Maugham book *The Summing Up* and Plato are what I'm concentrating on. Decker and I had a long philosophic exchange of ideas last night on everything from religion to free love. I've never been so avid for reading.

August 4—Lights on life jackets are a new addition. Have seen quite a few sharks, porpoises, and flying fish. Rained last night and had to rush below. Morale is very high.

August 7—Radio broke the news this morning of the atom bomb and its terrific destructive capacity. It looks like a real weapon. It raised morale even higher.

August 9—Today Russia entered the war vs. Japan and what a cheer went up on ship. It looks like it's about all over.

August 10—Pulling into New York harbor now. A little foggy. Here comes a boat covered with cheering women. There are "Welcome Home 10th Mountain" signs everywhere … "Welcome Yanks," etc. We have divisional and regimental banners all over us. Every ship in the harbor is blowing its horn. Ferries are cheering. What a madhouse. Press is all over the ship interviewing. There's the "lady with the lamp." A great thrill.

From boat to ship to shore. One woman slipped her little brown hand in mine and said, "Aren't you glad to be home?" and another said, "Welcome home, Yank."

Everyone excited over seeing cars running again and the people and the homes. What a difference from Europe.

The ship was indeed carrying twice the maximum number of passengers for which it was designed, a total of 3,149 men—all from the 85th Regiment.[10] Supposedly, when large numbers of the American troops in Europe were asked whether they would prefer to return with ships carrying their rated capacity, or double that amount—which would require trading off sleeping facilities (one man sleeping during the day and the other at night), the overwhelming vote was for double-loading.[11] And there is little doubt that if asked, we would have voted similarly. Nevertheless, the smells, together with the crowded sleeping conditions, drove me to the deck, and except when it rained, I spent all my nights sleeping in a lifeboat or raft. Fortunately, we had sunny weather most of the trip even though it was quite rough on occasion.

When the ship's radio broadcast the news of an atom bomb having been dropped on the city of Hiroshima at 8:15 A.M. on August 6, we recognized it to be an important event which some of us dared hope might save us from having to be sent to the Pacific to participate in the invasion of Japan. But initially we did not fully appreciate how powerful the bomb was, and we could not forget how many *"Tedeschi kaputt"* false stories we had been given before the hope in Italy turned into reality. Only 12 days earlier, at their Potsdam Conference (July 17–August 2, 1945), the Allied leaders had asked Japan for its unconditional surrender, but the demand had been refused two days before we sailed.*

We had read many accounts of how Japanese shipping had been virtually cut off, how our warships had been pounding their coastal cities, and how B-29's were carrying out terrible fire raids on their metropolitan centers. Historians Thomas Allen and Norman Polmar provide heart-stopping data in *Code-Name Downfall*, their recently published account of plans to invade Japan. They tell us that the first incendiary raid (against Tokyo on March 9, 1945) burned out 15.8 square miles of city, killed almost 84,000 persons, and left more than 1,000,000 people homeless. Before the raids ended, they destroyed about 40 percent of Japan's major metropolitan areas.[12]

Yet the Japanese continued their defiance, as demonstrated by the horrors they had inflicted on the American troops attacking Iwo Jima and Okinawa. The struggle to take Okinawa cost us over 49,000 casualties, with 34 warships sunk and 368 damaged. We could easily foresee far greater losses in the invasion.[13] All of this made us dubious about the impact the new bomb would have on the Japanese.

The War Department had planned to invade Japan itself, beginning in November of 1945 with the island of Kyushu. The invasion, code-named Operation Olympic, was to be followed in March 1946 with Operation Coronet, an assault on the Tokyo plain of Honshu, the principal home island. Before the atomic bombs were dropped, Washington was not convinced the Japanese were anywhere near surrender. On Okinawa, where they had fought almost to the last man, their military and civilian deaths exceeded the combined losses to come at Hiroshima and Nagasaki.[14]

Admiral Suzuki, who became Japan's premier following our invasion of Okinawa, told his people that Japan had "to fight to the last," and the War Guidance Council, "To underscore its resolve, ... approved a resolution, in Hirohito's presence, calling for 'supreme self-sacrifice' and 'the honorable death of a hundred million.'"[15]

Operation Coronet, the Honshu invasion, would employ troops from Europe, presumably including the 10th Mountain Division. The official Joint Chiefs of Staff history called it "this much dreaded operation," with good reason. Heavy shark-infested seas characterized the planned landing sites. According to Allen and Polmar, those scientists who studied the relevant beaches concluded that except on those rare occasions when there was very low surf, "an attempt to land on the beaches of Honshu would have been an amphibious disaster."[16]

In the hope of inflicting unacceptable losses of American lives in both

*Despite this refusal President Truman delayed using the bomb until August 6, hoping for a change in the Japanese position. It did not come.

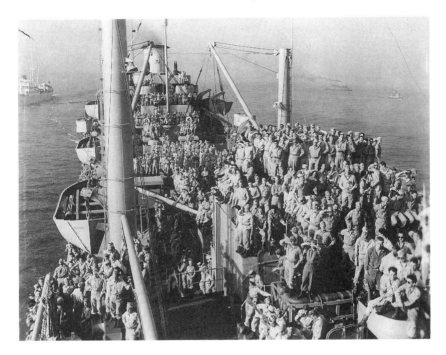

Author's 85th Regiment arriving in New York harbor, August 10, 1945 (courtesy National Archives).

island invasions, the Japanese anticipated having by early fall some 10,500 planes, hidden on scattered airfields and in caves, prepared for kamikaze action. The Japanese army had assembled some 560,000 troops on Kyushu by early August 1945, while the Japanese navy planned to have available over a thousand midget submarines. The navy was training hundreds of pilots for manned torpedo suicide missions and hoped to have 4,000 frogmen ready to operate as human mines by swimming out with explosives to contact landing craft.[17] Pentagon planners agreed it would be the bloodiest invasion in history, General Marshall estimating in response to President Truman's request that the casualties might reach 1,000,000 on the American side alone.[18]

Without the effective threat, if not the actual use of the atomic bomb, we were facing a potential blood bath. But when Russia declared war on Japan on August 8 and when the second atomic bomb was dropped on Nagasaki on August 9 before we landed, it did appear that a miracle had occurred and we would be spared the terrible loss of life we had anticipated as necessary to overcome the Japanese. Now it all seemed to be over. The day we thought at times would never come had come at last. Not only were we probably home for good, but we hoped we would soon would be out of the army and taste the freedom of civilian life again. While, as I noted, a great cheer went up aboard our ship, we experienced less a feeling of great exhilaration than one of deliverance or immense relief. The passage of the years would eventually diminish the horrors we had witnessed and even delude us at times into thinking it was an adventure not to have been missed, but none of us would ever be able to suppress the memory of our dead companions lying on the ravaged hills and roadsides of Italy. They could not share this day.

Given our state of euphoria, it is not surprising we didn't think about the long-term consequences of the atomic bomb. (President Truman, describing it on the day it was dropped, called it, "The force from which the sun draws its power,"[19] while the physicist Harold Urey said, "We need first of all to be thoroughly frightened."[20]) Our thoughts and memories were principally of the Italian campaign, however, and the losses we had borne. Commenting on the entire Italian undertaking, the *New York Times* editorialized: "Some day we will see [it] in its true perspective.... It has been a terrible front, the only one in this war where we had to claw our way rock by rock across an almost endless array of precipitous peaks."[21]

The casualties the Italian conflict had inflicted on our company were evidence of the price that was paid. Only one of our Company F officers who went over on the USS *West Point*—Lieutenant Wayne Mackin—came back with us on the *Marine Fox*.[22] Between January 8, when the 86th Regiment first went up to the front, and May 2 when the Germans broadcast their order to cease fire, a period of 114 days of combat, the 10th Mountain Division had 992 men killed and 4,154 wounded.*[23]

No other divisions in Italy sacrificed so many in so few months of battle. Even the highest ranking officers paid the price in unusual numbers. Both assistant division commanders (General Duff and Colonel Darby) were casualties, one being wounded, the other killed; two out of our three regimental commanders were wounded, with one replacement being wounded as well; and five of our nine battalion commanders were either wounded or killed, including one replacement. In short, 11 occupants of the 14 top infantry positions of command in the division—not to mention officer casualties experienced at the company and platoon levels—were killed or wounded during our time of slightly under four months fighting in Italy.

Naturally we took great pride in our accomplishments. In evaluating the Italian campaign, the last volume of the official history published by the Center of Military History of the U.S. Army concluded that one of the few tactical innovations developed during the campaign was the "ingenuity [shown] by the Fifth Army's employment of mountain troops to move across rugged terrain so rapidly as to confound the Germans, who did not expect such an Allied move."[24] The German commander, Generalleutnant von Senger, who signed the surrender documents for his country and who had experienced combat on three fronts, wrote in his diaries, "The 10th Mountain Division had been my most dangerous opponent in the past fighting."[25] British Field

*In actual fact, eight of those killed and four wounded were casualties preceding our engagement with the enemy, having occurred on January 6 from mines in a training area near the front.[26]

Marshal Alexander, his principal opponent, reacted similarly: "The only trouble with the 10th Mountain Division," he said, "was that the officers and men did not realize that they were attempting something which couldn't be done, and after they got started they had too much intestinal fortitude to quit. The result was that they accomplished the impossible."[27]

I only knew that the war was over. I had just turned twenty-one and had spent two years and four months in the uniform of the United States Army learning not only why freedom is to be cherished, but also to appreciate what Ernie Pyle called "the powerful fraternalism in the ghastly brotherhood of war."[28] Soon I would be my own master again, and that cherished freedom could not come swiftly enough.

Notes

Preamble. A Rendezvous with Death

1. Lawrence Boyajian, letter to author, 25 October 1992.

Chapter 1. From a Middle East Inferno to World War II

1. St. Clair McKelway, "The Presbyterian Pyramid System," *New Yorker*, 9 August 1952.
2. Peter Schwab, *Haile Selassie I: Ethiopia's Lion of Judah* (Chicago: Nelson-Hall, 1979), 165–72.
3. Frank Harper, *Military Ski Manual: A Handbook for Ski and Mountain Troops* (Harrisburg, Pa.: Military Service Publishing, 1943), 15.

Chapter 2. Ninety Pounds of Rucksack

1. Richard Thruelsen, "The 10th Caught It All at Once," *Saturday Evening Post*, 8 December 1945.
2. Rene L. Coquoz, *The Invisible Men on Skis: The Story of the Construction of Camp Hale and the Occupation by the 10th Mountain Division 1942–1945* (Boulder, Colo.: Johnson, 1970), 15.
3. Frank Harper, *Night Climb: The Story of the Skiing 10th* (New York: Longmans, Green, 1946), 126.
4. *Denver Post*, 6 April 1943.
5. Harper, *Night Climb*, 126.
6. William Johnson, "Phantoms of the Snow," *Sports Illustrated*, 8 February 1971.
7. *Denver Post*, 6 April 1943.
8. Louis E. Keefer, *Scholars in Foxholes: The Story of the Army Specialized Training Program in World War II* (Jefferson, N.C.: McFarland, 1988), 54, referencing a quote in Henry C. Herge, *Wartime College Training Programs of the Armed Services* (Washington, D.C.: American Council on Education, 1948), 27.
9. Ian V. Hogg, ed., *Jane's Infantry Weapons 1984–85* (New York: Jane's Publishing, 1984), 230–31.
10. Johnson, "Phantoms of the Snow,"; *Sports Illustrated*; Hal Burton, *The Ski Troops* (New York: Simon & Schuster, 1971), 136.

11. *Steamboat Pilot*, 11 February 1943.
12. Burton, *Ski Troops*, 122.
13. Nat Fleischer and Sam Andre, *A Pictorial History of Boxing* (Secaucus, N.J.: Citadel, 1987), 130–35.
14. Keefer, *Scholars in Foxholes*, 49–50.
15. Thruelsen, "The 10th Caught It All at Once," *Saturday Evening Post*.
16. *Combat Divisions of World War II* (Washington, D.C.: Army Times, 1946), 13.
17. Johnson, "Phantoms of the Snow," *Sports Illustrated*.
18. Shelby L. Stanton, *Order of Battle, U.S. Army, World War II* (Novato, Calif.: Presidio, 1984), 12, 93.
19. Curtis W. Casewit, *Mountain Troopers! The Story of the Tenth Mountain Division* (New York: Crowell, 1972), 20.
20. Johnson, "Phantoms of the Snow," *Sports Illustrated*.
21. E. J. Kahn, Jr., "The Philologist," *New Yorker*, March 11–April 1, 1950.
22. War Department, *Mountain Operations*, FM 70-10 (Washington, D.C.: USGPO, 1944), 198.

Chapter 3. Off to Heaven and Back to Hale

1. Louis E. Keefer, *Scholars in Foxholes : The Story of the Army Specialized Training Program in World War II* (Jefferson, N.C.: McFarland, 1988), 56.
2. Godfrey Ettlinger, letter to author, 28 December 1986.
3. Keefer, *Scholars in Foxholes*, 57.
4. Ibid., 92.
5. Ibid., 161.
6. Ettlinger, letter to author.
7. Keefer, *Scholars in Foxholes*, 117.
8. Henry L. Stimson and McGeorge Bundy, *On Active Duty in Peace and War* (New York: Harper & Brothers, 1948), 459.
9. Roger A. Beaumont, *Military Elites* (Indianapolis: Bobbs-Merrill, 1974), 179.
10. S. L. A. Marshall, *Men Against Fire* (New York: William Morrow, 1947), 15–17.
11. Keefer, *Scholars in Foxholes*, 221.
12. Charles Moritz, ed., *Current Biography Yearbook 1965* (New York: H. W. Wilson, 1965), 432.
13. Stimson and Bundy, *On Active Duty*, 459.
14. *Washington Post*, 1 March 1944, quoted in Keefer, *Scholars in Foxholes*, 180.
15. Keefer, *Scholars in Foxholes*, 271.
16. *Seattle Times*, 7 November 1993.
17. Frank Harper, *Night Climb: The Story of the Skiing 10th* (New York: Longmans, Green, 1946), 160.
18. Curtis W. Casewit, *Mountain Troopers! The Story of the Tenth Mountain Division* (New York: Crowell, 1972), 29.
19. Robert B. Ellis, scrapbooks.
20. Beaumont, *Military Elites*, 177.

Chapter 4. Poison Ivy and Cockroaches

1. Roger A. Beaumont, *Military Elites* (Indianapolis: Bobbs-Merrill, 1974), 183.
2. William Johnson, "Phantoms of the Snow," *Sports Ilustrated*, 8 February 1971.
3. Shelby L. Stanton, *Order of Battle, U.S. Army, World War II* (Novato, Calif.: Presidio, 1984), 10.

4. U.S. Senate Committee on Veterans' Affairs, *Medal of Honor Recipients 1863–1973* (Washington, D.C.: USGPO, 1973), 446; and Laurence Stallings, *The Doughboys: The Story of the AEF, 1917–1918* (New York: Harper & Row, 1963), 133.

5. Robert B. Ellis, scrapbooks; Curtis W. Casewit, *Mountain Troopers! The Story of the Tenth Mountain Division* (New York: Crowell, 1972), 38.

6. Richard Thruelsen, "The 10th Caught It All at Once," *Saturday Evening Post*, 8 December 1945.

Chapter 5. See Naples and Die

1. Alan Seeger, "I Have a Rendezvous with Death," in *The Best Loved Poems of the American People*, ed., Hazel Felleman (New York: Doubleday, 1936), 423.

2. M. R. Montgomery and Gerald L. Foster, *A Field Guide to Airplanes of North America* (Boston: Houghton Mifflin, 1984), 88.

3. Capt. John B. Woodruff, *85th Mountain Infantry Regimental History, 4 January–30 May 1945* (November 1945), A, 1. Woodruff was the regimental historian. This unpublished history, discovered in the National Archives in Suitland, Maryland was compiled by him in November 1945 from morning and battle reports and interviews with various soldiers. The history is divided into four separately dated parts and paginated within each part. I have arbitrarily designated these parts as follows: A (4 January–28 February 1945), B (1–31 March 1945), C (1–30 April 1945), and D (1–30 May 1945).

4. Ernest F. Fisher, Jr., *United States Army in World War II: The Mediterranean Theater of Operations; Cassino to the Alps* (Washington, D.C.: Center of Military History, U.S. Army, 1977), 417.

5. Woodruff, *85th Mountain Infantry*, A, 1.

6. *The Hachette Guide to Italy* (New York: Pantheon, 1988), 723.

7. Fisher, *Cassino to the Alps*, 231.

8. Ibid., 6.

9. Ibid., 536.

10. Ian V. Hogg, ed., *Jane's Infantry Weapons 1984–85* (New York: Jane's Publishing, 1984), 343.

11. *Hachette Guide*, 698.

12. *F Company Morning Reports, 85th Mountain Infantry Regiment, 1 July 1944–31 November 1945*, 16 February 1945. These unpublished, highly abbreviated daily reports concerning personnel and company activities and movements were prepared under the direction of the company's first sergeant.

Chapter 6. The Bastards Blew My Arm Off

1. Flint Whitlock and Bob Bishop, *Soldiers on Skis: A Pictorial Memoir of the 10th Mountain Division* (Boulder, Colo.: Paladin, 1992), 54.

2. Curtis W. Casewit, *Mountain Troopers! The Story of the Tenth Mountain Division* (New York: Crowell, 1972), 130.

3. Ernest F. Fisher, Jr., *United States Army in World War II: The Mediterranean Theater of Operations; Cassino to the Alps* (Washington, D.C.: Center of Military History, U.S. Army, 1977), 425–26.

4. Richard Thruelsen, "The 10th Caught It All at Once," *Saturday Evening Post*, 8 December 1945.

5. Albert Kesselring, *The Memoirs of Field-Marshal Kesselring* (Novato, Calif.: Presidio, 1989), 213.

6. Ibid.

7. Fisher, *Cassino to the Alps*, 428.

8. *Combat History of the 10th Mountain Division, 1944–1945*, 14–15. Author unknown. This history was found by Lt. James Hauptman in 1969 in the files of the Infantry School Library, Ft. Benning, Georgia, and was privately printed by his father, Charles M. Hauptman, in 1977.

9. *F Company Morning Reports, 85th Mountain Infantry Regiment*, 19 February 1945.

10. Thruelsen, "The 10th Caught It All at Once," *Saturday Evening Post*.

11. *Combat History of the 10th*, 18.

12. Capt. John B. Woodruff, *85th Mountain Infantry Regimental History, 4 January–30 May 1945* (November 1945), A, 10a.

13. Ibid., 12.

14. Thomas Parrish, ed., *The Simon & Schuster Encyclopedia of World War II* (New York: Simon & Schuster, 1978), 430.

15. Omar N. Bradley, *A Soldier's Story* (New York: Henry Holt, 1951), 41.

16. Bernard Fitzsimons, ed., *The Illustrated Encyclopedia of 20th Century Weapons and Warfare* (New York: Columbia House, 1971), 218.

17. Bradley, *Soldier's Story*, 322.

18. Paul Fussell, "The Real War 1939–1945," *Atlantic Monthly* (August 1989).

19. Fitzsimons, *20th Century Weapons*, 218.

20. James P. Orwig, combat notebook, 18 February–3 March 1945.

21. Ian V. Hogg, ed., *Jane's Infantry Weapons 1984-85* (New York: Jane's Publishing, 1984), 232.

22. Woodruff, *85th Mountain Infantry*, A, 14.

23. Woodruff, *85th Mountain Infantry* , A, 15; and *Combat History of the 10th*, 20.

24. Orwig, combat notebook.

25. Woodruff, *85th Mountain Infantry*, A, 17.

26. Orwig, combat notebook.

27. Woodruff, *85th Mountain Infantry*, A, 17.

28. *Combat History of the 10th*, 21.

29. Woodruff, *85th Mountain Infantry*, A, 18.

30. Ernest Hemingway, *Men at War: The Best War Stories of All Time* (New York: Crown, 1942).

31. Ernie Pyle, *Brave Men* (New York: Henry Holt, 1944), 149.

32. Woodruff, *85th Mountain Infantry*, A, 19.

33. S. L. A. Marshall, *Men Against Fire* (New York: William Morrow, 1947), 60–61.

34. Woodruff, *85th Mountain Infantry*, A, 20; and *Combat History of the 10th*, 22.

35. *F Company Morning Reports, 85th Mountain Infantry Regiment*, 23 February 1945. These unpublished, highly abbreviated daily reports concerning personnel and company activities and movements were prepared under the direction of the company's first sergeant.

36. Orwig, combat notebook.

37. Lawrence Boyajian, letter to author, 20 December 1993.

38. Laverne R. Staebell, letter to author, 17 September 1988.

39. Staebell, letter to author, 10 November 1993.

40. Albert H. Meinke, Jr., M.D., *Mountain Troops and Medics: Wartime Stories of a Frontline Surgeon in the U.S. Ski Troops* (Kewadin, Mich.: Rucksack, 1993), 182.

41. Whitlock and Bishop, *Soldiers on Skis*, 102.

42. Woodruff, *85th Mountain Infantry*, A, 20a; Fisher, *Cassino to the Alps*, 432; and *Combat History of the 10th*, 23–24.

43. Fisher, *Cassino to the Alps*, 432.

44. Roger A. Beaumont, *Military Elites* (Indianapolis: Bobbs-Merrill, 1974), 177.

45. S. L. A. Marshall, *Pork Chop Hill: The American Fighting Man in Action, Korea, Spring, 1953* (New York: William Morrow, 1956), 249.

46. *F Company Morning Reports*, 24 February 1945.

47. Woodruff, *85th Mountain Infantry*, A, 24.

48. *Combat History of the 10th*, 24.

49. *A Short History of the 85th Mountain Regiment* (November 1945), 22; and Woodruff, *85th Mountain Infantry*, A, 24. The 60-page *Short History*, with a foreword by Maj. Gen. George Hays dated 23 November 1945, was reprinted in 1989 by Curry Printing, Falls Church, Virginia. The author is unknown.

50. *Combat History of the 10th*, 26.

51. Orwig, combat notebook.

52. Erich Maria Remarque, *All Quiet on the Western Front* (New York: Fawcett Crest, 1987), 281.

53. Ibid.

54. Woodruff, *85th Mountain Infantry*, B, 6.

55. Fussell, "The Real War," *Atlantic Monthly*.

56. Farley Mowatt, *My Father's Son: Memories of War and Peace* (New York: Houghton Mifflin, 1992), 19.

57. Ibid., 124.

58. Ellis, scrapbooks.

Chapter 7. A Rat Walked Over My Face

1. Capt. John B. Woodruff, *85th Mountain Infantry, Regimental History, 4 January–30 May 1945* (November 1945), B, 2; and Ernest F. Fisher, Jr., *United States Army in World War II: The Mediterranean Theater of Operations; Cassino to the Alps* (Washington, D.C.: Center of Military History, U.S. Army, 1977), 433.

2. Woodruff, *85th Mountain Infantry*, B, 5–7; Fisher, *Cassino to the Alps*, 433; and *Combat History of the 10th Mountain Division, 1944–1945*, 33. Author unknown.

3. Ian V. Hogg, ed. *Jane's Infantry Weapons, 1984–85* (New York: Jane's Publishing, 1984), 268–69, 343.

4. S. L. A. Marshall, *Men Against Fire* (New York: William Morrow, 1947), 183.

5. *New York Times*, 17 March 1945.

6. Hal Burton, *The Ski Troops* (New York: Simon and Schuster, 1971), 164–65.

7. Fisher, *Cassino to the Alps*, 433.

8. Woodruff, *85th Mountain Infantry*, B, 10.

9. *A Short History of the 85th Mountain Regiment* (November 1945), 32.

10. Fisher, *Cassino to the Alps*, 434.

11. Robert B. Ellis, scrapbooks.

12. Albert Kesselring, *The Memoirs of Field-Marshall Kesselring* (Novato, Calif.: Presidio, 1989).

13. Chester G. Starr, ed., *From Salerno to the Alps: A History of the Fifth Army, 1943–1945* (Washington, D.C.: Infantry Journal Press, 1948), 380–84.

14. Ellis, scrapbooks.

15. Kesselring, *Memoirs*, 216.

16. Roger A. Beaumont, *Military Elites* (Indianapolis: Bobbs-Merrill, 1974), 12.

17. Donald Chrisler, letter to author, 5 February 1994.

18. Woodruff, *85th Mountain Infantry*, B, 24.

19. Ibid., B, 25.

20. Woodruff, *85th Mountain Infantry*, B, 32–33; and *Combat History of the 10th*, 35.

21. Ernie Pyle, *Brave Men* (New York: Henry Holt, 1944), 270.

22. Alta Macadam, *Blue Guide to Rome and Environs* (New York: W.W. Norton, 1989), 278.

23. Pyle, *Brave Men*, 102.

24. John Bartlett, *Familiar Quotations* (Boston: Little, Brown, 1955), 839.

25. Beaumont, *Military Elites*, 13.

26. Paul Fussell, "The Real War 1939–1945," *Atlantic Monthly* (August 1989).

27. Woodruff, *85th Mountain Infantry*, B, 29.

28. Ibid., B, 31.

29. *F-Company Morning Reports, 85th Mountain Infantry Regiment*, 13 March 1945, 15 April 1945.

30. Marshall, *Men Against Fire*, 38, 42, 153.

31. *Time*, 19 March 1945.

32. Kesselring, *Memoirs*, 222.

33. Woodruff, *85th Mountain Infantry*, C, 4.

Chapter 8. Packs On

1. Ernest F. Fisher, Jr., *United States Army in World War II: The Mediterranean Theater of Operations; Cassino to the Alps* (Washington, D.C.: Center of Military History, U.S. Army, 1977), 460; and *Time*, 26 March 1945.

2. Wendell Willkie, *An American Program* (New York: Simon and Schuster, 1944), 7.

3. Fisher, *Cassino to the Alps*, 456.

4. Robert B. Ellis, scrapbooks.

5. George Barrett, "The Jump Off," *Yank* (in Ellis, scrapbooks).

6. Capt. John B. Woodruff, *85th Mountain Infantry, Regimental History, 4 January–30 May 1945* (November 1945), C, 10–15.

7. *F Company Morning Reports, 85th Mountain Infantry Regiment, 1 July 1944–31 November 1945*, 14 April 1945.

8. *A Short History of the 85th Mountain Regiment* (November 1945), 37. Author unknown.

9. Fisher, *Cassino to the Alps*, 472.

10. Woodruff, *85th Mountain Infantry*, C, 12.

11. Richard Ben Cramer, *What It Takes: The Way to the White House* (New York: Random House, 1992), 102–5.

12. Ibid., 108.

13. Woodruff, *85th Mountain Infantry*, C, 12.

14. *Short History of the 85th*, 40.

15. *E Company Morning Reports, 85th Mountain Infantry Regiment*, 14 April 1945. Obtained from Wallace J. Huston, Jr.

16. *Medal of Honor Recipients 1863–1973*, 617; Hal Burton, *The Ski Troops* (New York: Simon and Schuster, 1971), 170–71; Flint Whitlock and Bob Bishop, *Soldiers on Skis: A Pictorial Memoir of the 10th Mountain Division* (Boulder, Colo.: Paladin, 1992), 136–37; and Katherine Halversen, enclosure in letter to author, 29 January 1995.

17. Fisher, *Cassino to the Alps*, 473–74.

18. Woodruff, *85th Mountain Infantry*, C, 19.

19. Ibid., C, 21.

20. *Short History of the 85th*, 45.

21. *F Company Morning Reports*, 15 April 1945, 19 April 1945.
22. Thomas R. Brooks, letter to *Blizzard* (newsletter of the National Association of the 10th Mountain Division), 4th Quarter, 1993, 13.
23. *F Company Morning Reports*, 19 April 1945.
24. Chester G. Starr, ed., *From Salerno to the Alps: A History of the Fifth Army 1943–1945* (Washington, D.C.: Infantry Journal Press, 1948), 406.
25. Fisher, *Cassino to the Alps*, 476–77.
26. Burton, *Ski Troops*, 171.
27. Fisher, *Cassino to the Alps*, 480–81.
28. Woodruff, *85th Mountain Infantry*, C, 36.
29. Fisher, *Cassino to the Alps*, 476.
30. Starr, *From Salerno to the Alps*, 407.
31. Woodruff, *85th Mountain Infantry*, C, 37.

Chapter 9. I've Never Seen Such a Madhouse

1. Ernest F. Fisher, Jr., *United States Army in World War II: The Mediterranean Theater of Operations; Cassino to the Alps* (Washington, D.C.: Center of Military History, U.S. Army, 1977), 479.
2. Ibid., 483.
3. Robert B. Ellis, scrapbooks.
4. *Combat History of the 10th Mountain Division, 1944–1945*, 58. Author unknown.
5. Fisher, *Cassino to the Alps*, 483.
6. *Combat History of the 10th*, 59.
7. Captain John B. Woodruff, *85th Mountain Infantry Regimental History, 4 January–30 May 1945* (November 1945), C, 45.
8. *Combat History of the 10th*, 59; Hal Burton, *The Ski Troops* (New York: Simon & Schuster, 1971), 176.
9. Woodruff, *85th Mountain Infantry*, C, 46–47.
10. Fisher, *Cassino to the Alps*, 489. The 100-yard figure is taken from a *New York Times* story by Milton Bracker headlined "April 24, 1945, With the Fifth Army Across the Po River." An AP dispatch datelined Rome, April 25, 1945, stated, however, that "The 10th's crossing was made where the river is 200 yards wide."
11. *Combat History of the 10th*, 60; and Ellis, scrapbooks. The number of people manning the boats is also taken from the *New York Times* story by Bracker, although the *Combat History of the 10th* claims the boats held twelve infantrymen as well as three engineers.
12. Burton, *Ski Troops*, 177.
13. Woodruff, *85th Mountain Infantry*, C, 49; and *Combat History of the 10th*, 60–61.
14. *New York Times*, 26 April 1945.
15. Woodruff, *85th Mountain Infantry*, C, 50.
16. Burton, *Ski Troops*, 178.
17. *Combat History of the 10th*, 62–63; Fisher, *Cassino to the Alps*, 501; and Woodruff, *85th Mountain Infantry*, C, 53.
18. Fisher, *Cassino to the Alps*, 500; and Roger A. Beaumont, *Military Elites* (Indianapolis: Bobbs-Merrill, 1974), 50.
19. Allen Dulles, *The Secret Surrender* (New York: Harper & Row, 1966), 239.
20. Trevor N. Pupuy and Molly R. Mayo, *The Military History of World War I: Campaigns in Southern Europe* (New York: Franklin Watts, 1967), 51.

21. Albert H. Meinke, Jr., *Mountain Troops and Medics: Wartime Stories of a Front-line Surgeon in the U.S. Ski Troops* (Kewadin, Mich.: Rucksack, 1993), 270–71.

22. *Combat History of the 10th*, 68; and Fisher, *Cassino to the Alps*, 510.

23. *The Hachette Guide to Italy* (New York: Pantheon, 1988), 802.

24. Franca Piazza, ed., *From Lake Garda to Sicily with Goethe* (New York: W.W. Norton, 1961), 9–11.

25. Fisher, *Cassino to the Alps*, 512.

26. Curtis W. Casewit, *Mountain Troopers! The Story of the Tenth Mountain Division* (New York: Crowell, 1972), 119.

27. Dulles, *Secret Surrender*, 254.

Chapter 10. We Who Are Left

1. Ernest F. Fisher, Jr., *United States Army in World War II: The Mediterranean Theater of Operations; Cassino to the Alps* (Washington, D.C.: Center of Military History, U.S. Army, 1977), 529–30.

2. Allen Dulles, *The Secret Surrender* (New York: Harper & Row, 1966), 246–47.

3. Fisher, *Cassino to the Alps*, 511.

4. Albert Kesselring, *The Memoirs of Field Marshal Kesselring* (Novato, Calif.: Presidio, 1989), 227.

5. *Combat History of the 10th Mountain Division, 1944–1945*, 76; and Captain John B. Woodruff, *85th Mountain Infantry Regimental History, 4 January–30 May 1945* (November 1945), C, 15–19.

6. *Blizzard* (Newsletter of the National Association of the 10th Mountain Division), 10 June 1945.

7. *F Company Morning Reports, 85th Mountain Infantry Regiment, 2 July 1944–31 November 1945*, 2 July 1945.

8. *New York Times*, 28 July 1945.

9. Omar N. Bradley, *A Soldier's Story* (New York: Henry Holt, 1951), 100.

10. Robert B. Ellis, scrapbooks.

11. Dwight D. Eisenhower, *Crusade in Europe* (Garden City, N.Y.: Doubleday, 1948), 422.

12. Thomas B. Allen and Norman Polmar, *Code-Name Downfall: The Secret Plan to Invade Japan—and Why Truman Dropped the Bomb* (New York: Simon & Schuster, 1995), 86–89.

13. Allen and Polmar, *Code-Name Downfall*, 110; and *New Encyclopaedia Brittanica*, 1993, s.v. "World Wars," 1024.

14. *Washington Post*, 15 April 1995, A 14.

15. Stanley Weintraub, *The Last Great Victory: The End of World War II, July/August 1945* (New York: Truman Talley/Dutton, 1995), 54.

16. Allen and Polmar, *Code-Name Downfall*, 244.

17. Ibid., 226–38.

18. Allen and Polmar, *Code-Name Downfall*, 266; and Roger A. Beaumont, *Military Elites* (Indianapolis: Bobbs-Merrill, 1974), 169.

19. *New York Times*, 7 August 1945.

20. Harold C. Urey, *Speech on the Atomic Bomb*, 3 December 1945.

21. *New York Times*, 23 April 1945.

22. Introduction to *F Company Morning Reports*.

23. Hal Burton, *The Ski Troops* (New York: Simon & Schuster, 1971), 183.

24. Fisher, *Cassino to the Alps*, 543.

25. General Frido Von Senger Und Etterlin, *Neither Fear Nor Hope* (Novato, Calif.: Presidio, 1989), 307.

26. *Combat History of the 10th*, 3.

27. William Johnson, "Phantoms of the Snow," *Sports Illustrated*, 8 February 1971.

28. Quoted by Studs Terkel, in Foreword, xii, to David Nichols, ed., *Ernie's War: The Best of Ernie Pyle's World War II Dispatches* (New York: Random House, 1986).

Author's Military History

8 December 1942	Enlisted in Army Enlisted Reserve Corps but remained on inactive duty while attending the University of Chicago.
11 March 1943	Notified of acceptance as a volunteer for the Mountain Troops and assignment, upon induction, to the Mountain Training Center, Camp Hale, Pando, Colorado, for basic training.
7 April 1943	Entered on active duty in Chicago, Illinois, with the rank of Private (Serial No. 16169350) and reported to the Recruit Reception Center at Ft. Sheridan, Illinois.
16 April 1943	Reported for duty at the Mountain Training Center, Camp Hale, Colorado, and was assigned as a rifleman to Company L, 86th Mountain Regiment.
26 May 1943	Reassigned to Company M, 86th Mountain Regiment, as a member of a .30-caliber Light Machine Gun squad.
26 July 1943	Reassigned to Company F of the newly formed 85th Mountain Regiment where continued service as a machine gunner.
20 August 1943	Set regimental record for machine gun accuracy on the range at the 85th Mountain Regiment School for Machine Gunners.
20 August 1943	Application was approved for Languages and Foreign Area Study in the Army Specialized Training Program (ASTP).
19 October 1943	Completed Non-Commissioned Officer School, Camp Hale, Colorado, and promoted to Corporal.
21 October 1943	Reduced in rank to Private because of transfer to ASTP, and departed for the ASTP Specialized Training and Reassignment (STAR) Unit at the University of Nebraska, Lincoln, Nebraska.
17 March 1944	Returned to Company F, 85th Mountain Regiment, Camp Hale, following the closure of the Languages and Foreign Area Study part of the ASTP program.

247

5–26 April 1944	Participated in the winter "D-Series Maneuvers" of the 10th Light Division.
21 June 1944	Moved with the Division to its new post at Camp Swift near Austin, Texas.
21 December 1944	Left with the 85th Mountain Regiment of the newly renamed 10th Mountain Division, now commanded by Maj. Gen. Hays, for Camp Patrick Henry, Virginia, to prepare for departure to the Mediterranean Theatre via the nearby Port of Embarkation at Newport News.
4 January 1945	Departed on USS *West Point* for Naples, Italy, to join rest of Fifth Army in combat against the Germans.
28 February 1945	Promoted to Sergeant to replace one of two dead and wounded machine gun squad leaders.
11 May 1945	Awarded Bronze Star for action on 14 April 1945 near Monte della Spe, Italy.
27 June 1945	Offered appointment to the U.S. Military Academy at West Point but refused.
30 July 1945	Departed Naples, Italy, on the Liberty ship the *Marine Fox*, for New York City and home leave before retraining as flatland infantry for the invasion of Japan.
19 September 1945	Arrived Camp Carson near Colorado Springs, Colorado, to await discharge.
24 November 1945	Discharged from Army of the United States at Ft. Logan, Colorado.

Index